GUIDE TO OLD RADIOS

Pointers, Pictures and Prices

GUIDE TO OLD RADIOS

Pointers, Pictures and Prices

Second Edition

David and Betty Johnson

Krause Publications
Iola, Wisconsin

Published by Krause Publications
Iola, Wisconsin 54990

Interior design by Jerry O'Brien
Cover design by Anthony Jacobson
Cover photo by Mark Jenkins

Manufactured in the United States of America

Library of Congress Cataloging-in-Publication Data
Johnson, David, 1933–
    Guide to old radios: pointers, pictures and prices/David and
Betty Johnson.—2nd ed.
        p.   cm.
    Includes bibliographical references and index.
    ISBN 0-87069-740-4 (pb)
    1. Radio—Receivers and reception—Collectors and collecting.
  2. Radio—Receivers and reception—Conservation and restora-
tion.
  I. Johnson, Betty.   II. Title.
  TK6563.2.J64   1995
  621.384′18′075—dc20   95-14943
                                                             CIP

On the cover: Majestic "Melody Cruiser," model 921, from the collection of Dave Christiansen. Wood body with metal sails, 1946,
$300–$400.

2 3 4 5 6 7 8 9 0   0 9 8

We dedicate this book to Hugo Gernsback
—who made the impossible seem possible even before it was possible.

LOOP AERIAL →

LOUD
TALKER

RECEIVER
AND
AMPLIFIER

TUNER
BATTERIES

"Here is the 'Radiotrola', which will take the place of the phonograph in our homes soon. It could be so designed that only one adjustment would be necessary to tune in music, news, etc., which could be sent at the same time on different wave-lengths" (Radio News, December 1921). Hugo Gernback felt that radios would have to be easy to use to make them popular. Looking at the 1921 sets, it's easy to see why he felt this way.

CONTENTS

ACKNOWLEDGMENTS

We want to say "thank you" to many people who helped us with this book. Some of these people are radio dealers, others are radio collectors. Some are primarily antiques dealers. There are corporations, as well as individuals, who permitted us to photograph radios at radio swap meets. Also to those people who wanted to remain anonymous. But they all were necessary; without them, this book would not have been possible.

Ed and Irene Ripley
John Wilson
Shirley Olson
Delayne Rand
Dave Christenson
Virgil Byng, "The Byng Studio"

Charles Auenson, "The Studio"
The Antique Center of LaCrosse Limited
Gene Harris Auction Center of Marshalltown, Iowa
General Electric Company
Radio Corporation of America
McGraw Hill Publishing Company
Zenith Radio Corporation

We also want to acknowledge the women and men who have made the restoring and collecting of old radios the fast-growing and exciting hobby and business that it has become these last 15 years. We have learned from many of those people and we hope that we have helped many others to know and enjoy those wonderful old radios.

INTRODUCTION

Back in 1872, Joshua Coppersmith was arrested in New York City. The charge: He was attempting to extort money from gullible people by convincing them to invest in an instrument that he said would transmit voices over wires. He called it a *telephone*. Coppersmith may or may not have been a con man. Within four years, however, Alexander Bell did send a voice over wires and did call it a telephone. What is interesting is the reaction of the Boston paper that reported the case. "Well-informed people," it said, "know that it is impossible to transmit the human voice over wires...(and) were it possible to do so, the thing would be of no practical value." What would that writer have said about something that seemed even more impossible—transmitting voices without wires!

Let us define terms. Transmission of code through the air was common in 1920. This transmission without wires was called *wireless*. It had an ex-

MY WIFE CAN'T SAY I'M IRRELIGIOUS NOW !!

citement of its own, with an aura of mystery surrounding its operators. It enabled people, even in smaller towns and cities, to keep in regular touch with the world, but required someone to interpret those dots and dashes and convert them back into something that anyone could understand.

Radio, on the other hand, is the transmission of *voice* without wires. Anyone who could get a radio working could actually listen to voices from Pittsburgh or New York City, even though they were thousands of miles away.

In 1920, the very idea of plucking a voice or music out of the air from hundreds or thousands of miles away still had a magical quality that is very hard for us to imagine today. At this time, newspapers in cities could keep their readers up to date because they received the news by wireless. But for the person living in a small town or on a farm, current news might be a week or more old. Trips to town, often by horse, were a weekly rather than a daily event for many people. There was no daily mail delivery for farmers, so the only time to catch up on the news was on those weekly trips. Entertainment at home was a wind-up phonograph or a piano in the parlor. No wonder people took to radio with enthusiasm.

In spite of the difficulties of early radio, people gathered around tinny-sounding horn speakers or sat with earphones clamped to their heads, with a rapt look on their faces, as they listened to those voices from the sky. Houses and apartments sprouted huge antenna systems. Thousands of kids put together crystal sets and simple one-tube sets to the amazement of their parents

and relatives. Never had anything caught the imagination of the science-oriented young person the way radio did. A few years ago we saw this same kind of enthusiasm in the way kids took to the computer. Radio was as radical to most people in the 1920s as the computer was just a short time ago—and just as fascinating to the young!

Yes, radio was the miracle of the age. Now we simply consider it another appliance, and give it as little thought as a toaster, a washer, or an electric razor. Part of the joy of collecting old time radios is the discovery of some of that earlier excitement and awe. The old radio magazines and advertisements from the 1920s make fascinating reading, as you watch their enthusiasm about things we now take for granted.

The first decade of radio (1920–1929) was one of its most fascinating times. Things were happening with great rapidity. Something consid-

The romance and enchantment of radio in the early 1920s is revealed in this ad for Frost-Fones (Radio News, June 1922).

Sometimes radios were free if a child wrote for the Free Radio Plan.

ered impossible at the start of the decade (non-battery-operated radio, for instance) was common by the end of it. From being a home-built concoction, radio ended the decade in a place of honor in the living room. Instead of broadcasting studios operating out of the men's room or women's cloak-room, network broadcasting covered the entire United States.

The second decade (1930–1939) saw the maturation of the broadcasting business and the acceptance of the ra-

A 1921 Brandes headset made a perfect Christmas present.

"Above them all"

TRESCO

TRESCO

Seven Years in Radio
—*Think What That Means!*

TRESCO
SECTIONAL UNIVERSAL
Licensed Under Armstrong U. S. Patent No. 1,113,149

The Tresco Tuners were among the first ever made under the Armstrong Patent. They are found in all parts of the world, giving satisfactory service. The sectional idea is original with us.

The instruments are identically the same as those we have been manufacturing for seven years—but we have made their casings on the plan of the sectional bookcase—each a separate unit which, when put together with a top and base, forms one complete section.

The set consists of three units:

1. **Tuner and Detector.**
2. **Two-Stage Amplifier.**
3. **Case for "A" Storage Battery.**

The sections are of oak, finished in French gray, making an extremely attractive piece of furniture—something you will be proud to have in your home, beside your phonograph or piano. No wires or battery on the floor.

PRICES

Tuner and Detector Unit without vacuum tube, head set or "B" Battery	$ 50.00
Two-Step Amplifier Unit without vacuum tubes or "B" Battery	35.00
"A" Battery Unit for holding "A" Battery	9.50
Top and Bottom, which, when added to the three other units, make a complete section all in one. Each, $5.00; both	10.00
Complete set of five units—Total	**$104.50**

The units when assembled make a cabinet 40 inches wide, 15 inches high and 10 inches deep.

We do not furnish vacuum tubes, batteries or head sets.

TRESCO SECTIONAL UNIVERSALS are being supplied to dealers and jobbers just as fast as possible. Order from your local dealer. If he cannot supply you, we will fill your order upon receipt of prices as given.

Dealers and jobbers are rapidly finding out that TRESCO is one of the very few manufacturers who are actually in position to take care of large volume orders for immediate shipment. Liberal discounts are given to jobbers and dealers for quantity orders. We do not furnish vacuum tubes, batteries or loud speakers.

TRESCO RADIO
Used All Over The World
J. Matheson Bell, Sales Mgr.
Davenport Iowa. U.S.A.

1922 Tresco Sectional Universal tuner; original price $100.00.

dio and its entertainment into millions of homes. Radio indeed came of age in the 1930s.

It was a time of impressive growth. If we look in greater depth at the components of radio during the 1920s and 1930s—technical improvements, usability and appearance, and broadcasting—we will gain a better understanding of early radio.

PART ONE

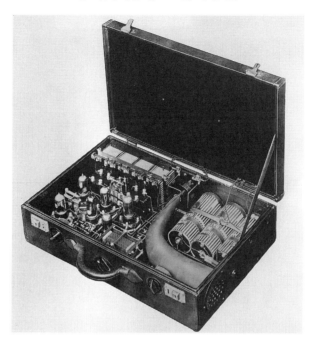

BACKGROUND
FOR THE
COLLECTOR

SOME RADIO BASICS

To collect, enjoy, and appreciate old radios, those "miracles from the past," you do not have to understand everything about their workings. It is helpful, though, to have some idea of what happens in the broadcasting and receiving process. Let's look at a drawing.

With all the technical jargon removed, we'll try to break a complex task down into a few simple ideas. Broadcasting begins at the sending end, the *radio station*. A sound (voice or music) is converted by a microphone to an electrical signal, which in turn is converted by the transmitter to a radio signal and sent into space through the antenna. That radio signal, or radio wave, will travel thousands of miles through space at the speed of light (which is an almost inconceivably fast 186,000 miles per second).

When we get to the other end of that radio signal, we see that the *radio receiver* works in a way exactly the opposite of the way the transmitter works. The radio receiver's antenna captures a portion of that radio signal, its internal electronics convert this back into an electrical signal, and the loudspeaker produces the sound you hear.

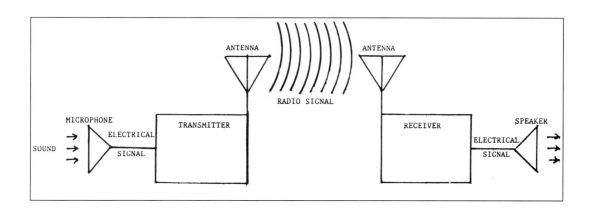

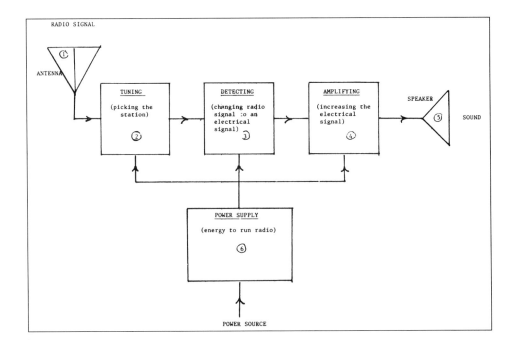

This is the simplest picture we have of what happens. Unfortunately, the receiving end isn't quite that simple. To judge the radio receiver we're examining or buying, it is good to know a little more about radio reception. Let's take a closer look at that radio receiver.

Again, we will ignore electronic theory and stick to what happens in plain language. We see there are six basic parts in the receiver.

1. The *antenna* gathers the weak radio signals. There are dozens of different signals from as many stations, all crowding into the radio through the doorway of this antenna. The antenna will be a wire of some sort. It may be a wire outside the house, carefully insulated from everything but the receiver. It may be a short wire that you attach to your receiver. It may be hidden inside the radio as a "loop" wound on a flat cardboard frame. In one form or another, your radio has an antenna.

2. You must select the particular signal you want through a process that is called *tuning in* the radio. To understand why this is necessary, you need to know that each radio signal has a frequency and a wavelength. The *frequency* is the rate at which the signal changes its character, measured in cycles per second, kilocycles (1000 cycles) per second, or megacycles (1000 kilocycles) per second. Every station on the air will have an assigned frequency. The usual broadcast band of frequencies is 550 kilocycles to 1600 kilocycles per second. This is usually called the standard broadcast band (shortened to BC) or the AM (amplitude modulation) band. Just to make things confusing, the word *cycle* has now been replaced by *hertz*. This means that what was once called "kilo-

1926 loop antenna made by Eclipse Radio Laboratories; a basketweave antenna could be rotated easily on its pivot.

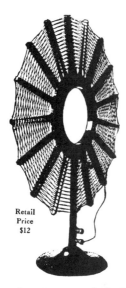

Retail
Price
$12

1925 spiderweb antenna made by Paramount.

The Loop That Solves
So Many Radio Problems

Warren Radio Loop

1922 Warren loop antenna proved that you could take radio with you.

cycle" (kc) is now called kilohertz (kHz). Most old radio literature talks of kilocycles.

Since each of these radio signals travels out at a rate of 186,000 miles per second, you can also measure a signal in terms of its *wavelength*. The wavelength is the length in meters of one cycle (or one complete change in character and back) that the signal travels in a second. If you want to move between the two ways of measuring, you can do a little algebra. The formula is frequency (in kilocycles) times wavelength (in meters) equals 300,000 ($F \times W = 300,000$).

You will find stations identified by either their frequency of transmission or the wavelength. Again, the tuning section of your receiver does the selecting of the station you wish to receive when you turn the tuning knob or knobs on the outside of the set.

3. The sound you want is encoded in the radio signal. Your radio must *detect* this sound signal, extracting an electrical image of the sound from the radio signal.

MARBLE ANTENNA

COMPLETELY replaces all ordinary wire aerials and outside wiring.

Connected to light-socket anywhere (alternating or direct current); fool proof and perfectly safe; uses no current, hence cannot blow fuses and will not interfere with Electric Lighting System.

Local static overcome and lightning proof; acts equally well with cheapest as with most elaborate instruments. A beautiful ornament suitable for office or library; taken anywhere it makes your Receiving Set useful at all times and in all places.

IN U.S.A. POSTPAID $3.00

CANADA $4.00

Packed complete in box with instrument cords and 2-piece light socket plug. Full directions.

MARBLE ANTENNA COMPANY
MINNEAPOLIS, U.S.A. 510 N. Y. LIFE BLDG.   EDMONTON CANADA   CATTISTOCK BLK.
"The Canned Aerial"

COPYRIGHT 1922

The manufacturer bragged about the marble, but it was only for looks; a capacitor actually coupled the antenna to the power lines.

RADIO ANTENNA TOWERS

Simple. Sturdy. Easy to erect. Built of galvanized steel. Will last for years. 100 ft. high or less. Fitted to take pipe mast at top. Immediate shipment. Write TODAY for prices.

Radio Department
STOVER MFG. & ENGINE CO.
FREEPORT, ILLINOIS

A tower's height made a tremendous difference in the number of stations that could be received.

4. This weak electrical image must now be *amplified* (increased) to the point where it is strong enough to operate the loudspeaker.

5. The *loudspeaker* converts the electrical signal into sound waves that resemble the original sound at the radio station. Your ears do the rest.

Radio News for December, 1922

RADIO SCHOOL

Send at once, if you are interested in obtaining a license, for our catalog explaining how and why, during the last two years, we have graduated and placed more licensed operators than any other school in New England.

MASSACHUSETTS RADIO and TELEGRAPH SCHOOL, Inc.
18 Boylston St.   Boston, Mass.
G. R. ENTWISTLE, Radio Director
Formerly Boston School of Telegraphy. Est. 1903

Radio schools were a great boon for the ambitious.

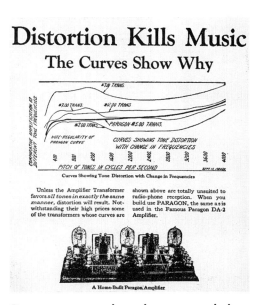

Distortion Kills Music
The Curves Show Why

Curves Showing Tone Distortion with Change in Frequencies

Unless the Amplifier Transformer favors *all tones in exactly the same manner*, distortion will result. Notwithstanding their high prices some of the transformers whose curves are shown above are totally unsuited to radio-phone reception. When you build use PARAGON, the same as is used in the Famous Paragon DA-2 Amplifier.

A Home-Built Paragon Amplifier

Response curves have been around since 1922, as seen in this Paragon ad.

6. Electrical energy is needed to operate the radio. This is provided by the *power supply*. A power supply can be a group of batteries or an electrical circuit that provides the correct energy levels from an outside power source (usually the electrical outlet in the wall).

That's all there is to it. The complex and differing ways that various radios have of accomplishing their mission can provide you with many hours of study. Some people find it fascinating work to understand and fix the old sets.

If you want to service old radios, you will need to learn radio theory. Trying to skip this important step is futile and unsafe. Learning the theory of tube sets becomes a do-it-yourself project, since schools no longer teach it. Books that will help you to understand radio circuitry and teach you how to repair tube-type radios are available. Some of these books are listed in the section entitled "Further Reading."

CHAPTER 2

POWERING THE FIRST RADIOS

adio in the 1920s was a new field and, as such, it had major limitations. Radios were unwieldy, especially since most of them required both external batteries and an external speaker. It was at this time (1922) that Hugo Gernsback made a strong argument that radio would never become successful if it couldn't be used easily and attractively in the living room, by anybody. "The telephone would never have become as popular as it is to-day if you had tried to sell each man an instrument he had to connect himself, and in order to do so learn all the 'how and why' of telephony." The easier it was to use, he felt, the more necessary it would be in everybody's lives.[1]

To better understand radios, their

---

[1]Hugo Gernsback was one of the major forces in making radio popular. He was more of a futurist than an inventor, and could see practical applications of scientific knowledge. He wrote and edited books and magazines about radio, science, and science fiction. Always practical, he ran the earliest radio supply company. See his article entitled "The Radiotrola" in *Radio News*, December 1921.

workings, and some of the peripheral problems arising from the use of batteries, it's good to have a little background about radio in the 1920s.

CRYSTAL SETS

Admittedly, the earliest radios didn't require batteries and certainly couldn't supply enough power for a loudspeaker. These crystal sets did require a great deal of fiddling to receive the station properly, and anyone listening was forced to use headphones.

Oddly enough, a crystal set today would be thought of as a "solid state" set. What is more solid state than an electrical reaction taking place in a mineral? The crystal was, of course, a mineral that was receptive to radio waves. It took all of its energy from the radio frequency signal of the transmitter. Since the crystal could not amplify or increase the energy (loudness) of the received signal, it required a large antenna and a good ground to get the most out of it. Even with this help, you could only receive a station no further

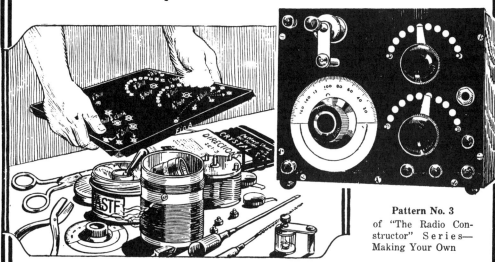

An example of a fairly sophisticated crystal set. This Radio Phone was available as a pattern only (Radio News, October 1922).

Typical 1922 crystal detector.

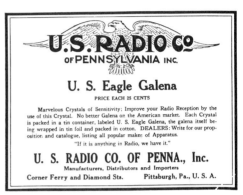

*Certain crystals were better than others for
bringing in stations. Million Point Mineral
(top) claims to be the "world's greatest" but
doesn't mention what type of crystal it is.
Generally, the galena crystal was preferred.*

than a few miles away. Exceptional distances were occasionally received—advertisements sometimes claimed 1000
miles—and were certainly bragged
about.

EARLY TUBES

The development of the vacuum
tube triode (Lee DeForest's Audion)
made it possible to amplify the intensity of any electrical signal fed into its
control grid. This characteristic was
used to build a practical radio receiver.

Vacuum tubes, though, need
power (energy) to work. There has to
be a supply of electrons made available
by a heated filament. The "A" battery
is used to heat the filaments.

To pick up the electrons sent by
the filament, the tube has a plate which
attracts the electron stream because it
has a strong positive (+) charge. Since
the charge of electrons is negative (−),
the electrons are attracted by the positive plate. The intensity of the flow is
controlled by the grid (the third part
of the tube). The positive charge for
the plate of the tube is supplied by the
"B" battery, which has the higher voltage (22 to 135 volts) needed to do this
job.

Some amplifying circuits need to
put a certain negative voltage on the
grid in order to operate well. When
this is necessary, the battery providing
the voltage is called the "C" battery.

The voltages a tube needs may
come from either batteries or another
power supply. The tube doesn't care,
so long as the right amount of power

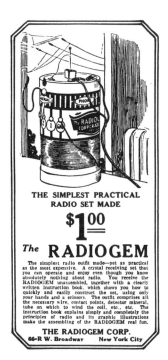

1925 Radiogem crystal set; available only as a kit and designed for the youthful builder, it is a simpler set than the Radio Phone.

at the right polarity (+ or −) reaches it. All batteries supply DC (direct current), which flows in one direction, from the − to the + connections. Later, when alternating current became the power source for homes, radio design made batteries unnecessary.

BATTERIES

Zinc-Carbon Batteries. The basic cell, called the zinc-carbon cell, is still commonly found in ordinary flashlight batteries. (The currently popular, better quality alkaline battery has a different composition.) A zinc-carbon cell obtains its electricity by a chemical process that gradually destroys the zinc metal casing. Once the zinc casing develops enough holes, the chemicals inside the battery dry out and the cell dies.

Batteries are made up of a group of dry cells, usually connected in series to provide a voltage that is some multiple of the dry cell's 1.5 volts. Thus B and

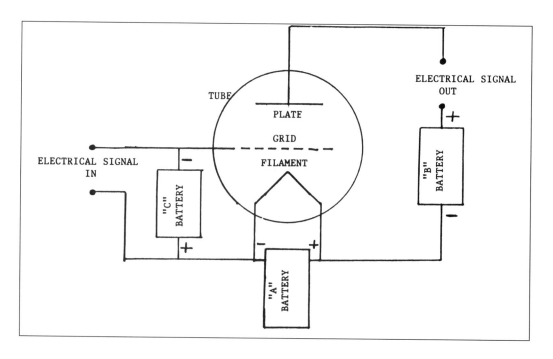

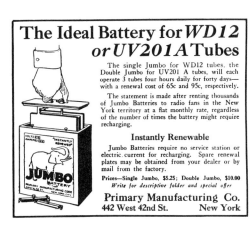
Instead of taking the entire battery in to be recharged, the owner of a Jumbo could remove just the plates from the case and replace them with fresh ones.

Tube rejuvenator brings back tubes to "full efficiency," especially in the summer when tubes are working at higher voltage.

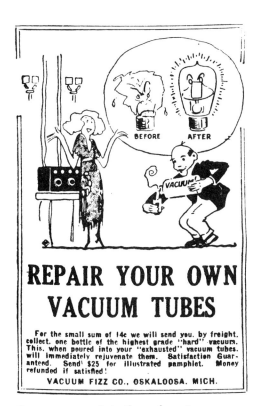

BEFORE   AFTER

VACUUM

REPAIR YOUR OWN VACUUM TUBES

For the small sum of 14c we will send you, by freight, collect, one bottle of the highest grade "hard" vacuum. This, when poured into your "exhausted" vacuum tubes, will immediately rejuvenate them. Satisfaction Guaranteed. Send $25 for illustrated pamphlet. Money refunded if satisfied!

VACUUM FIZZ CO., OSKALOOSA, MICH.

There were spoofs in those days, too.

C batteries are simply groups of cells and provide voltages like 3, 4.5, 6, 7.5, and so on.

The earliest radio sets using batteries were one-tube designs. The tube is an amplifying detector which changes the radio frequency signal from the transmitter into an increased audible signal for the listener. Sometimes a crystal detector was even used with a tube and the tube simply amplified the signal.

These early sets generally had tube filaments designed to run on about 1.1 volts. This was done so the common and cheaply available "No. 6 Cell" zinc-carbon cells could be used. (The 6 in the number means the battery is 6 inches tall.) These big single cells were used for doorbells, local telephones, and even automobile ignitions. They

A built-in switch allowed voltage adjustment for best results.

A typical early 6-volt A battery in a wood container.

A typical replaceable B battery.

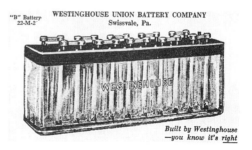

Rechargeable B batteries were never very popular; they required a special charger.

were relatively long-lasting and readily available. The cell supplied 1.5 volts, which was reduced to 1.1 volts by an adjustable resistor which could be changed as the A cell got older and its voltage dropped. This adjustment could be made from the front of the set using one of its knobs. In some cases, there was an adjustment for each tube.

Since these early sets were something of a novelty, they weren't used a great deal. The simple A cell was satisfactory, and the B battery lasted a long time in such use. However, as multi-

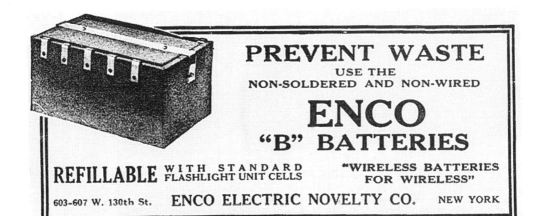
This B battery was filled with standard flashlight batteries.

tube sets, and particularly loudspeaker sets, became popular, the use of non-rechargeable A batteries became too expensive and a cheaper source of filament power was sought.

A better nonrechargeable A battery was developed by Eveready during the early 1930s. This was a miracle battery called the Air Cell. Basically this Air Cell was a zinc-carbon cell, but an imaginative method was used to prevent hydrogen buildup on the carbon center electrode, a problem with any zinc-carbon cell.

The Air Cell promised longer life at a steadier voltage than the regular cell. It had one fault. If it was overloaded (if more current was drawn from it than it was designed to supply at one time), it was quickly ruined. It also was more expensive than its simpler competitor, and it didn't succeed.

Lead-Acid Batteries. Again designers looked to readily available sources of power. The 6-volt lead-acid battery was just coming into use in automobiles. It was used for starting the car as well as the rest of the electrical

Radio batteries, like car batteries, had to be tested.

system. The battery had many faults: It was heavy, could have a foul smell, sometimes bubbled over or spilled corrosive sulfuric acid, and was expensive. However, it did have two excellent qualities. It was rechargeable, and it could supply a great deal of power.

Looking at the shelves of many old radio tables, you will see the results of spilled batteries in the acid burns on the shelves.

Because of its chemical composition, a lead-acid cell puts out about 2.2 volts. In the normal auto battery, 3 cells were packaged in a wood box (lined with tar to protect the wood) or, later, in a hard rubber container.

Nickel-Iron Batteries. Another rechargeable cell was designed by Thomas Edison. Used in Edison's electric trucks, it was able to supply about 1.2 volts per cell. It had several advantages: It supplied an even output voltage as it discharged, was not touchy about overcharging or storage, had a steel case that was indestructible, used a liquid alkaline electrolyte which was far less corrosive than the acid in the lead-acid battery, and could be recharged more times than a regular battery. So why didn't it succeed? It was much more expensive than the already high-priced lead-acid rechargeable battery.

Tubes. Tubes were designed to use the new filament power source. Now they had 5-volt filaments. Again it was decided to use adjustable resistances to cut down the voltage from 6.6 volts. As the battery discharged, its voltage dropped slowly, and the adjustable resistance would be reset to keep the voltage on the tube filaments at the correct level.

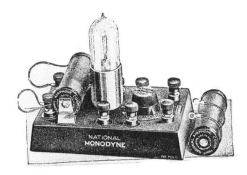

1923 National Airphone; one-tube set on a base; no cabinet; original price $10.00.

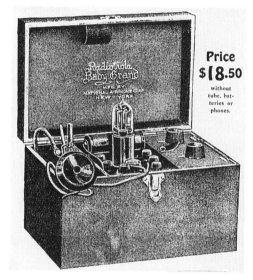

1924 Radiotrola Baby Grand made by National Airphone; one-tube set, with space for headphones; original price $18.50.

This adjustable resistance knob could be used as a crude volume control to reduce the loudness of the radio on closer stations. It also meant that it was possible to run the filaments at too high a voltage in order to get just a little more power on weak stations, which shortened the life of the tubes.

Among the new tube types created by RCA (the preeminent tube design

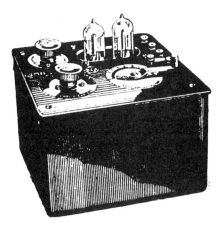 

1924 RCA Radiola III and Radiola III Balanced Amplifier, each housed in boxes. The combined model is the Radiola IIIA. Original prices: III, $35.00; amplifier, $30.00.

and manufacturing company) were the 201A, the 200A, and the 212A. Together these three types made more powerful radios possible.

Battery Charging and Chargers

Battery Charging. That big 6-volt A battery eventually had to be charged. There were "Charging Stations" in many towns and cities, to which the battery had to be taken to be recharged at a cost. There were a number of problems with this procedure. The heavy battery had to be physically taken to the station. Recharging cost money. If the battery was kept overnight, it meant another charged battery would have to be available in order not to miss favorite radio programs. There was no way to tape the broadcasts at your neighbor's house back then.

If you had electricity (110 volts AC) coming into your home, you could purchase a battery charger for your A battery. There were chargers for rechargeable (lead-acid) B batteries,

but they never became very popular. Recharging a B battery was not cost-effective. Rechargeable C batteries were not used, since C batteries lasted for years anyway.

The battery chargers of the time were not sophisticated in design. If you were not cautious, you could overcharge your battery. Then it would give off fumes, heat up, and sometimes bubble over. Overcharging also shortened the life of the battery.

A typical 6-volt A battery charger.

HOMCHARGE *your* Radio Battery *for a nickel!*

A battery charger allowed recharging in the home. The ad also shows the problems of hiding the battery and battery charger.

Battery Eliminators. For those with "wired" homes (those on 110-volt AC lines), battery eliminators came in all sizes and types. These were top-selling accessories in the late 1920s. You could do away with A batteries or with all of the batteries (A, B, C) together. Getting rid of the A battery was most important. The B lasted for several months of normal use and the C lasted for years.

Battery eliminators were not perfect. They often added some "hum" (buzz) to the sound heard from the receiver, because the DC produced was not as smooth as that from a battery. They were expensive, but for heavy radio users they made sense.

Experimenters who had a 110-volt AC line into their houses tried to do without the A eliminator altogether. Using a simple voltage-changing transformer, such as a doorbell transformer,

they reduced the 100 volts to the 5 volts AC that would operate a tube safely. It would operate a tube safely, but not successfully. The light weight of the filaments in tubes designed for battery use (needed to conserve batteries), coupled with the audible rate of

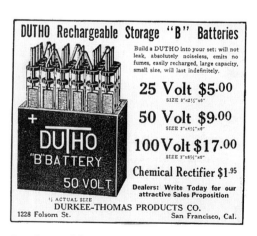
A rechargeable Dutho B battery; this is one of the more unusual-looking ones.

change in the AC current direction (60 times a second) produced a buzz that made the system—unless very carefully balanced—unlistenable.

ALTERNATING CURRENT TUBES

What was needed now was a tube designed for AC on the filament. The theory said that a tube shouldn't care what kind of current (AC or DC) is used to heat the filament. The designers set to work.

Any vacuum tube requires direct current on the plate to amplify, since a steady positive voltage must be present to attract the electrons from the filament. By necessity, the grid voltage (C) had to be DC as well. The AC coming into the grid was the signal that had to be amplified. So a radio still had to contain a B eliminator or power supply to provide the necessary DC voltages. The C voltage was usually produced in the radio itself, directly from the B supply.

It was much cheaper to heat the filament wire with AC. It did mean that the filament wire would have to be heavier than for DC tubes. This was done successfully in tubes like the 26 and the 45.

In another design, the *cathode* (electron emitter) was insulated from the filament (now called a *heater*). The cathode would be heated enough to provide the needed electrons. Common early types of this sort of tube were the 24A and the 27.

The AC-operated radio soon replaced the battery set in homes where AC was available. The radios were heavy and, in their early years, expen-sive. However, they performed well and were inexpensive to run.

LATER BATTERY SETS

Battery sets are still being manufactured today; these are our portable radios. There are probably few people, however, still using them as home radios.

Technology kept improving the battery systems available for (primarily) rural homes. Until the Rural Electrification Agency came along in the 1930s, most farmers never expected to be on an AC line. Because electricity was important not only to their comfort, but more importantly to their farming operations, many farms had some sort of power plant. The Delco system that often is referred to was a 32-volt DC system that charged its batteries with a gasoline engine. Radios that ran on 32 volts were available for this system.

It was possible to avoid the B battery completely. Using a 6-volt car battery and a *vibrator* power supply, these radios could be used in nonelectrified areas. A number of Zenith radios during the 1930s were 6-volt radios.

There was never any doubt that farmers would bring in AC power when it was available. Allied Radio catalogs in 1938 advertised not only AC radios and battery radios of various voltages, but also AC/battery radios. The assumption was that AC power would reach farms during the lifetime of these radios, and the farmer could easily switch over his radio without having to go out and buy another one. Crosley also made radios designed to operate as either battery or AC radios.

It is impossible to know when battery radios stopped being used in homes. They were produced until sometime in the early 1950s; Philco was advertising "Farm Radios" into the late 1940s in farm magazines. Many rural areas didn't get electricity until after World War II was over; the plans to bring light to the farms of America had been shelved for the duration of the war. It was almost 1950 before some parts of hilly, southwestern Wisconsin were hooked up to electric lines, for example, and it was probably still later in other parts of the country. Hence, farm radios remained around for a long time.

THE CHANGE FROM BATTERIES TO AC

Assuming that line power was available in a city in the 1920s, the change from battery radios to AC ones was rapid. As has been seen, batteries were pesky, expensive, short-lived, messy, and altogether a thing people were eager to get rid of.

There were, for instance, those dratted holes in the carpet. If one were unfortunate enough to spill the battery acid while moving the battery around, there would be a large burn hole. If the battery charger were unsupervised and the liquid started to bubble, small acid burns would be found in the rug. Because of this, many housewives tried to limit the location of the radio to the attic, where the spots wouldn't show. Inevitably, there would be an important broadcast that many of the family would want to hear. If the set was brought down to the dining room table, "just once, mind you," it generally remained downstairs. Clustering

around the loudspeaker or sharing the headphones brought a bit of the outside world to the family. Once people sampled radio, they didn't want to give it up.

Trying to hide the big and cumbersome batteries was another problem. It would be like hiding today's car battery in the corner and hoping that no one would see it. Radio tables were developed that were long enough and narrow enough to hold one of the mid-1920s sets, with a shelf underneath to hold the batteries. Some of the tables had oak or wicker fronts to hide the batteries and make them more attractive. This meant getting behind the table to remove the battery for recharging, with the possible problem of spilling the battery acid.

Batteries had a bad habit of dying at important times. Numerous cartoons and advertisements from the late 1920s had men coming home from work and telling their wives that they had invited the Smiths in that night to listen to the radio, only to have the wife or child lament, "But the batteries are dead! I listened to the radio this afternoon." It must have happened often enough to make a point to the readers.

Then there was the constant cost of keeping up those batteries. As radio became more important to the family, the family started planning its life around certain programs. The radio was used more and more often, and for more and more hours.

The manufacturers and dealers were not at all reluctant to encourage this high regard for radio. The ads from the late 1920s implied, if not stated, that modern families used modern radios. There were many ways to get peo-

Here's the *Simplest* Way

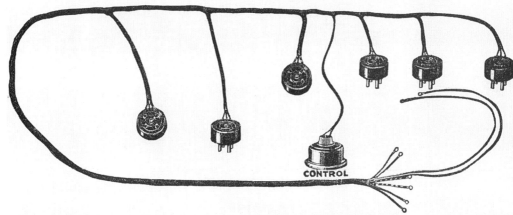

To Change DC Receivers to AC

Absolutely no Rewiring Necessary on Standard Sets

The Eby AC Adaptor Harness can be used in practically any standard five or six tube set equipped with separate B battery and C bias feeders for the last AF stage *without changing the wiring in any way*.

An AC adapter harness; this wiring harness allowed the use of the new AC tubes in earlier battery sets.

General Electric Tungar charger (reprinted with permission).

"Sorry, but we won't be able to listen in tonight. My "B" batteries are dead".

This embarrassment need never happen to you again.

The PERMANENT POWER UNIT FOR RADIO

RADIOBATS

This battery eliminator removed the problems of B batteries.

ple to turn in their old, "obsolete" battery sets and get one of the new, modern AC sets. Just in case the point was missed, National Radio Week in 1929 used a number of gimmicks. In Milwaukee, there was a parade, complete with decorated floats and trucks, that led to a giant bonfire where the old trade-in sets were destroyed. In St. Louis, nearly 3000 old sets were burned. The mayor himself lighted the fire in Buffalo. "The agreement on the trade-in allowances, the special window displays, the generous use of newspaper space, and propaganda of obsoles-

cence—by these many means the dealers, acting together, gave these campaigns a cumulative force to which the fire itself was a fitting climax."[2]

The AC set had won.

[2]Collectors of old battery sets flinch at the thought of this mayhem, but *Radio Retailing* proudly boasted of this coup. "Clearing the Way with Fire!" was the title of their article, which went on to state that National Radio Week "inspires many dealer associations to 'burn the bloopers'." For further information see page 72 of *Radio Retailing*, November 1928.

THE 1920S—FIRST STATIONS AND STATION FIRSTS

Radio history doesn't only include the history of radio technology and radio manufacturers, but it also includes the field of broadcasting—what was broadcast and how. Broadcasting is an increasingly popular field of radio history. Museums grow and clubs meet to listen to old programs and read aloud original scripts. When the fates are kind, they may even get a member of the original cast to join in one of these readings.

While the 1930s are considered the golden age of broadcasting in terms of programming, the mechanics of broadcasting itself already had become settled. During the 1920s, almost anything could happen, and sometimes did. There were no established standards, so each station tried to define broadcasting in the best way possible for its own particular audience. Trial and error played a large part as the stations learned on the air.

1921 Westinghouse model RC includes both the RA and DA in the same box; battery set sold by RCA; original price $125.00 (Gene Harris Auctions).

BROADCASTING: AN IMPORTANT PART OF RADIO

Probably the first question people ask about broadcasting is: What was

1922 RCA Aeriola Sr. made by Westinghouse; popular one-tube set (John Wilson).

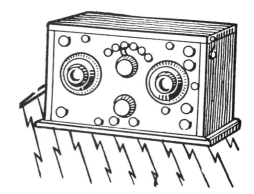

1922 Tuska type 224; original price $35.00.

1923 Telmaco one-tube receiver; original price $25.00.

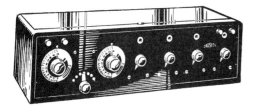

1922 Crosley model X; one of the larger Crosley models. Crosleys were famous for their low prices; even so, this model comes in a mahogany cabinet; original price $55.00.

the first station? The answer to that depends on exactly what we mean by the question. The first station to broadcast voices? The first to broadcast a regularly scheduled program? The first to be licensed?

KDKA (Pittsburgh) has the honor of being the first station in the United States licensed not for experimental or amateur use, but for broadcasting un-der the 1920 federal regulations. Frank Conrad, Westinghouse's chief engineer, had been making experimental broadcasts from his garage since 1916. The broadcasts were to the Westinghouse plant in East Pittsburgh, where the Radio Engineering Section was working on developing radios better than the crystal sets of the day. Although the Department of Commerce suspended all amateur broadcasting licenses as a security mea-

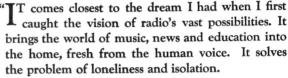

When Marconi heard the AERIOLA GRAND

© UNDERWOOD & UNDERWOOD

Look for this trademark at your dealer

"IT comes closest to the dream I had when I first caught the vision of radio's vast possibilities. It brings the world of music, news and education into the home, fresh from the human voice. It solves the problem of loneliness and isolation.

"The Aeriola Grand is at present the supreme achievement in designing and constructing receiving sets for the home—a product of the research systematically conducted by scientists in the laboratories that constitute part of the R C A organization."

G. Marconi

1922 RCA Aeriola Grand; testimonials were just as important then as now.

sure once the United States became involved in World War I, Conrad's test station was exempted. He continued to use it during the war, with government approval, to test military equipment for Westinghouse.

When the ban was lifted after the war, Conrad resumed his amateur broadcasting. World War I had pushed the whole field of radio into rapid development. The advancement of vacuum tubes during the war was remarkable, giving radio greater sensitivity and volume. Along with the tests he was conducting, Conrad occasionally played phonograph records. Letters arrived from listeners delighted with this type of programming. The Hamilton Music Store saw that there were advantages in radio broadcasting and provided the records in return for a mention on the air. The record concerts became a regularly scheduled event, once a week at first, but soon on a

daily basis. Until this point, those who listened were primarily experimenters and amateurs. But public attention was drawn to Conrad's broadcasts when the Joseph Horne Department Store ran an ad mentioning the broadcasts as an aid in promoting their new wireless department.

Harry Davis, a Westinghouse vice-president (and the reason for the "D" and the "A" in KDKA), saw the public relations value of a station. If you

Broadcasting the Engagement by Wireless

Up-to-date surely is the one who chooses radio as the basis of an engagement party.

A radio instrument may furnish the evening's entertainment. Then at the supper table the centerpiece and serving cups carry out the idea. Attached to a ribbon which comes from the receiving wires is a card on which is written "Hear the News." On the reverse side are the names of the engaged couple.

Radio was a cute idea for a party.

Tresco model W receiver and amplifier; not listed in Tresco literature.

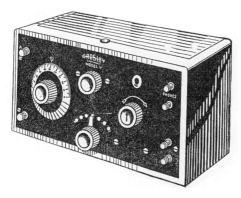

1923 Crosley model VC. This is a model V with an engraved front panel. One month later, in June 1923, it was being advertised as the Ace Model V, "formerly known as the Crosley VC;" original price $20.00.

could broadcast interesting programs, people would buy your radios. With new federal guidelines in effect for licensing broadcasting stations, Westinghouse applied for a license and received it in only eleven days, on 27 October 1920. KDKA went on the air with the results of the Harding-Cox presidential election on 2 November 1920, less than a month after it had applied for a license.

What about the first voice broadcast? Certainly it was earlier than 1920? On Christmas Eve, 1906, Reginald

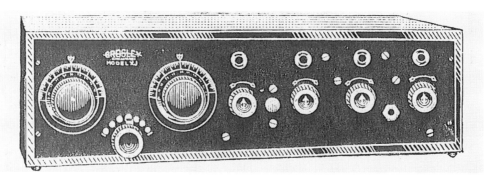

1923 Crosley model X-J; original price $65.00.

Specifications
Regenerative Tuner.
Vernier Control of wave length adjustment.
Detector and 1 stage Amplifier.
Two telephone jacks.
1 Pair Brandes Head Telephones.
3 Flash Light batteries.
2 B Batteries.

Price $97.50

1925 RCA Radiola II.

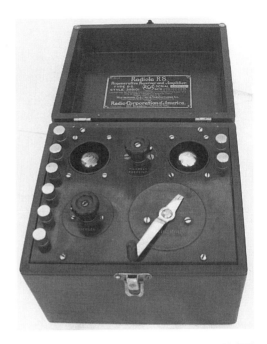

1923 Radiola RS; manufactured by Westinghouse; sold by RCA; original price $87.00.

Fessenden broadcast a program from Brant Rock, Massachusetts, that started with the "CQ, CQ" of Morse code and then switched to a human voice. There are no words that can adequately describe the surprise, shock, and amazement of shipboard radio operators who suddenly, at sea, heard a woman singing in their radio rooms. At that time, remember, wireless was all in code. The surprised operators didn't hear just an isolated song, either. In addition to the woman singing (taken from a phonograph record), someone read a poem, there was a violin solo (played by Fessenden himself), and a speech. It was a complete Christmas program. Fessenden then asked people listening to write him and let him know how far the broadcast had carried. The following New Year's Eve program was heard as far away as the West Indies.

Many other stations claim various firsts, but the first regularly broadcasting station (Fessenden didn't broadcast on a regular schedule) has to be KQW (San Jose, California), which was

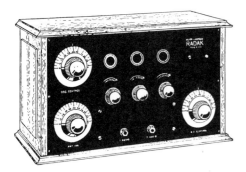

1923 Radak model C23; made by Clapp-Eastham; original price $125.00.

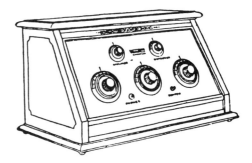

1924 Work Rite Air Master model; original price $160.00.

1924 Fada kit; original price $25.00.

started by Charles Herrold in 1909. It wasn't known as KQW then—this was before there were call letters. In fact, this was before there were any regulations regarding broadcasting stations. The station announcement was "This is San Jose," followed by the address of the college of engineering Herrold had started. Herrold, a self-trained engineering genius, at once made radio the focus of the college, with voice transmission his immediate goal.

At first Herrold made only occasional experiments, but soon voice broadcasts were a regular feature. Every Wednesday night the station was on the air with news bulletins and phonograph records (provided by a lo-

cal store). Anyone with a crystal set in the area planned on listening to these programs. Unfortunately, they didn't always hear the end of them. Herrold carefully planned the entire program, but pushed so much power (15 watts) through his carbon microphone that the program sounded more and more mushy as the evening went on. Often he had to simply stop and shut down. The next week he would apologize for the incident, but often the same thing would happen again. New Year's Eve, 1915, he decided to welcome in the new year with a blank shot from an old Army pistol. There was a sharp sound, and he was off the air again.

Herrold shut down the station during World War I. When he started it up after the war, he was unable to repeat his earlier success. Eventually he sold the station to a Baptist church, and it finally got call letters and became KQW. After several other sales, the station ended up as KCBS, the Columbia Broadcasting System station in San Francisco. Lee DeForest said in 1940 that KQW could "rightfully claim to be the oldest broadcasting station in the entire world."

There were others—lots of oth-

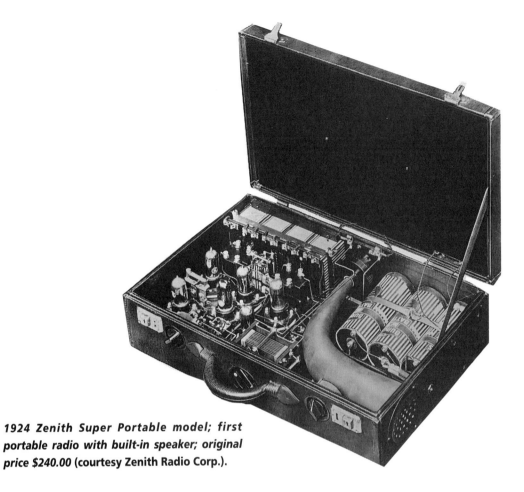

1924 Zenith Super Portable model; first portable radio with built-in speaker; original price $240.00 (courtesy Zenith Radio Corp.).

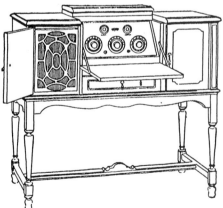

1925 Work Rite Aristocrat model; designed to look like a buffet when the radio and speaker compartments are closed; original price $350.00.

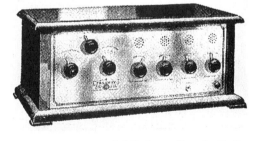

1924 Faraway model F. According to Radio Collector's Guide, Faraway made only four models. The light-colored front panel is different from most other sets of that date; original price $59.50.

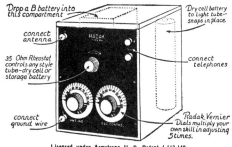

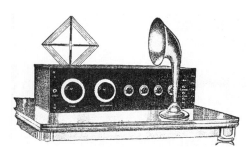

1924 Radak model R-4. The diagram shows that this is a self-contained small radio, including even the batteries; original price $25.00.

1924 Mu-Rad model MA-18. Notice the Radio Map on the wall—apparently the listener has been marking the stations he has picked up; original price $110.00.

1924 Ultradyne; available in kit form; made by Phenix Radio Corp.; original price $24.50.

1924 Mu-Rad model MA-15. This ad reflects the excitement and mystery of radio.

ers—who had various claims to being first. Canada considers that the first scheduled broadcast in North America occurred over station XWA (Montreal) on 20 May 1920, over five months earlier than KDKA's. Europe was developing its own broadcasting. This is why the question we asked originally has to be carefully phrased. There are so many answers. Everyone wants to be first, and the words "radio broadcast" or "regularly scheduled" can have many interpretations.

By the way, the firsts that took place the first year after KDKA began are awesome. Everything was a first, and the stations were willing to try just about anything. This list is selective and incomplete. There are certain to be other stations claiming some of these records:

1924 Zenith model Super-Zenith VII; original price $240.00 (Courtesy Zenith Radio Corp.).

31 August 1920
First election returns, Detroit primary (WWJ in Detroit)

October 1920
First World Series (WWJ)

2 November 1920
First national election returns (WWJ, KDKA)

31 December 1920
First New Year's Eve celebration (WWJ)

2 January 1921
First church service (KDKA)
First remote broadcast was of this same church service.

3 January 1921
First weather forecasts given by voice (WHA in Madison, Wisconsin)

11 April 1921
First boxing match, Johnny Dundee and Johnny Ray (KDKA)

9 May 1921
First live broadcast from theater stage (KDKA)

4-6 August 1921
First Davis Cup matches (KDKA)

5 August 1921
First play-by-play baseball (KDKA)

16 October 1921
First radio section started by a newspaper (*Newark Sunday Call*). Although not a broadcast first, these newspaper departments were important in making people familiar with radio.

11 November 1921
First live opera performance (KYW, Chicago)

These first years of broadcasting were exciting. No one really knew where radio was going, nor how it would get there. But everyone was convinced that radio was a great benefit for mankind.

An article in *Radio News* in December 1922 said:

"There will be concerts such as we really want to hear, college courses for the boy who could

1924 Magnavox model TRF-50. Elaborate doors cover the workings of this table set; original price $150.00.

1924 A&P. "The most beautiful and efficient neutrodyne set in the world," it claimed; original price $97.50.

1924 Halldorson. The company made three models in 1924. Originally it was a transformer manufacturing company.

not go as far as the university, business information in condensed form so that dad will not have to ruin his eyes and fill all his home time with reading. All will be systematized and on time like the visits of the postman. Probably we shall have individual receiving sets for the different members of the family, so each can hear what he wishes. They will be cheaper and more efficient than they are now, and simpler to operate. Radio will not take the place of the telegraph or the telephone, the newspaper or the magazine, the theatre or the moving picture show. It is just one more marvel of modern science that enriches our lives and fills [them] with pleasant, useful entertainment."

Radio Studios

In the beginning, radio studios weren't even primitive, they were nonexistent. They provide a perfect example of learning through trial and error, since there was no real information about what was necessary to produce a clear, understandable radio program. Accounts of early stations leave one wondering how the programs ever got on the air.

Take, for instance, the way KDKA developed its studio. Broadcasting the election returns was easy, with one man sitting in front of a microphone. When they tried to broadcast the Westinghouse band from a hall, they ran into acoustical problems they had never foreseen. Placing so many instruments inside a large room led to such reverberation that the broadcast sounded like bedlam. Up onto the roof of the building they went, and the broadcast went just fine. When rainy weather came, a tent was erected to protect the musicians. Finally a strong

1924 Day-Fan. This cabinet can be either the OEM-7 (4-tube, original price $98.00) or the OEM-11 (3-tube, original price $90.00).

wind blew the tent down, and they went back inside again—but this time they erected the tent inside the building. The tent softened the room acoustics and allowed the broadcasts to sound good. As time went on, the tent was replaced by hangings to do the same job.

The WJZ studio in Newark, New Jersey, was also on the roof of a Westinghouse building there. It put its new transmitter in a shack on the roof, reachable only by an iron ladder and through a hatchway. An Edison phonograph, which they were planning on using to play records, was too big to go through the hatchway to the

1924 Thompson Parlor Grand model; original price $145.00.

1924 Colin Kennedy model XV-430; TRF, battery set; original price $142.50 (Gene Harris Auctions).

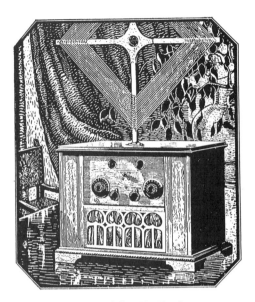

1924 De Forest model D-12. The loop antenna fits into a hole in the top of the cabinet. This particular model was available for either dry batteries or storage batteries. The case was gray-and-black Fabrikoid or two-tone mahogany. Original prices were from $161.20 to $195.00.

1924 Pfanstiehl model 7 Overtone. A bit of a radio table shows at the bottom. Not much wider than the radio itself, this table had a shelf on which to place the batteries; original price $150.00 (radio only).

The DAYRADIA

1924 Day-Fan model 5107 Dayradia; slant-front radio with enclosed speaker; original price $225.00.

roof. Instead it had to be hoisted up the outside of the building. After several weeks of tests and receiving letters of praise from people who were excited about this new entertainment, they began regular programming. A few performers made it up the ladder to the shack, but it soon became very evident that the studio should be easily accessible. Draping part of the ladies' cloak room with flannel was the solution to the problem.

Another example of how primitive early broadcasting could be was seen at what later became the Columbia flagship station, WOR (Newark). Their first programs were broadcast before there was a completed studio. With no studio, they needed a soundproof room to monitor the first day's programs. They ended up using the men's room.

There were some ambitious opening shows for stations. KYW (Chicago), another Westinghouse station, took advantage of the expertise Westinghouse was developing in radio to begin its broadcasting with the most

1925 RCA Radiola model 26; portable, loop antenna; battery operated; beautiful wood case with gold-colored dials; original cost $225.00 (Gene Harris Auctions).

ambitious project one could think of: a live production of the Chicago Opera Company. The opening show was immensely successful and nightly broadcasts of the opera continued to the end of its season.

In an attempt to look elegant (and incidentally to hide the dirt), WJZ dyed its flannel red. Studios in the early 1920s tried hard to look like living rooms or front parlors. Since most of the performers were used to a live audience in an unamplified room, they were intimidated by the microphone. With no audience present for whom they could perform, many of them suffered "mike fright." To overcome this, studios went to great extremes to hide what they were. Photographs of early studios show many popular decorative ideas of the times. There were those elegant-looking draperies (made of flannel or burlap), a great way to disguise a plain room as well as to deaden the reverberations. Oriental carpets covered the floor, not only giving a comfortable

feel to the room, but also muffling footsteps. Pianos were a necessity, of course, to accompany the many soloists who appeared; like the piano at home, it was covered with a paisley scarf. Potted plants gave the room a nice, homey feel. Amplifiers could hide in innocent-looking, commonplace phonograph cabinets. There was still the microphone to handle. It had to be hidden to keep the performers from becoming nervous. Suddenly the studios had ornate, floor-standing "lamps" with the fringed lampshade carefully disguising the microphone. The feeling that comes from looking at the pictures is one of an over-elaborately decorated, tasteless, middle-class parlor.

Glorious 1922! Radio was booming, stations were starting, and performers were delighted to be on the air. No one thought about wage scales and hours. WJZ, located across the river from New York City, had early access to a large number of performers. There was a problem in getting them, since the Westinghouse station was located in a factory district on the wrong side of the river. Undaunted, WJZ had limousines meet the artists at the ferry, a doorman to greet them at the studio, and an announcer who appeared in a

1924 Ozarka (no model number); original price $39.50.

1924 Crosley model 3R3 Trirdyn Special; original price $75.00; with tubes and earphones $90.75.

1925 Jones model J-75. This set was made by Joseph W. Jones (New York City) rather than the Jones Radio Co.; original price $75.00.

tuxedo or, occasionally, white-tie-and-tails. Artists wanted to come to perform on this new medium. It was modern; it was exciting.

The euphoria didn't last long, however. Soon stations in New York City were broadcasting. Without the need to bribe the performers to come, the amenities soon declined. The performers also learned that there was money to be made from radio and that performing for the thrill or the publicity was no longer necessary.

Advertising on the Air

Early broadcasting had certain ethical problems. One was the matter of advertising or not advertising on the air. Nowadays it seems impossible that radio seriously considered being advertising-free. There was a possibility—remote to be sure—that it would be limited to announcements such as public radio uses today ("This program has been brought to you by the XYZ Corporation, a leading manufacturer of widgets, located at 123 State Street.") This wasn't likely to last long, since businessmen already knew the value of the printed ad.

Back in 1916, the chief engineer of Western Electric had said, "We [do] not think it seemly to advertise on radio." Even at the first Washington Radio Conference in 1922, Herbert Hoover, then Secretary of Commerce, said, "It is inconceivable that we should allow so great a possibility for service to be drowned in advertising chatter." An attempt was made in 1925 to pass a law to prohibit advertising, but it failed. As time went on, the talk wasn't about banning all advertising, only "direct advertising." The lines grew less distinct all the time.

Even before radio advertising was acceptable, corporations found that they could gain early recognition of their products by naming the show after the company. Atwater Kent was sponsoring "The Atwater Kent Hour" as early as 1925. Kent felt that the extra cost of radio advertising was well worth the money, although it cost almost twice as much each week to put on the program as the entire year's cost for printed advertising. The Stromberg-Carlson Sextette, on weekly over the Blue Network, was "definitely designed to aid the dealer in selling Stromberg-Carlson receivers," according to an ad they ran in *Radio Retailing* in May 1928.

DE FOREST F-5 AW

1925 De Forest F-5 AW; original price $90.00.

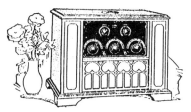

DE FOREST F-5 M

1925 De Forest F-5 M; enclosed speaker; original price $110.00.

1925 Gilfillan model GN-2; introduced in 1924; original price $140.00 (without the horn).

Not everyone questioned the merits of advertising. American Telephone and Telegraph began station WEAF (New York City) in 1922. Since they had no radio equipment to sell, unlike most of the other parent companies, they weren't particularly interested in broadcasting. They were used to handling toll charges for telephones and telegraphs, however. It wasn't a big jump for them to conceive of the idea of "toll broadcasting," an opportunity for anyone who was willing to pay the time rate to basically own that period of time to do with it what he wanted. An indication of where this all was going came in WEAF's first paid program. On 28 August 1922, Mr. Blackwell of the Queensboro Corporation gave a ten-minute talk. The announcer who introduced him mentioned Nathaniel Hawthorne and his ideals about a healthful home life. Then Mr. Blackwell began. After a token mention of Hawthorne and those ideals, he got right to the point. The Queensboro Corporation was selling a group of apartments (in "Hawthorne Court," naturally). They exemplified Hawthorne's dreams about healthful living and, for the rest of the ten minutes, Mr.

Blackwell gave unarguable reasons for buying into this great opportunity.

The battle against advertising was really lost almost as soon as it began. With the exception of educational and public radio, there was no way that broadcasting could remain unsullied by commercialism. Today there's a feeling that this is happening even to public radio, as sponsors not only give their names and locations, but also include some sort of slogan or short spiel.

Early Regulations

Radio grew. What had begun in 1920 as almost an experiment was by

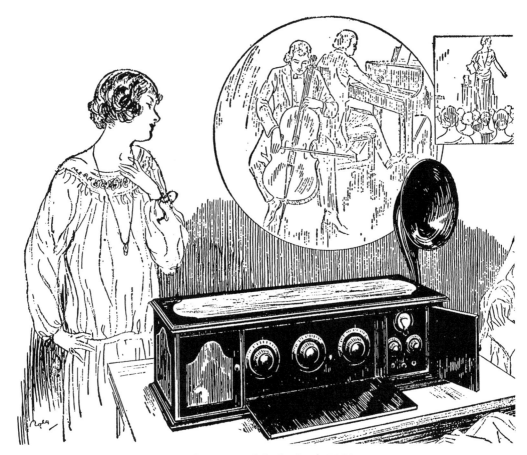

1925 Gilfillan model GN-1; introduced in 1924; original price $175.00.

1925 Mohawk model 110, consolette version. With its curved top, this table-top radio is highly styled; original price $175.00.

the end of the decade a vast, established business. David Sarnoff, of RCA, gained a reputation as a prophet for accurately predicting the growth of radio. His prediction was made early in 1920, before there were any licensed stations on the air. He visualized that the "Radio Music Box" could be made for $75 per set, and that the first year there would be sales of $7,500,000, the second year $22,500,000 and the third year $45,000,000. RCA didn't believe these figures and so was caught unprepared when KDKA went on the air and radio began booming. A shake-up the next year made Sarnoff the gen-

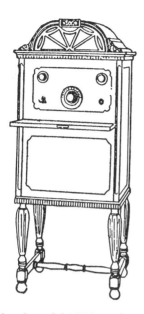

1925 Mohawk model 115 Console; same as the 110, but with a floor cabinet instead; original price $225.00.

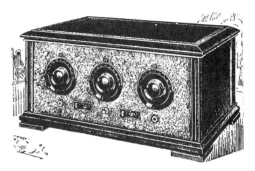

1925 Eisemann model 6-D; introduced in 1924; original price $125.00.

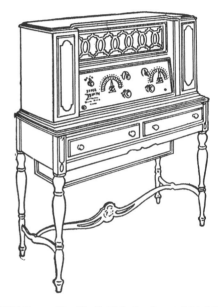

1925 Super Zenith X. This horizontal highboy concealed the speaker in the top of the compartment; available as either an AC set or a battery set; original price $550.00.

eral manager, while RCA rushed to make up lost time. The first year that RCA sold radios, they grossed $11,000,000. The second year they matched the prediction, while the third year they sold $50,000,000. This consolidated RCA's position in the field and Sarnoff's reputation as a visionary.

KDKA went on the air in 1920. By the end of that year, three stations were licensed. Nine months later, there were 451 stations, broadcasting from every state except Wyoming. Immediately a major problem arose. All of the stations (except those broadcasting governmental reports such as weather or crop news) were licensed at 360 meters. Crop reports and weather were to be found at 485 meters. A station would use 360 meters for entertainment and news, then switch to 485 meters for its weather reports. As soon

as two stations in the same area were broadcasting, some sort of compromise was necessary. The government had not allotted any broadcasting time periods, so it was up to the stations to make their own arrangements. With no supervision, a station could exceed its time and make life difficult for its companion station. Some sort of allocation

1925 Standardyne model B5; original price $60.00.

1925 portable Operadio; very early Deco style.

of the radio band was going to be necessary.

Meanwhile, every group wanted to be on the radio. Newspapers started their own stations, stores developed them to help sell radios, colleges and universities wanted them to help educate people in the remote parts of their states, and churches saw them as a method of expanding their ministries.

As the decade progressed, reassignment of radio frequencies was common, as was sharing a frequency with one or more other stations. The smaller stations were limited to certain hours of certain days, making it difficult for them to develop their own listening audiences. Since new listeners wanted to be able to brag about hear-

ing one of the large stations (KDKA, WJZ, or WWJ, for instance), it was necessary to do something about the local stations that were broadcasting on the same wavelength. At first there was "Silent Night," one night a week when the local station would stay off the air and its listeners could try to catch one of the major stations. Different nights were chosen in different parts of the country. For a while it worked, but the local stations eventually became tired of losing revenue for that night, and the idea slowly died.

Stations were still starting up haphazardly, and something was going to have to be done about the chaos. When several stations were sharing the same frequency, it became a major undertaking to tune in any one of them clearly. The government attempted to solve the problem in 1922 when the Commerce Department added a 400-meter band for broadcasting, with strict limitations. It was for Class B stations, who would operate on 500 to 1000 watts and were prohibited from playing phonograph records. Those that couldn't meet these terms (the Class A stations) were fated to stay at the 360-meter band. Listeners liked this, as did all those who favored a few powerful stations rather than a pleth-

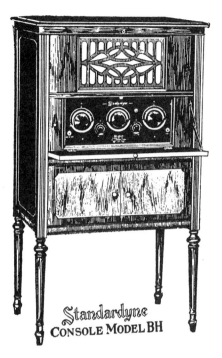

1925 Standardyne model BH; original price $135.00.

Wolper model RS5; slant-front radio in very deep case, with stepped-back enclosed speaker; mid-1920s. The radio is sitting on a separate table (Paul Johnson).

ora of smaller ones. The 400-meter stations were relatively safe from overcrowding, at least for a while.

But the Class A stations saw no improvement in their situation. In fact, since there was still virtually no regulation of the airwaves, the plight of the smaller stations was becoming worse than ever. This predicament encouraged them to wander off their given frequency in the hope that somehow or other they could be picked up more easily by the listener. Voluntary time sharing wasn't working out. The Commerce Department was forced to assign frequencies and allocate time in an effort to bring some order out of this, even though there was no certainty that the law specifically permitted these actions.

1925 Mohawk model A5. Some applied wood trim decorates this rather conventional slant-front cabinet; original price $115.00.

The WorkRite
CHUM
$75

1925 WorkRite Chum model; introduced in 1924.

$60 85
CABINET EXTRA

1925 Hammarlund Roberts.

Although regional stations were located over more of the broadcast band, there were still 86 stations operating at 360 meters in 1924. To spread these out, an arbitrary decision was made—stations operating at 500 watts or more were assigned to the regional sections of the band, while those of less power were lumped together in still more time-sharing plans.

An example of this involved station KMA of Shenandoah, Iowa, the station of the Earl May Seed Company. Earl May purchased a 500-watt Class B transmitter and went on the air in the fall of 1925. Although it had a large enough transmitter to qualify as a Class B station, it was assigned Class A status and ordered to share its frequency (252 meters) with Western Union College of Le Mars, Iowa. Western Union would be broadcasting only once a week, while KMA was permitted to be on the air an hour at noon, an hour in the evening, and two hours on Tuesday and Thursday evenings. Like so many other stations, KMA didn't stick to the letter of the law about these hours.

Shenandoah was a town with two major (although Class A) radio stations. The Henry Field Seed Company had beaten KMA to the punch and gotten on the air earlier with KFNF. Now the two friendly competitors were assigned the same channel (461 meters). Each station would broadcast for an hour or two, then go off the air to let the other one broadcast. The two stations looked around, found different little-used spots on the dial, and each began broadcasting at nonassigned frequencies.

It was inevitable that Congress would have to vote power to some organization to regulate radio stations. They established the Federal Radio Commission (FRC) in 1927. Herbert Hoover, then Secretary of Commerce, warned against channel jumping, citing (among others) KMA and KFNF of Shenandoah. The two stations decided that it was too risky to play around now and stayed at their newly assigned (in early 1927) weak frequency of 270 meters. With the situation in Washington, this didn't remain unchanged for long. In August 1927, KMA was offered a new frequency (740kc) if they would share it with a Shreveport, Louisiana, station.

This meant that KMA had four different frequency assignments in three years, and had shared time with a college station, a competing seed company station, and finally with a rabidly anti-FRC station in Louisiana. Unlike many others, KMA's story ended happily. They are still broadcasting today.

Networks

Network broadcasting started seriously in 1923. American Telephone and Telegraph (AT&T), which owned the telephone lines, began developing "chain broadcasting." Through experiments, they found that the normal telephone lines were not good enough for radio broadcasting. Special circuits would be needed, as would cable de-

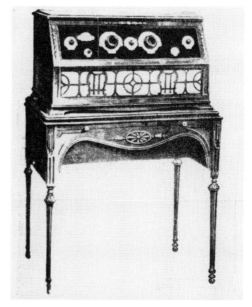

1925 Music Master model 215; spinet desk style; original price $215.00.

1925 Brunswick kit (no model information) sold by Radio Shack; original price $39.49 (kit without the fancy illustrated dial).

veloped for this purpose. On 31 July 1923, the first transcontinental hookup took place between San Francisco and New York to broadcast Warren Harding's speech on his return from Alaska. At this point, chain broadcasting was a monopoly of AT&T. They had a rate card (ranging from $150 per hour for Davenport, Iowa to $500 per hour for their flagship station, WEAF) that let the sponsor choose which cities he wished to cover with his advertising.

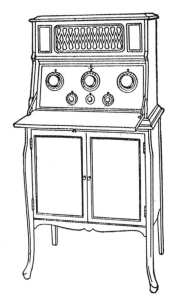

1925 Kodel model C-13; original price $28.00.

1925 Kodel model C-14; original price $32.50. The battery storage cabinet and horn speaker were extra.

1925 Fada; model 185/90A Neutrola Grand. The slant-front radio sits on a base with doors; enclosed speaker; original price $295.00.

1925 Kodel model C-11; original price $10.00.

As chain broadcasting developed for AT&T, other companies became interested. RCA, General Electric, and Westinghouse formed a new company, National Broadcasting Company, in 1926. This company bought out AT&T's stations and network broadcasting, as we know it today, began on 15 November 1926. This network, anchored by WEAF (New York), became NBC's "Red" Network. By the first of the new year, station WJZ (Newark) led the "Blue" network, the second NBC network.

A question always arises about how NBC named its networks. "Red" and "Blue" aren't the sort of names we expect. There are two different stories about how this took place, both of them plausible. According to one of them, radio engineers knew it wouldn't be good to send out a "Blue" network program on the "Red" network, so there had to be some way to keep these straight in the control room.

1925 Pfanstiehl model 10 Overtone; original price $155.00.

1926 Showers console model; gold-painted front; original cost $60.00. (Gene Harris Auctions).

The plugs on the patch cords were accordingly colored red or blue to aid in clarification. The other story says that this issue was decided even before the network was on the air. A group of NBC personnel, sitting on a train and trying to figure out what stations were being linked with either of the anchor stations, used a red pencil line for the one and a blue line for the other.

The Columbia Broadcasting System didn't start with the resources of three major communications companies behind it. Its original name was the Columbia Phonograph Broadcasting System, since the Columbia

1926 Westingale single-dial set; interesting design painted on the front panel; original price $57.00.

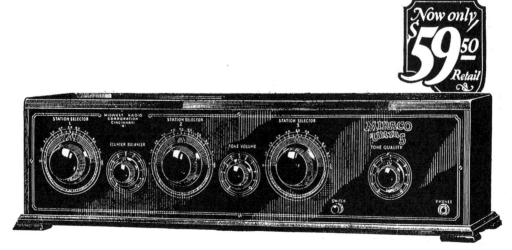

1925 Miraco Ultra 5.

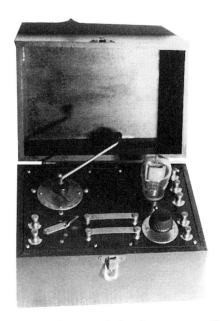

1926 Masterphone made by the Boston Radio Manufacturing Co. (John Wilson).

1926 MODEL

$60⁰⁰

1926 Somerset model 5.

A radio-clock to straighten out the confusion of time zones. It could be taken out of its cabinet and installed in the panel of the receiver.

Phonograph Record Company was the parent company. In the late 1920s phonograph companies had lots of money, but due to radio, faltering sales. It was logical to consider getting into the new action. The first CBS program was broadcast on 18 September 1927, but financial disaster soon loomed. The company owed AT&T $40,000 for rental of telephone lines and the Columbia Phonograph Record Company declined to put any more money into the network. Some fast footwork found enough money to keep the network afloat until it was refinanced in 1929. At that time William S. Paley became its president. For the

1928 Grebe Synchrophase Five; mahogany cabinet with mahogany Bakelite panel; original price $105.00 (less tubes).

1928 Grebe model Synchrophase A-C Six; mahogany cabinet with burled walnut panel; original price $197.50.

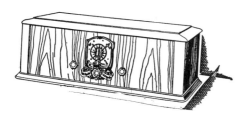

1929 A.C. Dayton Navigator model AC-98; walnut table with inlaid veneer top; original price $98.00.

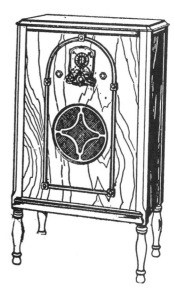

1929 A.C. Dayton Navigator model AC-9960; walnut lowboy; matte, not gloss, finish; original price $148.50.

1929 Sparton model Equasonne 301; ornate highboy; elaborate applied decoration on both the doors and the back panel; original price $274.00.

next five decades, CBS no longer had financial problems.

It wasn't until World War II that someone realized that NBC was actually two networks and was thus subject to anti-monopoly laws. Either the Red or the Blue network would have to be

1929 A.C. Dayton Navigator model AC-9970; wood lowboy with sliding doors; original price $165.00.

1929 Caswell PowerTone; a phonograph designed to be placed on top of a radio and blend in with it; original price $49.50.

sold. The Red network was NBC's most important one, with the best shows and strongest stations. Obviously, it would be the Blue that went. As the time for the sale came, the two networks divided up stations, equipment, and personnel. The Blue Network, its legal name at this time, was sold in 1943 and became the American Broadcasting Company.

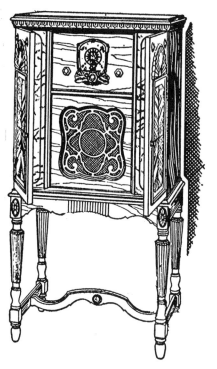

1929 A.C. Dayton Navigator model AC-9990; wood highboy with cabinet doors; original price $188.00.

$142^{50*}_{\text{Less Tubes}}$

1929 Stewart-Warner model 900; "Approved Jacobean cabinet No. 35." Cabinet was made by Louis Hanson Co. (Chicago) or Burnham Phonograph Corp. (Los Angeles); original price $142.50 with cabinet.

1929 Fada model 35-B; original price $255.00.

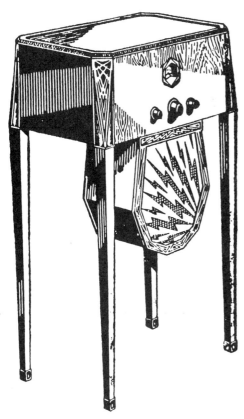

1929 Crosley model 34-S; original price $116.00–126.00.

1929 Crosley model 31-S; original price $56.50–$65.85. Legs were an additional $5.00.

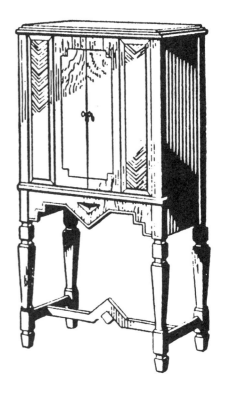

1929 Crosley model 82-S; original price $160.00 (less tubes).

1929 Crosley model 33-S; walnut veneer; original price $112.00 (less tubes).

1929 Colonial model 32 Cavalier AC; original price $268.00.

CHAPTER 4

FITTING IN AND LOOKING GOOD

A radio is not only a technical gadget, it's something the owner has to live with every day. One of the problems that early battery sets had was their looks. There was no truly satisfactory way to decorate a long, narrow box that required either a table, another box, or some floor space to stash the necessary batteries. Adding to the decorating worries was a good-sized horn speaker that stood on top of the radio or next to it.

Making the radio fit in with the rest of the living room was important. In a room already crowded with things, the cumbersome radio was a lot to cope with. As late as the 1920s, most people were still influenced by the Victorian front parlor, wherein every square inch of table and wall space was occupied. This crowding left rooms with a feeling of clutter.

SPEAKERS

Very early on, attempts made to improve the radio's looks often focused on the speakers, which were the most noticeable part of the radio. Early speakers were horn speakers, using the technology that had gone into phonograph horns. (By the way, the same problems of decorating affected the phonographs; people were delighted to get enclosed horns and not have to cope with that external one.) The first magnetic cone speakers were produced around 1923, but it wasn't until 1927 that more cone speakers were sold than horn speakers.[3] It was hard to get around the fact that most horn speakers looked exactly like a horn—curved, perhaps, but still with a narrow neck and a large bell. Ordinary cone speakers resembled a bowl-shaped piece of heavy paper standing on edge and held in a metal ring. Sometimes the cone speaker was enclosed in some sort of a metal box that, round or square, looked remarkably like everyone else's metal box.

[3]The best authority on horn and cone speakers is Floyd Paul. Much of the information in this section came from ads he has accumulated, as well as articles he has written. His book is listed in the section entitled Further Reading.

1922 Magnavox horn speaker, type R-3.

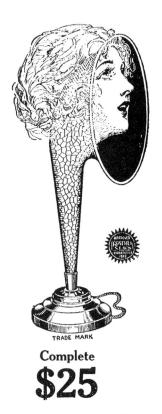

TRADE MARK

Complete

$25

Atlas Radio-Reproduction Loud Speaker.

An attractive horn speaker was harder to design than a cone speaker. Attempts were made to either glamorize the horn or to hide it. Probably the easiest way of hiding it was to build it into a speaker table. Now the horn was hidden in a long, narrow table, and there was enough space on the top of the table to place the radio itself. However, the speaker table was never as popular as the radio table. They look similar, the difference being that a speaker table incorporates the speaker into the table, while a radio table holds the batteries on a shelf under the table. Until batteries disappeared, it was more important to find a place for them than to hide the speaker. The physical design of a horn speaker (long neck and large bell) also created prob-

lems for anyone trying to design a table around it. Probably this is why there are few speaker tables shown for horn speakers.

Another design possibility was to stop trying to hide the shape and, instead, turn it into an asset. Take the horn, straighten its neck, cover the bell with a grille and grille cloth, and place it on the floor. Immediately it becomes a decorative column, 40 inches or so high, which might fit into the decor of a room better than a plain horn.

Victorians had always been in love with seashells. In England, where trips to the sea were a recognized holiday even for working people, the over-crowded parlor often housed a seashell as a souvenir from the beach. This

Amplion Dragon horn speaker model AR-19. A classic of speaker design, the horn is made of wooden sections; original price $42.50.

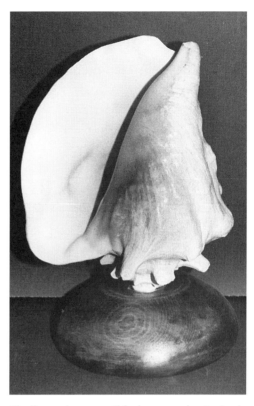

Shell speaker, possibly homemade. A single Brandes headphone is glued in the bottom.

wasn't as true in the U.S., where the distance to the beach from much of the country made trips there impractical. Thanks to innovation, it was possible to display a decorative seashell that also housed a speaker. Some of these speakers were installed in real conch shells. Because nature doesn't create shells to measure, the advertisements indicated size ranges (12 to 13 inches, for instance). There certainly would have been something striking about a mounted shell that stood 16 inches tall.

Perhaps the family wanted a more modern, less naturalistic shell and did not want to spend money on a loudspeaker. Sheltone (the name certainly explained its product) made a smooth-looking shell out of Pyralin (a Dupont celluloid) that saved the purchaser

money, because he or she never had to buy a speaker at all. The Sheltone simply amplified the sound that came through the headphones of a set. Put the headphones in the correct location, and the shell shape did the rest.

If natural shells weren't formal enough, and plastic shells appeared a little cheap, Florentine Art Productions made a fantastic, artistic shell out of "Italian gesso." Gesso is something like papier-mache, is made with plaster instead of ground paper, and molds beautifully. These characteristics of gesso allowed Florentine to come up with the "Voice from the Sky"—a Grecian figure with flowing robes standing in front of a shell-shaped

1922 Madera horn speaker made from papier-mâché by the American Art Mache Co.; original price $25.00.

Radialamp speaker. It used the "lamp base" and the shade to create a horn speaker. This strategy neatly hid an eyesore, since horn speakers tended to dominate a room.

horn. Available in walnut, mahogany, or ebony, this artistic figure would certainly have been the focal point in any room—after all, it stood 24 inches high.

Another great way to hide a horn speaker was in a speaker lamp. Designed to look like normal table lamps, many of them actually could be used as lamps, while others were simply speakers. The speaker lamps were designed to fit with many different decorating styles. Most commonly, they had heavy fringe around the edge of the shade, making them suitable for the Victorian front parlor. At least one company (Bel-Canto) made a speaker that would have fit well into a mission-style room. Others were typical 1920s lamps. A floor model version was the

1928 Sterling Vari-tone speaker model R-2; original price $25.00.

1928 Sterling cone speaker; original price $75.00.

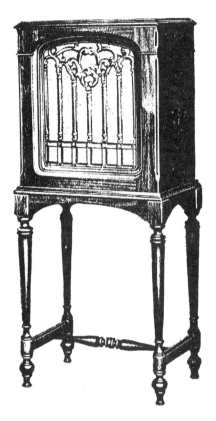

1928 Sterling speaker; floor model; original price $90.00.

Speak-O-Lamp. It had an 11-inch-deep shade, either hand-painted or silk-covered. Still another model, known as the "DeLuxe," had a silk-pleated shade over a double silk-lined shade, trimmed with lace to match. But hiding your speaker did cost money; the "DeLuxe" model was $65.00.

Cone speakers were not as difficult to place in an average living room. Although they took up space, they were relatively shallow. Because of that, companies didn't seem to spend as much time trying to hide the fact that a speaker was there. They spent more effort using the cone shape for decorative purposes.

There were still speaker tables. A cone speaker could be easily attached with screws to a hole in the front of a speaker table. The grille and grille cloth made the speaker less noticeable. It also gave a place on which to put the radio and, since tables could be found to harmonize with most living room styles, it kept the radio from overpowering the room.

Otherwise, most of the decoration involved the cone itself or the metal framework surrounding the cone. At its simplest, it meant painting some sort of design (a Greek key, for instance, or a fleur-de-lis) around the edge of the convex cone. Sometimes the decorations were more elaborate, such as the silhouette of a young woman with a branch or a painting of a full-rigged ship.

Ships gradually replaced shells as a major decorating theme. The full-rigged ship was more often seen cast with the metal frame of the speaker than painted on the cone. Tower, Vitalitone, and Timmons all used sailing ships. The ship sails across space with the speaker cone as background.

1927 Zenith model 11; walnut veneer; original price $110.00 (courtesy Zenith Radio Corp.).

Because a cone speaker is relatively flat, it is possible to hang it on the wall, something that could never be done with a horn speaker. It also meant that a very large cone could be used.

The eventual solution to the decorating problem was to enclose the speaker in the same cabinet as the radio. When this happened, visible speakers disappeared until the advent of high fidelity in the late 1940s.

RADIOS

The earliest radios were table models. They were utilitarian-looking sets, with lots of knobs and dials housed in a long wooden box. They were nothing too terrible, but nothing very glamorous either. Sets eventually became more simple, one-dial tuning

came in, and tube voltages didn't need to be reset, but the cabinet remained the same. It was inevitable that someone would step into the gap and design a set to appeal to the women in the family.

In 1928 *Radio Retailing* pointed out the advantages of having the customer buy a good cabinet. For one thing, everything could now fit inside. The cabinets were being made of good wood (walnut, mahogany, oak, and gumwood) and were well constructed. The workmanship could be as good as that of conventional furniture, and hand carving was possible. Cabinets could harmonize with whatever style the homemaker had. Last but not least, customers could put $200 to $500 into a cabinet, knowing that a replacement radio could always go inside the

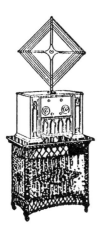

Wicker radio table. The batteries were hidden behind the solid wicker panel.

Radio table. Note the batteries in a drawer that opens from the front.

same cabinet. (This view changed rapidly. In 1930, after the stock market crash, manufacturers predicted that separate cabinets and speakers were no longer going to be strong sellers.)

Cabinets were generally being made by companies other than the radio manufacturer. For example, Atwater Kent made its first console set, the model 52, in 1928. Previously they had manufactured wood or metal table models. If an early Atwater Kent shows up at an auction in a fancy wood cabinet, the first thought may be that someone is trying to pull a fast deal, but this isn't necessarily true. Even though the company itself wasn't producing furniture, other companies were. They were even designing their cabinets to fit particular models of the Atwater Kent. In 1928, there were a number of ads in *Radio Retailing* in which Red Lion, Pooley, Bay View, and others advertised that their cabinets were designed to house the Atwater Kent. In fact, Red Lion advertised itself as "the authorized furniture for all Atwater Kent radios." Other

1928 model 820. Grebe sold this impressive cabinet to fit any of their radios; original price $97.00 (console only).

1928 Grebe power amplifier table; shown with the Grebe Synchrophase A-C Six; original price $227.00 (without tubes or radio set).

1928 Grebe speaker table model 2250; shown with the Grebe Synchrophase Seven A-C; original price $24.50 (table only, no speaker or radio).

cabinets were produced for sets of different manufacturers who were still making only table radios. Certain cabinet manufacturers created cabinets that, even today, aid in selling a radio. A Pooley cabinet, for instance, is often mentioned in ads.

The cabinet most prominently mentioned in this era was the Kiel table. The Kiel table was six-legged and six-sided. It usually housed an Atwater Kent (either model 55 or 60) in the front skirt of the table, although it could handle other brands as well. The radio was hidden behind a door; when the door dropped down, the radio controls were within easy reach. The speaker was inside the table, pointed down toward the floor, and gave a smooth, non-directional sound.

The left rear leg housed the antenna and the ground wires, while the right rear leg housed the power cord. The ads truthfully said, "No unsightly wires." With a marquetry design in the hexagonal top, these tables are still attractive pieces of furniture.

Many companies had decided by this time to sell their radios in their own cabinets. Various elaborate cabinets were designed. Splitdorf had marketed one of their radios in 1928 in a model called "The Winthrop," a corner secretary including a desk, radio, and bookcase, and retailing for $600. Sparton had highboys that not only had applied pressed-wood trim on the

Left to right: 1936 Zenith chairside, model Portola, manufactured by United Air Cleaners for Zenith; 1931 model 64, original price $370.00; 1930 model 40A, original price $850.00 (notice push button tuning to right of dial on these two models); 1929 model 60, original price $145.00 (courtesy Zenith Radio Corp.).

doors covering the cabinet, but also a panel down the back to the floor, also with pressed-wood trim.

Radio as furniture was disappearing in late 1929. The first of the midget sets (midget by the standards of the day) were arriving. Cathedrals were coming into style. Now that everyone had a radio, there wasn't the necessity to have the set be a showpiece. The neighbors weren't being invited in any more; they had their own sets. The Depression meant that the radio became a workhorse and was no longer a stylish thoroughbred. Utility was more important than looks.

These fine cabinets from the 1920s didn't disappear. People didn't throw a good cabinet like that away. The radio was used until it broke, and then the cabinet was saved. Sometimes it was saved in a barn, where the moisture and mice didn't do it any good. With luck, it stayed in the house. Often it was converted into a bookcase or a bar or a desk. So often at auctions now, one of these radio cabinets shows up, but minus a radio.

THE 1930S— A DECADE OF CHANGE

Radio began as a novelty. It was the "techies" of the 1920s who put sets together from parts, sat around wearing headphones, fiddled with several knobs to get the station tuned in, and were willing to spend one hundred dollars or more to have the fun of listening to a station miles away. Fortunately, radio developed quickly into what would now be considered a "user-friendly" operation.

There were many reasons why radio became so popular in the 1930s. For one thing, people became comfortable with it. They didn't need to know how it operated. Anyone could go to a store, buy a set, bring it home, plug it in, tune it with only one knob, and sit back to hear favorite programs. The radio was now simple enough for anyone to use.

Radios were available at many different stores, making it easy to buy one as an impulse purchase. They also came in a large variety of styles. Table mod-

els, floor models, in wood or plastic, with curved or straight lines—there was something for everyone.

Programming was now nationally transmitted and received. Not everyone could receive all of the programming, of course, but by using special telephone lines, the broadcasts were brought to stations in many parts of the country. If you visited a large city, you could expect to hear the same network programs you heard at home.

The networks used the AM band. Radios, however, often came with shortwave and police bands. Shortwave let you listen to foreign countries, and the police band kept you in touch with your own town (much like a scanner does today).

At first glance it doesn't make sense, but lack of money was another reason radio became popular. With little money to spend for entertainment during the Depression, people were careful how they used it. A family go-

Tatro. Cabinet model is CR-557, which may or may not be the radio model. An extremely plain lowboy, c. 1930.

1930 General Electric. The model is actually called "Lowboy." Because it's wider than the normal lowboy, it looks quite impressive.

ing to a movie would have a good time, but, afterwards, there was nothing to show for it. If they bought a radio instead, the entire family could enjoy listening to it for years to come.

Development of new tubes and plastic cabinets meant that radios became smaller. These developments lowered the cost of radios. A single radio could be carried from room to room in the house, keeping the housewife company in the kitchen during the day and entertaining the family in the living room after supper.

By the end of the decade, radio became so much a part of daily life that it was taken everywhere. There were portables for a picnic and car radios to entertain while driving there.

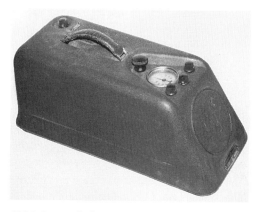

1934 General Electric auto radio model B-52; operates at both 6 volts and 110 volts; brown crackle finish metal. This radio could be placed on the front seat; the dial would face the driver.

WHERE TO BUY THAT RADIO

During the 1930s, radio sales changed. When radio became popular in the 1920s, prominent department stores established radio sales departments; many stores even had their own broadcasting stations. These departments were impressive, and the radios they sold were expensive. Other people went to the local radio shop for ever-necessary batteries. The owner would try to sell the right set to each customer, since he would be the person who heard the complaints and did the repairs when things went wrong.

As the demand for radios increased further, large chain stores began selling radios. Not only did they sell various makes of radios, they sold their own brands as well. These were not manufactured by the retailer, but were bought from a manufacturer with the store's house brand nameplate on the front. Montgomery Ward had Airline, Sears Roebuck had Silvertone, Firestone had Airchief, Western Auto had Truetone, Spiegel's had Aircastle, Gamble's had Coronado, and Coast to Coast stores had Musicaire as house brands. The consumer found it easier to buy a radio while doing general shopping. People were already in these stores, so many sets were probably impulse purchases. A respectable small table set from Wards in 1941 cost only $7.49. With easy credit terms, a person with little money could buy a $50 radio for only $5 a month. The small weekly or monthly payment made it easier to own a good radio.

The small radio shop had to change if it wanted to stay in business. Small retailers couldn't match the prices that the chain stores offered. Large stores got a better discount from the manufacturer and had a larger variety of sets than that little corner store. In addition, a small store would have problems handling credit sales, which would tie up too much of the owner's already-short supply of cash. Even the retailer in a small town wasn't safe. He had to look around for ways to make money, since Wards and Sears were as close as the local post office. In order to survive, many small radio shops phased out radio sales and offered radio repair as their primary occupation. It might be cheaper to buy a radio at a big store or through the mail, but getting it fixed was better done close to home.

THE NEW LOOK IN THE FAMILY RADIO

Now the family had decided it needed a radio. But what should they buy? Obviously, the wooden-box radios of the 1920s were outdated. Consoles of that time were big wooden boxes placed on their ends with turned legs holding them up. Doors were added and fancy "carving" was done on their fronts to make them look less like boxes. The radio of the 1920s was a featured piece of furniture in the living room; but it still was a box. Table radios were smaller boxes (although still large by our standards), with several knobs on the front. They were larger if they housed batteries, or, if they were AC like the RCA Radiolas, they were very heavy. They certainly couldn't be carried from room to room easily.

These styles might have continued

1930 Sentinel model 15. "Gothic design, superbly ornamented;" original price $137.50 (less tubes).

1930 Stewart-Warner, St. James model; solid walnut front "with artistic genuine carving;" original price $197.50 (less tubes).

MODEL 11

well into the 1930s if it hadn't been for the Exposition Internationale des Arts Decoratifs et Industriels Modernes in 1925, commonly, although incorrectly, thought to be the start of the Art Deco period. The asymmetrical curves of Art Nouveau styling—the acanthus leaves and flowing draperies—now were out of style. Art Deco stressed symmetry with angular and tubular shapes.

Although the exposition did not really mark the start of Art Deco (it

1930 Sentinel model 11; deco style; original price $130.00 (less tubes).

1930 Gloritone model 27. Gloritone took a totally different approach to building cathedral radios. Strong angles were used instead of pointed arches. There is another version of this model with rope-like trim (John Wilson).

1937 Grunow model 1183; wood console with telephone dial; original price $149.95.

had been developing for several years), it did focus attention on the style and made it internationally known. It featured artists and craftspeople who made unique items or ones with small production runs. Such works were not suitable for mass production, and, since they also were expensive, were not readily marketable to the Depression-strapped masses.

The exposition did create a new image, however. "Modern" was the thing. Various styles were derived from Art Deco and applied to mass-produced items. In the United States, for example, skyscrapers and streamliners were the style-setters. These de-

signs were strongly influenced by Art Deco.

Radio cabinets followed this American interpretation of Art Deco. Both consoles and table models used the stacked look of skyscrapers. The Arvin Rhythm King 1127 is an example of the skyscraper influence. (For a picture of the Rhythm King, see *Flick of the Switch*, pg. 58.)

Much more common was the streamliner motif. Streamliners were trains designed with aerodynamic concerns in mind. From the locomotive to the last car, train designers used smooth curves and avoided sharp angles. Radio cabinets, both console and table, fol-

1930 Crosley New Buddy. The front is rep-wood, a type of molded wood (Ed and Irene Ripley).

1932 General Motors model 252. A sliding door pulls up to cover the dials when not in use. It's an unusual radio because the speaker faces out the bottom of the set.

lowed this design. Large, rounded curves replaced the front corners of the cabinets. Rounded shoulders, with a much smaller radius curve, replaced the top edges. The most "streamlined" of all was the waterfall front, where the top curved down into the front in one large, sweeping curve. None of this would have been possible without the use of plywood. The cabinet frame could be built of mismatched pieces of solid wood; with the top surface covered by a thin layer of good plywood, however, it looked like a radio of high quality. These pieces also held up well, since there were no sharp corners to get chipped and pitted.

The Modern-style radio didn't replace the large box of the 1920s quickly. The two styles overlapped for several years. Until 1933 or so, both styles were being produced. As the decade continued, Modern triumphed.

There was more variety in table radios than in consoles. Table radios were less expensive, and it wasn't necessary to buy a radio that would last for years and look important during that time. Table radios featured many short-lived styles. There was the "tombstone," which originally was a high table radio with rounded corners. Now the term has come to refer to any tall, vertical table radio. (The Philco 70B is a tombstone radio.) The most common radio from the 1930s is the horizontal table radio; this shape was carried over from the 1920s, but curves and smoothness were added while its size became smaller. Cathedral radios were popular for three years (1931-1933), with or without a sharp

1930 Philco model 20B; one of the traditional Philco cathedrals (Ed and Irene Ripley).

1932 Crosley model 125; cathedral radio (Ed and Irene Ripley).

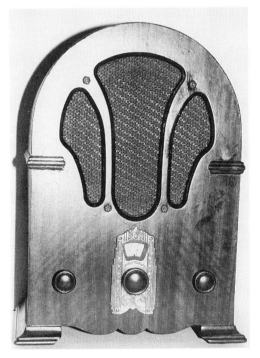

1931 RCA model R5, the "Radiolette;" cathedral style (Ed and Irene Ripley).

point at the top of the arch. These were made of wood or plywood, but even more modern and different were the plastic radios that arrived in quantity in the mid-1930s.

It is important for radio collectors to know the difference between plastics such as Bakelite and Catalin, the two major plastics used in radio cabinets. In today's market, Bakelite radios tend to be inexpensive, while Catalin radios are always expensive. The difference in the prices makes it essential to know something about these plastics.

Bakelite, a thermosetting phenolic resin, is the trademark of the Bakelite Corporation (now a part of Union-Carbide). A thermosetting resin is heat-hardened; application of heat to the plastic forms its final shape. Because of this, high temperatures don't bother it. Bakelite radios could

1933 Philco model 81; a simple cathedral (Ed and Irene Ripley).

1938 Emerson model BA-199; brown Bakelite.

1933 Philco model 16B. The cathedral arch has disappeared, leaving only a slightly pointed top. This set is almost a console, with 11 tubes and a 10″ speaker.

be manufactured successfully only in brown or black. If a Bakelite radio is colored (often ivory), it is by paint applied to the original dark cabinet. Other manufacturers made a Bakelite-type plastic that tends to be lumped together under the Bakelite name.

While other heat-set plastics also were used in the manufacture of radios, these are not Bakelite and don't resemble it at all. Two of them are found in radio cabinets.

Urea is a thermoset plastic that has the advantage that it can be colored. When colors are mixed in the plastic, they create swirled or mottled effects. Unlike Bakelite, however, urea does not stand up well under use. Urea cabinets today often will be found with warps or cracks.

Styrene plastic is another heat-set plastic, but it does not use the same procedure as Bakelite. In styrene's case, the heat to set the plastic comes from a reaction in the compound itself. Instead of being thermoset, styrene's process is "endothermic." Styrene was stable, could be colored in just about any imaginable way, and was inexpensive to make. It became the plastic of choice in the late 1950s and 1960s. It handled color beautifully, so bright red or orange radios could be made. Extremely colorful swirl designs were possible. Styrene's only major fault is that it scratches easily.

The other type of plastics used in radios were cast phenolic resins. Instead of needing heat to set up the plastic, it was simply poured into molds and allowed to harden. Catalin was the king of radio cabinet plastics. It took wonderful colors and had a depth like alabaster. It also was expensive to make, because a lot of hand labor was required to finish it for use. It was used only for a short period before and after World War II and thus is rare as well as beautiful. Catalin changes color with time. The butterscotch color so popular today really began as an off-ivory. Catalin sets are lovely to look at and expensive to buy. Even the simplest and most common sets sell for hundreds of dollars today.

Plastics changed the look of radios. Wooden radios needed a square frame which really held the shell together. Even the curved radios from the 1930s are basically rectangles with curves added. Plastics could stand alone. Plastic radios could have fanciful curves, compound curves, and narrow louvers covering the radio grille. If a mold could be designed, the radio could have that shape.

Plastics also meant that radios no longer had to be brown. They could harmonize or contrast with the color scheme of any room. Although the common Bakelite color was brown or black, other models of the same radio

1939 Sentinel model 195ULT. This is a butterscotch Catalin radio with burgundy trim. Pushbuttons are on the top on the right side.

could be painted any color. Since styrene and Catalin mixed the color into the plastic, they allowed even more variations.

NETWORKS AND BROADCASTING[4]

Networks were the dominant force in broadcasting during the Depression. They created national exposure for their performers and made national advertising a fact of life. By the 1930s, there were two dominant networks: CBS and NBC. NBC actually had two networks, the prestigious Red and the Blue. Attempts to start competing networks, in the most part, failed. Since CBS and NBC had the high-powered stations in the large cities, there wasn't much left over for the others. Of the competitors, Mutual Broadcasting

[4]For a truly interesting, in-depth, and well-written account of the networks' battle, read Erik Barnouw's *The Golden Web: A History of Broadcasting in the United States 1933-1953* (Oxford Press, 1968).

System was the only national network to survive. Regional networks were started, but most of them were nothing more than outlets for regional sponsors and were no real competition to the big two.

Until the mid 1930s, NBC had been the major network. It was the first one, it had money, and it captured the primary classical musicians and the foremost vaudeville stars; because of this, it also got the largest corporations as sponsors. William Paley at CBS wasn't satisfied to be second-best. Paley began by attacking the NBC method of distributing its programs to its stations. NBC sold its nonsponsored programs to the local stations (irritating the smaller stations who didn't have a lot of money to spare) and paid stations to carry its sponsored programs (making the large stations unhappy because they weren't getting enough money for the programs). Paley allowed the CBS affiliates to carry all of its programs free with a proviso that CBS could, with notice, preempt local programs for a network presentation. With this, CBS gained effectual control over prime-time broadcasting on its stations. The local stations weren't unhappy. When CBS had a sponsored broadcast, the local station would receive a percentage of the advertising rate, and it didn't have to do anything extra for the money. By 1935, both networks could claim to be first: CBS had more stations, but NBC had greater wattage.

The major networks broadcast comedy, drama, variety shows, educational and cultural programs, children's shows, sports, news—much the same mix that TV uses today.

There were both stand-up comedi-

ans and sitcoms. Jack Benny could deliver a monologue that would nearly convulse listeners. His vaunted miserliness, his Maxwell, the continuing jokes with Rochester, and his everlasting thirty-ninth birthday made families chuckle, laugh and howl. *Fibber McGee and Molly* was a classic sitcom, the same characters doing the same things every week, but somehow it was funny. Fibber's closet (which always was stuffed to overflowing and would naturally spill out noisily whenever he opened the door) was a joke everyone understood. *Amos 'n' Andy* were visitors in innumerable homes, with the whole family sitting around and listening to their blackface humor.

Soap operas were the afternoon version of drama. The continuing saga of someone who had more problems than the listener was relaxing to people who were fighting the problems of the Depression. *Life Can Be Beautiful* was everyone's hope. *Ma Perkins* and *David Harum* and *Our Gal Sunday* were a regular part of the daytime schedule for many housewives. (Soap operas got their name, naturally, from the number of soap companies sponsoring them.)

Detective stories, suspenseful dramas, and westerns were evening and Sunday staples. *The Shadow* had "the mysterious power to cloud men's minds." *The Lone Ranger* rode out of a West that never was, along with his "faithful Indian companion, Tonto." Together they brought law and order to the West, and a great feeling of familiarity when, at the end of the show, someone would say, "Who is that masked man?" We all knew it was the Lone Ranger.

Plays were popular. *Lux Radio Theater* and *Screen Guild Theater* were well-done promotions for current Hollywood films. The drama most people think of from the 1930s, however, was the 1938 broadcast of *War of the Worlds*. Orson Welles and the Mercury Theater produced this frightening tale of an alien invasion of the United States. It was more frightening than the book, since it sounded like a "live" broadcast. People trusted the radio; if they missed the opening announcement, they had no idea that what was being broadcast was not a real event happening at that time. People were already nervous about the war in Europe. An invasion in New Jersey and Washington, D.C., was too close for comfort. The show was an excellent drama, so well-conceived and presented that it panicked much of the country.

Variety shows had their roots in vaudeville. Music and jokes were intermixed on these shows, with Kate Smith, Rudy Vallee, and George Jessel headlining.

Networks also broadcast educational and cultural shows on a weekly basis. CBS and NBC were in a battle for first place. When CBS moved ahead, NBC started "covering" the CBS shows. If CBS had a poetry show (*Norman Corwin's Words Without Music*), NBC would have to have one, too (*Fables in Verse*). When CBS had the New York Philharmonic Orchestra, NBC came up with the idea of having its own orchestra, with Arturo Toscanini conducting. *The American School of the Air* got competition from *University of the Air*. Not only were both networks producing competing shows, they were broadcasting them at the same time. However, the listener had many opportunities to learn from leaders in a particular field and enjoy cultural events not available in small towns.

Children's programs, usually fifteen minutes long, featured the ongoing stories of Jack Armstrong, Captain Midnight, Little Orphan Annie, Roy Rogers, and others. They were there by the dozens and loved by millions of kids. Local programming of children's material was common as well. But the network shows had adventures and prizes you could send for, and these shows usually became the ones that people remembered when they grew up.

News broadcasting in the early 1930s was practically nonexistent. NBC Red (the leading network) didn't have a single daily news broadcast. NBC Blue had commentator Lowell Thomas. CBS had occasional commentaries from H.V. Kaltenborn (and couldn't find a sponsor for them.) Bad news was not supposed to be broadcast. WLW, a 500,000-watt station that covered the Midwest, had a policy that no mention of strikes, including school strikes or walkouts, would be made. Afraid of alienating sponsors, the networks and stations left news reporting in the hands of the press.

In 1933, this changed. NBC started a one-man news department that gathered news using a telephone. Local NBC affiliates were expected to let the network know if something newsworthy happened in their city. CBS took up the challenge. They developed a news department, primarily of "stringers," that was so good that newspapers began boycotting the network. Eventually the networks promised the news services that they would limit their newscasts to two five-minute newscasts a day, both scheduled after people would have read the morning or evening editions of the local papers. They also promised to report only news at least twelve hours old.

Naturally, competition to the network news services, designed to be used by local radio stations, followed. Local stations began broadcasting news using Transradio. Corporate sponsors appeared, and the agreement fell apart when UP (United Press) and INS (International News Service) started making their news services available to radio.

TECHNOLOGY KEEPS IMPROVING

During the 1930s, technology advanced to make radios more useful and more powerful. They were easier to use, smaller, and the quality per-dollar was much higher. Radio tubes were the primary reason for these striking changes. Tube design had improved rapidly. New tubes were developed for special purposes, such as the oscillator-mixer tube in the superheterodyne. When several tasks were built into one tube, it meant that one tube could take the place of two. Surprisingly, the shrinking of the radio didn't worsen the quality; thanks to better tubes, the whole operation improved.

The quality of the loudspeakers also improved greatly as designs improved. The dynamic speaker (cone and voice coil) was more efficient and gave a smoother sound and wider range than the horn speakers of the 1920s. This is the same basic design used today in radios and stereo systems.

Finally, the superheterodyne became the exclusive receiver design. It was easy to tune, received many stations, and didn't drift once it locked on a station. This also is the same basic circuit that is used today.

Other improvements contributed to ease of use and sound quality. Green tuning eyes became popular in the later 1930s. Although it only took one knob to tune in a station, it might be difficult to get the clearest sound. The tuning eye helped locate a station accurately. When the green light came together and formed a circle, the station was at its clearest. People who grew up with radios during the 1930s still remember the fun of tuning in the eye.

Push-button tuning made it easy to find often-used stations. Today it's often possible to find the original location of one of these radios by what local stations are set on the push buttons. Sound quality could be adjusted using tone controls. Multi-band sets with several shortwave bands and a police band opened new worlds to the radio user. Combining phonographs and radios into the same cabinet gave another dimension to the entertainment value of the radio.

Portables and Car Radios

As improvements in design and tubes made radio better, they also moved radio out of the home and onto the beach and into the car. In the mid 1930s, car radios became so common that automakers began designing space for them in the dashboard. Previously they were loaded onto the running board, along with their cumbersome batteries. The dash-mounted radio didn't require separate batteries; they would be powered by the car battery.

By the end of the 1930s, portable radios were becoming popular. They carried their own batteries, and the better models could pick up shortwave stations. The basis for this popularity was the newly designed tubes. These became so efficient that radios could operate with batteries small enough to fit inside the set itself, while the set was still light enough to be carried easily. Some very small personal portables weighed only a pound or two. By 1940, the larger portables would run on batteries or could be plugged into a wall.

The Depression made radio an important part of any home. They were an affordable luxury. It was possible to get a 1932 Wards Airline table radio for $24.95. A large console was $72.50. (For comparison: by 1950, a small superheterodyne cost $9.95 from Sears. For that, you got a better radio than you would have gotten even ten years earlier, and it cost less.) The radio became a center around which the family gathered. Networks supplied

General Motors portable; late 1930s; called a "plug in portable." The middle control switches from AC to battery operation.

programs that would entertain an entire family, whether it was comedy or music. There was enough cultural programming to justify the expense to some people.

The Depression helped radio become a major component of family life. If it weren't for the Depression, people would have gone off in separate directions, as cars were readily available. As it was, the family stayed home and listened to the same programs, laughed at the same jokes, enjoyed the same bands. Radio became indispensable to most American families during the 1930s.

CHAPTER 6

AFTER 1940— CHANGE AND GROWTH

During the mid 1930s it seemed that everything that could have been done to improve radio had been done. Radios were economical, popular, and better than ever. Even before World War II, however, it became apparent that radio wasn't stagnant. Frequency Modulation (FM) was in its infancy, although no one knew how important it would become. Television was just becoming available. The war gave a push toward the development of better communications technology.

THE RADIO

Radios just prior to World War II and immediately after the war looked very similar. During the war there were not enough radios available to satisfy consumers. The manufacturers had little time to worry about consumer interests. They spent the war producing equipment for the armed forces, although by 1944, with the end of the war in sight, companies were beginning to advertise that radios soon would be available. Hence, radios for the home showed little change during this period. Their cabinets were similar to the prewar models; even the insides hadn't changed much. This wasn't a time for redesigning. In 1946, the goal was to get radios out to consumers as quickly as possible. People were delighted to buy a new radio to replace the one that had been around since 1940 or before. People bought radios whether or not they were stylish or modern. If they looked like the ones from 1940, no one complained. They were new and they worked.

Within the cabinet, however, things had improved. While working with the military during the war, manufacturers improved tubes and other parts. Very High Frequency (VHF) and Ultra High Frequency (UHF) radio was more efficient. Tubes were designed that worked at high frequencies.

This Philmore crystal set was highly popular.

High frequencies led to the invention of new circuits and the development of better-designed insulators, resistors, capacitors, and inductors. This engineering applied directly to the new fields of FM and television.

Military communications engineers perfected VHF; it was more secure than conventional AM radio, and it provided greater protection from enemy eavesdropping because of the way the signal traveled. Large amounts of radio band space became available with wartime radio research and design, and it was practical to use it. Much of this development came in the realm of Frequency Modulation (FM) instead of the normal radio Amplitude Modulation (AM).

It's important to know the difference between AM and FM. AM uses a transmission technique that varies the power of the high frequency RF carrier wave at different rates. The rate of variation of the power is the pitch of the sound. The amount of variation is the loudness. It is easy to get rid of the RF carrier wave, leaving only the sound of varying volume. This system uses little band space (space on the dial), so well over a hundred stations fit into the standard broadcast band of 550 kHz to 1600 kHz. Until recently, AM did not provide high-quality sound. It was easily disturbed by storms, electric motors, and other interference, resulting in buzzes, whistles, and static that made it hard to hear a station.

The search for a better system led Edwin Armstrong to develop FM. Here the frequency of the RF carrier varies at a rate equal to the pitch of the sound; the amount of variation reflects the loudness of the sound. This discovery resulted in many advantages. The sound quality was much better than AM, it had three times the audible range of AM radio, and there was almost no interference or background noise.

There were also disadvantages. First, FM didn't travel nearly as far as AM, going only 40 to 50 miles as opposed to the 1000 miles of AM. Second, it took a lot of RF frequency band space. The standard broadcast band had space for more than 100 AM stations. Five FM stations would fill that same amount of space.

Armstrong ended up in a battle

A selection of Philmore crystal sets from the World War II era (John Wilson).

1940 RCA Victor model 45X11; brown Bakelite (Ed and Irene Ripley).

BAKELITE MODEL

Novel midget crystal radio with self-contained earphone. Very neat and compact. Complete set is housed in polished mahogany-color bakelite cabinet of modernistic streamlined design. Earphone fits conveniently into compartment in case. Average range is about 25 miles. Has extremely sensitive fixed crystal; one tuning knob controls reception. Weighs only 5 ounces; measures but 4x2½x 1⅝". Supplied complete with earphone, aerial wire, and full instructions. Wt., 2 lbs. **$1.62**
B9314. NET......

This set from 1941 is designed to look like a modern small plastic radio. It comes from a 1941 Allied Radio catalog.

1940 Stewart-Warner model 0751H (Ed and Irene Ripley).

1942 General Electric model JCP-562. Cabinet has been refinished.

1941 General Electric model L-916; large console with pushbuttons; AM/2SW.

with David Sarnoff of RCA when he felt that RCA was neglecting FM for the more glamorous television. Without the active support of a major manufacturer, FM was still something of an experiment. There were only a few stations in the East (primarily in New York City) broadcasting in early 1939. When more license applications arrived than available space, the Federal Communications Commission (FCC) realized that it was necessary to rework the broadcast bands. There really was a channel 1 on television before this happened. In 1939, channel 1 was taken away from TV and given to prewar FM (42-50 MHz). There wasn't much growth in FM listening during the war, however. FM couldn't get more listeners when people could not buy a radio that would pick it up.

With development of radio during the war, band space was opened up and technology improved. In 1945, broadcasting space was revised. FM got a new bandwidth (88-108 MHz), where there would be space for an amazing one hundred stations. One hundred stations shouldn't be a problem; since FM could only travel small distances, this seemed like all the space it would ever need. (This new band could have handled 20,000 of the old-style AM stations.) Several radios right after the war came with space on the dial for both the old and the new FM bands.

FM still had problems after the war. There were few sets. The FCC permitted identical broadcasting on both AM and FM, which eliminated innovative programming as a reason to buy the new-style radio. But the quality of FM broadcasting was so superior to AM that people began buying the sets. Around 1950, FM/AM radios became the standard, and sets with only the AM band became the inexpensive ones.

At the same time that FM was becoming strong, the high-fidelity boom began. Hi-fi made quality sound some-

This large 1931 calendar advertises Majestic radios.

Cookie jar and salt and pepper shakers are styled like an RCA 65X1 radio.

Kennedy model 63 cathedral radio.

Little Wonder and Little Radio Mike (toy microphones attached to radios).

This radio is styled after a 1928 Lincoln Town Car.

Weston DC voltmeter from 1930 (radio testing equipment).

A collection of novelty radios, featuring a gas pump, Snoopy, ladies' shoe, and the Dukes of Hazzard.

Santa Bear lunch box and radio, a Dayton-Hudson company promotion.

Coke bottle radio with box, and Coke dispenser radio.

Frankoma advertising ashtray and a mug advertising a radio shop.

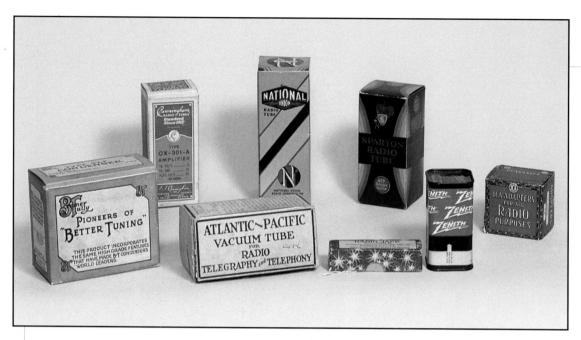

Collection of like-new
old radio parts in original
boxes, with tuning
condenser, tubes, and
other small parts.

Fleischmann's Gin bottle and
Malibu Rum bottle radios.

Champion spark plug radio.

This "Soundmobile" Volkswagen van will play an LP record by driving in circles.

Advertising pieces. Back row: Permoflux (loudspeaker) ashtray, Atwater Kent playing card deck, and Newsette radio that receives only WTMJ from Milwaukee. Front row: Emerson radio bank, Philco Medallion, Sears WLS sharpening stone, and a Zenith logo for counter display.

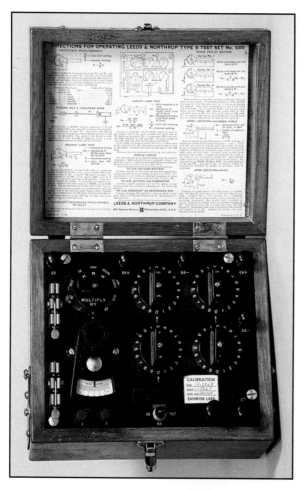

Leeds & Northrup test bridge (radio testing equipment).

1942 Philco model 42-KR3; white painted wood radio.

thing most anyone could afford. FM tuners became part of a hi-fi system. But hi-fi is really another story.

Television was also around before the war, but it took the technical improvements from the war years to make it practical for home use. TV uses high-frequency RF bands, and the modern FM band is now tucked into the middle of the TV space. That's why television antennas make good FM antennas as well.

The next big change in radio technology was a quaint little device invented in Bell Telephone Laboratories in 1948 called the "transistor." This had the promise of doing most of the

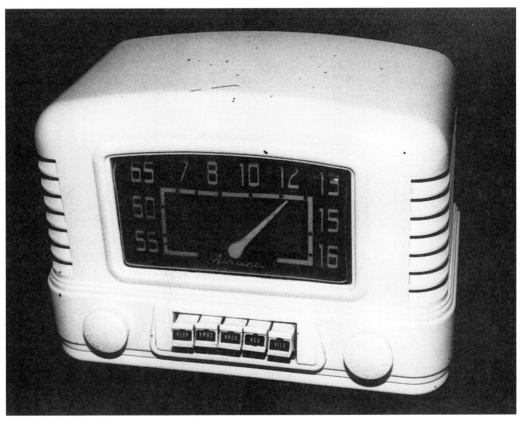

1946 Airline model 54BR-1506A. The dramatic dial makes this ivory Bakelite radio stand out (Ed and Irene Ripley).

things a tube could do, while using less than 1/100th of the power and at a fraction of the tube's size. More powerful and smaller transistors made possible the pocket radio.

By the end of the 1950s, the transistor was fast replacing the tube in most electronic equipment. In time, it came to do everything a tube could do and do it better.

Styles didn't change much during the 1940s. Those that were around in the late 1930s were still around in the late 1940s. Wood table radios became less attractive. Plastics appeared in a blaze of color and became more popular. Catalin and styrene plastics made an unlimited variety of colors and shapes possible. Many plastic radios in the late 1940s were based on the striking models designed before the war. There was a strong similarity between the two eras. Shortly before the war consoles had become large, long pieces of furniture with a phonograph side by side with the radio instead of beneath it. After the war, this became the common style. Several companies even had elaborate consoles that included a television set built into the same cabinet. E. H. Scott produced some truly monumental consoles.

THE PROGRAMS

Programming was much the same before and after the war, continuing with the same mix of serious programs and lighthearted entertainment.

There was one exception: the news. With the threat of World War II, people bought and used shortwave sets. Shortwave allowed Americans to get the distressing news from Europe

1946 Zenith model 6D029; one of the most unusual shapes found for a dial (John Wilson).

at the same time as the Europeans. We could also worry along with Europeans on the status of the war.

Network news reporting in the early 1930s had been a farce. As the decade progressed, the networks became interested in having news departments. War and rumors of war caused the networks to expand their European news staffs. News coming out of much of Europe was censored, but Americans wanted to hear it anyway. Reporters were no longer anonymous voices. Eric Severeid, William L. Shirer, Charles Collingwood, and Lowell Thomas were names and voices everyone knew. But the one reporter who made the most impact was Edward R. Murrow. Broadcasting directly from the rooftops of London during a blitz, he gave the nation a close-up glimpse of what war was really about. The war was in our living rooms and our lives even before we joined it.

All broadcasting during the war reflected America's total involvement in the war. The music portrayed the loneliness of those in the service and the concern and love of those on this side

1946 Air King model 4604-D; AM/SW. Reverse painting on dial is flaking off. Watch out for this when buying a set.

of the ocean. Even the comedies were colored strongly by the war effort.

The war, and the years following it, changed broadcasting. There were now three different networks instead of two. NBC, which had the Blue and the Red networks, was required to sell one of them. After negotiations, NBC Blue was sold in 1943 and became the American Broadcasting Company. Red was dropped from the NBC name.

Television was gaining new viewers. Shows that had been on radio were making the switch to TV, leaving gaps in the radio schedule that had to be filled. Canned music and the disc jockey became important, and radio tended to become a background to whatever people were doing. When they wanted to pay attention, they watched TV.

Public radio—that is, noncommercial radio—grew in importance. Back in the 1920s colleges, universities, and even churches owned their own stations. As the in-fighting continued in the late 1920s, many of these institutions gave up their stations. But some of them held on. WCAL, in Northfield, Minnesota, was a small station affiliated with a small Lutheran college. After the war it became one of Minnesota's earliest FM stations and a founding member of National Public Radio (NPR). KSJN, a similar station in Collegeville, Minnesota, became a founder of Minnesota Public Radio. College and university programming generally was more cultural and educational than what was available on commercial stations. College courses, some-

1947 Emerson model 547A (Ed & Irene Ripley).

1948 Emerson model 541.

1948 Arvin model 358T; beige plastic (Ed and Irene Ripley).

1949 Stewart Warner model C51T1; ivory Bakelite with blue dial (Ed and Irene Ripley).

1949 RCA model 8-X-71; brown Bakelite.

times with credit, were offered to people who couldn't attend classes.

During the 1950s public radio became important. Many states developed their own public radio networks, which tended to broadcast on FM. Wisconsin, one of the first, developed a network that eventually covered the entire state. Living in the boondocks didn't mean that you had to give up good listening.

The public radio movement reached its height when National Public Radio became almost a nationwide network. Excellence in news and commentary continue to be its greatest strengths. Today there are also a number of smaller networks providing specialized programming to public stations all over the country. One example dedicates itself to news of native Americans and their concerns. Small noncommercial stations, unaffiliated with NPR, produce special-interest broadcasting for their listeners. WOJB in Reserve, Wisconsin, a station on the Lac Court Oreilles Indian Reservation, broadcasts Native American news and powwows, as well as many programs from NPR and some entertaining local programming.

Radio also changed as big entertainment moved to television. It became more of a traveling companion to Americans on the move. Their radios became smaller as transistors became affordable, making it easy to take radio with you. But that, too, is another story.

WHEN WAS THAT RADIO MADE?

he best way to date a radio is, of course, to know the model number of the particular set. With this information, it is moderately easy to come up with an approximate date. Through the use of service manuals, instruction books, and advertisements in magazines, a given radio can *usually* be dated within one year. The qualification in that sentence covers those exceptions that inevitably occur. Some companies reused the same model number for totally unrelated radios two or three times over a period of years. Here a general idea of the age of the set helps immensely. Some brands or models never seem to have made it into the service manuals, which eliminates one of the better sources, so the only thing possible is a rough dating. Advertisements were built around specific, highly salable radios, and ignored the vast majority of run-of-the-mill sets.

But, all things being equal, these sources should permit dating of the vast majority of radios.

Trying to make a rough guess is more difficult. Like anything else for the house, designs came and went, overlapped each other, and always tried to be new and different. In spite of this, it is possible to come up with some general guidelines. Why is this important? In the case of a model number showing up several times during a company's production, it makes it easier for anyone fixing the radio to find the service information. Someone may describe to you a radio they want to sell. Knowing how to roughly date the radio from a verbal description saves unnecessary trips to see unsuitable radios. At an auction, a clever buyer can sometimes pick up a good buy simply by having a better understanding of how old, and possibly how valuable in general, a certain radio may be. In none of these cases is an exact figure essential—a good ballpark figure gives a solid place to start.

The following rough dates for various styles are exactly that—rough. They make no claims to accuracy. All rough dating must take into account that eras overlapped. Battery sets were finished by the 1940s, but some were

1934 Powertone sold by Reliable Radio Co., New York; original price $9.95 (4 tube); $12.95 (5-tube). (Both prices without tubes.)

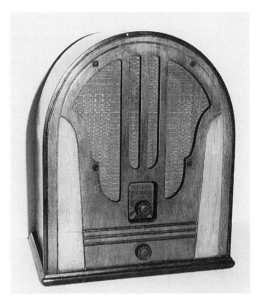

1934 Philco model 84B. The later cathedrals tended to modify the pointed arch (Ed and Irene Ripley).

1934 Grunow model 750.

1934 Reliable Treasure Chest model sold by Reliable Radio Co., New York; original price $9.50 (less tubes).

made into the 1950s. Highboys went out around 1932, but someone didn't tell RCA. They made one model in 1934. Nothing is cut and dried. Practically every style started before there was a demand for it and lasted until after most people had switched to something different.

Regardless of the style or its popu-

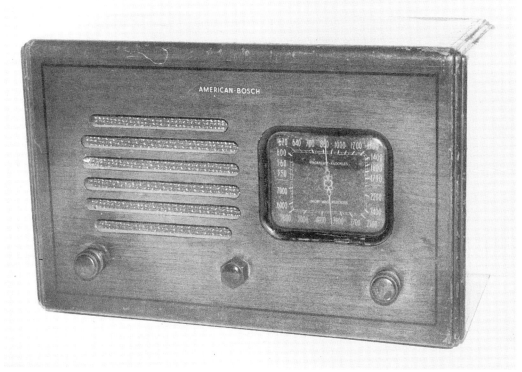

1935 American Bosch model 604. Note that the center knob is not original.

larity, people eventually became tired with it. Change is different and exciting and has always been a factor in the radio industry.

DIALS

Multi-dial sets. These were common from the beginning of radio until 1927. In all but one-tube sets, two or more dials were necessary to adequately tune in the radio. Generally there were three dials for tuning in the station and two knobs, one that controlled the detector filament while the second controlled the filaments of other tubes. The tuning scale wasn't marked with the 550 to 1600 kc we use today. Instead there was a linear scale (0 to 100) on each dial. All of the dials would be set at approximately the same place, but not exactly. For instance, one dial might be at 20, the second at 22, and the third at 18. To avoid the nuisance of fiddling with all the dials each time the station was tuned in, and trying to remember where exactly each was set, a log book was kept with the radio. In it the listener noted the numbers where the station had come in, and started with those the next time. It still might require a little more tinkering to come up with a clear station, but at least he was close when he started. (By the way, some early radios still have their logbooks. Whether used or unused, these are a plus when buying a set.)

One-dial tuning. One-dial tuning came onto the scene around 1925. There was an overlap of several years

1935 Crosley model 555; AM/SW.

St. Regis miniature cathedral; no model identification; no year known.

Garod model 769; AM/SW; pushbutton; mid-1930s.

from this feature's arrival to the time when multi-dial tuning was out. One-dial tuning simplified radio, making it possible to tune in a station by ear. Remembering the station location using one number was much easier than keeping three numbers straight.

Airplane dial. The airplane dial appeared about 1934. This feature was reminiscent of airplane instruments, with a round dial housing a pointer that went around in a circle. The de-

sign was still around after World War II. Zenith made a design statement out of the airplane dial by making theirs very large (dominating the entire front of the set) and coloring it black. Big Zeniths are easily recognized by this feature. If big and round was stylish, then the new style would have to be very different. It was.

Slide-rule dial. The slide-rule dial became popular around 1938. This dial is a long rectangle with the pointer moving straight across the scale to mark the stations. The slide rule dial is still found on stereo systems today.

Telephone-dial tuning. In 1936 telephone-dial tuning was developed. Put a finger in the hole, just like on a telephone dial, and turn it until it stopped; the station would then be tuned in. It seemed much more up-to-date than turning a knob and watching a pointer move. It was replaced quickly with easier to use push buttons.

1935 Coronado model 686; 3-band.

1935 American Bosch (paper label is missing). This unique set was sold by the German American Bund to raise money for the 1936 Berlin Olympics.

GEC model 8336; made by General Electric Co. (England), c. 1936.

FLOOR MODELS

Floor models have gone through several styles. There was the highboy of the 1920s, the lowboy of the 1920s and 1930s, and the to-the-floor con-

1936 RCA model 13K; 4-band console.

1936 Zenith model 6B129; a 6-volt farm radio.

1936 Crosley model 167; cathedral radio (Ed and Irene Ripley).

1936 Grunow model 1291, chassis 12B; tele-dial; 12-tube, 4-band (Gene Harris Auctions).

1936 Airline model 62-425; wood table model with decorative grille (Ed and Irene Ripley).

1936 General Electric model E-52.

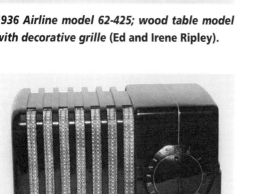

1936 Silvertone model 4500; black Bakelite; first plastic radio offered by Sears (Ed and Irene Ripley).

1937 Wells-Gardner model 108A1-704; wood table with telephone dial.

1937 Clarion model 691; wood table with telephone dial; original price $49.95.

sole of the 1930s and 1940s. Another striking style was the long, horizontal console of the 1940s. There were variations to each of these major styles.

Highboy. The height of popularity for this style was 1927 to 1932. The highboy is, by definition, a radio on legs where the legs are approximately one-half the height of the radio. (This is not what the term means in the antique furniture field. As with many terms, manu-

1937 Troy model 100; wood table with telephone dial; original price $32.50.

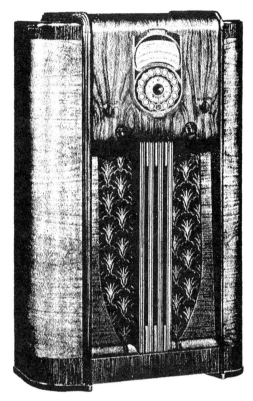

1937 Fairbanks-Morse model 9AC-4; wood console with automatic tuning; original price $105.00.

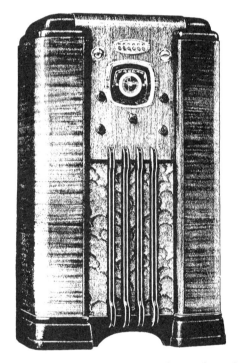

1937 Sparton model 1068; wood console with push-button tuning.

facturers took it to mean what they wanted it to mean. There was no industry standard defining a highboy.) Highboy radios usually had four legs. It wasn't until it looked like radio was here to stay, and particularly after AC radios became common and found a place in the living room, that people began putting money into an attractive cabinet, rather than into the radio itself.

Lowboy. This style began at approximately the same time as the highboy. These two styles were the first of the nontable, floor-model styles to become popular. The lowboy continued in popularity longer than the highboy, lasting until about 1934 (although sets were built like this until the end of the 1930s). The lowboy by definition has legs that are anywhere from 6 inches high to half the height of the cabinet, with four or more legs. Many lowboys

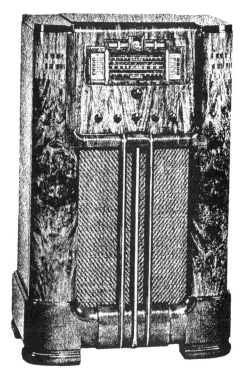

1937 RCA-Victor model 811K; wood console with automatic tuning; original price $150.00.

1937 Motorola model 10Y; wood console; original price $99.95.

had six legs, and there is at least one model (Stewart-Warner, model 51) that had five. The vast majority of early floor model radios will be lowboys. They won't all look alike, since the proportions of the cabinet to the leg height can be very different.

Highboy or lowboy with doors. These styles were popular from 1927 to 1931. Doors to hide the radio were popular at the beginning of the radio era, just as they were with early television sets, when many sets came with doors to close off the screen from the room. Later, when the sets became commonplace, no one felt they had to hide them. The same appears to be true of radios.

Console. What we consider the floor model or console became popular around 1932 and continued to be in vogue through the 1940s. The console has sides that go to the floor, or it has feet less than 4 inches high. The word "console" in the 1920s could refer to all floor radios in general but, by the end of the 1930s, it had come to mean this style. Because of World War II, when all radio building for the home ended, these radios stayed around until nearly 1950.

Console radio-phonograph. These were popular from just before World War II (approximately 1938) to 1942. The phonograph was built into a console radio, either rolling out to play or, more usually, tipping out.

1937 Stromberg-Carlson model 249-R; fancy, unusual, semicircular Deco design; original price $197.50.

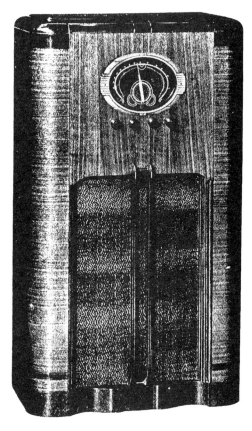

1937 Belmont model 840; all wave, with tuning eye included in dial design; wood console.

Remember that this phonograph will be a 78-rpm record changer only. If it's a three-speed changer, either the changer has been replaced or the radio was made in 1948 or after.

Phonographs had been built into radios since the 1920s. They appeared in highboys, lowboys, and some massive affairs that seem to defy mere words to describe them. However, unlike the radio-phonograph consoles of the late 1930s, they never were a dominant style. If one of them shows up, date it by its cabinet style.

Horizontal radio-phonograph console. Although the horizontal style was around from before World War II, it became important after the war. These radio-phonographs had the phonograph side-by-side with the radio, making them as wide as or wider than they were high. They came in all sorts of styles to harmonize with the living room. Virtually the same arrangement could fit into a blond modern living room or a Chippendale room. All it took was a change of wood color and trim.

Chairside. The chairside, popular from 1936-1941, started with Philco

1938 Philco model 38-7.

1938 Zenith chairside model 7-S-240; walnut finish, large black dial; 3-band (courtesy Zenith Radio Corp.).

in 1933 and gained renown quickly. By the middle of the 1930s, the chairside was an important style, with the dial right in the table, making changing a program exceptionally easy to do. This style is defined by its function (chairside) rather than its looks. The chairside came in rectangular shapes, as well as oval and semi-circular ones. Bookshelves or magazine storage was often built into the chairside cabinet.

TABLE RADIOS

It all began with table radios and, long after television has become dominant, it is table radios that we still use today. They have lasted this long because of their immense practicality.

Slant-front wood table radios.

1937 Clarion model 770; AM/SW; wood table; original price $19.99.

The slant-front table radio, popular from 1924 to 1926, was an attempt to dress-up the original plain wooden table radio. Looking at pictures of the early sets, it isn't surprising that they needed to be glamorized. There was nothing exciting about the cabinets of most of the sets. They were sensible wood boxes

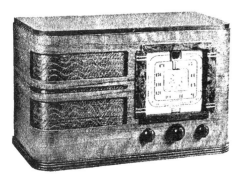

1937 RCA model 87-T; AM/SW; wood table; original price $49.95.

1939 Firestone Air Chief model S-7403-4; small wood radio with angled wood grille.

1937 Freed-Eisemann model FE-28; wood table; AM/SW; original price $29.95.

designed to hold the necessary apparatus to permit radio listening. In a slant-front set, the panel (of Bakelite, Formica, or the like) was angled back from the front of the set instead of being set in vertically, creating a more dressy look. (Philco revived this style for both large table and console models in the 1940s. Again, the general style of the radio itself will clearly show that it is from the 1940s, not the 1920s.)

Metal table radios. Metal table radios appeared in two different eras: 1926 to 1928, and 1940 to 1948. The earliest ones were the bright idea of

Atwater Kent. He was fascinated by the new steelmaking technology, and he couldn't see why it shouldn't be adapted for radios. Metal radios made a clear statement that radio was Modern, a technology come of age. It had a real benefit, as well, in providing electrical shielding to the set, which permitted it to work better. The cabinet was simply a metal box in which the radio chassis was placed and fitted with a metal cover. The finish was often brown crinkled paint. Atwater Kent, Crosley, RCA, and Philco all produced metal sets. The style only lasted for three to four years.

In 1928, for one year only, Philco decorated its plain metal sets with hand-painted floral designs to appeal to women. Their ad stated they "are offered in a variety of hand-decorated, softly modulated, two-tone effects... which (are) enhanced with color effects by Mlle. Messaros, one of the foremost colorists in the decorative arts. The colors are applied *by hand* under her personal direction."

The later metal table radios (from the 1930s and 1940s) were midget

1939 Arvin model 502. This radio is in a metal cabinet that looks very much like the plastic cabinets of 1939.

1937 Philco cathedral model 37-93. By this time, cathedrals had become much simpler. The peak was gone, and so was much of the wood trim (Arie Breed).

sets, usually inexpensive, always small, and in appearance like normal radios. They are very similar to the small plastic sets of the same period. Where the earlier metal sets had removable tops to permit servicing the radio chassis, the later ones slid the chassis in through an open back.

Wood midget set. From 1930 onward, wood midget sets were available. These sets were shaped like a normal horizontal table radio. They became popular because their timing was right. The first ones were manufactured just before the Depression. When money became tight, the midget sets continued to sell well, while sales of the large, impressive sets sagged. In 1931, midgets were still considered as stopgaps by the larger manufacturers. Predictions were made that "midget radios will never replace the console receiver as the major radio installation." As time went on, midgets became smaller and smaller. Midget sets from 1930 would seem to be very large table radios to people in

the late 1950s. Usually the sets were varnished or lacquered, although some of them were painted. (These radios are considered traditional and inexpensive by people over fifty. Under fifty, the traditional set would probably be a plastic table radio.)

Cathedral radio. The cathedral style came onto the scene around 1930 to 1934—just before the Depression wiped out the market for more prestigious sets. They weren't expensive at the time, and as such could substitute for the more-expensive lowboy. They were certainly more impressive than the plain wood table radios. Because they stayed popular for many years, there were style modifications. Some versions had very pointed, Gothic arches; others had rounded arches

1939 Firestone model S-7403-8; AM/2SW.

1937 Zenith model 6S229; AM/2SW.

where the basic proportions (height to width) remained the same as the pointed arch models; and there were models where the curve of the top was completely removed and straight lines were substituted. The almost square (height equals width), rounded-top beehive (1933) is usually included in this last category. In all cases, there was a lot of overlapping of substyles. The manufacturers, by the way, never referred to them as "cathedrals," but instead called them "Gothic."

Cathedrals not only looked impressive, but they also could sound that way. In some of the large cathedrals, such as the Philco 90B, the same radio chassis was used as in the large consoles.

Upright wood table radio. Upright wood table radios appeared between 1933 and 1940. Taller than they are wide, these, too, include many substyles. Rounded-corner tomb-

stones, stacked-top Deco sets, even cathedrals would fit into this classification. The emphasis was on the Modern look of an upright table radio as contrasted with the Gothic look of the cathedral. By World War II, the upright wood table radio had been replaced in turn by the conventional horizontal wood and plastic table radios. Once money was freer than during the Depression; anybody who wanted to buy an impressive radio bought a console instead.

Table radio-phonograph. Starting about 1938 and lasting until 1950, these large square boxes held both a 78-rpm phonograph and a radio. After 1948, they might have a two- or three-speed changer instead of a single-speed 78-rpm one. They usually had wood cabinets but occasionally were housed in Bakelite. They were designed to go into a living room or a recreation room and look nice, while not taking up valuable floor space. High-fidelity systems eventually replaced these sets.

Plastic table radios. Plastic table radios have been around since 1931. Plastic was still a novelty when first used in radios. Although plastics had been around for 50 years, to date they hadn't

1941 Zenith model 5F134; farm (6-volt) set; AM/3SW bands.

1939 Zenith model 6D414; brown Bakelite; inverted Bakelite chassis.

1939 Belmont model 636; brown Bakelite.

been usable for radio sets. The earliest plastics (celluloid, for instance) would soften and melt when hot. This wouldn't do for a radio, in which the tubes produced much heat. The advent of thermoset plastics (Bakelite, Catalin, and urea) was a boon for radios. These plastics, unlike some others, won't soften or melt in heat. Even leaving them on the back shelf of a car on a 100-degree day won't faze them. Once set, the plastic retains its shape until it is hot enough to simply burn, and it takes a bonfire to get that much heat. Plastics became the set of choice for a number of reasons. First, molding a cabinet of plastic is cheaper than the manual work of gluing a cabinet together and putting a finish on it. Second, the particular properties of thermoset plastics meant that the heat buildup inside a tube set

was no longer a problem. Third, because various plastics could be used in making radios, many colors could actually be molded into the radio. These colors may alter with age, but they won't chip off the way paint does. (Remember, though, that Bakelite radios in light colors are painted, and have all the same problems with chipping that a wood cabinet would have.)

STYLING DETAILS

Sometimes it is the little things that help to date a set. So often a cabinet

1938 Howard model 368; 3-band.

1939 General Electric model HJ-624; pushbutton.

1938 RCA model 86T; 3-band; curved wood.

1939 Majestic model 1A-59.

1939 Stewart Warner model 03-5C1-WT.

1939 Zenith portable; chassis no. 5416; battery only.

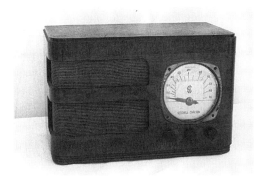

1939 Setchell Carlson model 588.

style lasted over most of a decade or more. But many of the styling details were around only briefly. This makes dating a set relatively easy.

Pressed-wood fronts. Pressed-wood fronts were available in 1933-1934. Crosley loved using pressed-wood fronts on its table radios. This gave a lot of detail and interest to an otherwise plain set. This had been done earlier, in the 1920s, when additions of carved or pressed-wood moldings had made highboys and lowboys more expensive looking. But rarely had the pressed-wood design dominated the set as it did with Crosley's.

1939 Firestone Air Chief model R-3051; 2-band **(David Tuttle).**

1940 Philco model 40-120. The handle is for convenience only. This is not a battery radio.

1940 Philco model 40-155; 3-band table radio.

1940 RCA Radiola 520; maple finish (Ed and Irene Ripley).

Continental model 1000; striking lines; c. World War II (Ed and Irene Ripley).

Deco. From 1933 to World War II, the Art Deco style was popular. This was inspired by the Chicago World's Fair (1933-1934), with reinforcement of the style found at the New York World's Fair (1939-1940). The style had started in Europe with an exhibition in 1925, but the Chicago World's Fair popularized it in the U.S. While the style didn't dominate radio design of this period, it made an impressive statement. Deco radios reflected the spirit of the Deco movement. They could be angular cathedrals, stacked-top upright radios, or radios with wrap-around modern grilles. They were found in both plastic and wood. Radio design relied much on fronts curved boldly into one or both sides, emphatic vertical or horizontal straight lines, and strong contrasts of color (chrome against dark wood, two-tone plastic, two-tone wood). For a short period, strongly designed chrome grilles were used. Probably the best adjective to describe the Deco style is *bold*.

Chrome-plated grille. Chrome-plated grilles, available in 1934, primarily were popular for one year. This extremely Deco-styled detail seems to have been inspired by the Chicago World's Fair.

Mirror radios. Another short-lived (1935-1936) Deco fad, mirror

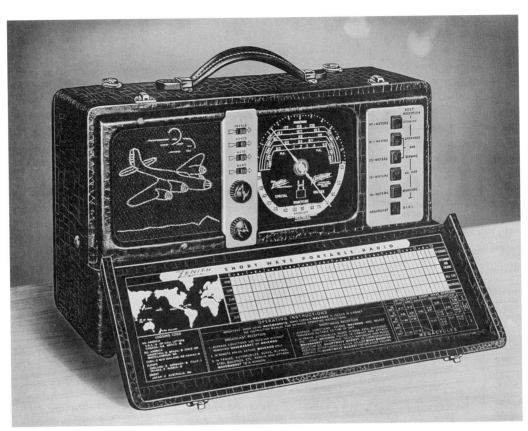

1940-41 Zenith Trans-Oceanic portable model 7-G-605; black leatherette (courtesy Zenith Radio Corp.).

1940 Philco Transitone model PT33; brown Bakelite (Ed and Irene Ripley).

Airline; c. 1940; made by Belmont (Ed and Irene Ripley).

Airline; no model identification on this radio—the paper label generally found has disappeared. c. 1940 (John Wilson).

1941 Airline model 62-476; available in both white and brown Bakelite; complete with both a tuning eye and a telephone dial. There are leaves embossed on the top, and pillars on the sides (Ed and Irene Ripley).

1940 Motorola model 41A; brown Bakelite. Grille looks like an auto's; 1½ and 90 volts. This particular radio was given a battery eliminator sometime in its past.

1941 Airline model 14WG-806A. Curving the grille out from the front of the radio adds design interest.

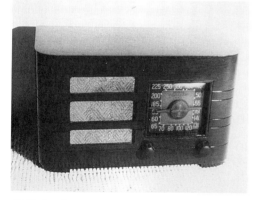

1941 Crosley, probably model 52-TG (label is partially gone); (John Wilson).

1941 Zenith model 6R631; tone controls on left, station pushbuttons on right.

1941 Admiral model 4204-B6; interesting lyre-shape grille.

1941 Emerson portable model FU-427.

1941 Zenith portable model 6G-601-M; cloth-covered.

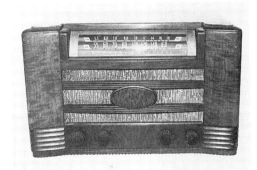

1942 General Electric model L-641; AM/SW (John Wilson).

1941 Airline model 14BR-522A; white plastic radio with simple lines.

1942 Philco model 42-321 (John Wilson).

1942 Philco model 42-350. The large curves give it a heavy modern look.

1946 Farnsworth model ET-067. The distinctive feature of this wood radio is the grooves on the top of the case. The log scale on the dial gives the impression that this set has more than just the broadcast band.

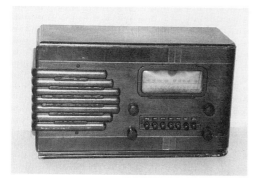

Musicaire (model unknown), straightforward wood table radio with interesting grille; probably made around World War II (pre- or postwar).

radios ranged from mirrors basically screwed on to flat panels to the highly collectible Sparton "Bluebird" and "Nocturne," where the radio was of secondary importance to a large round mirror. In the 1930s colored mirrors were popular, and many of these radios came with blue or peach mirrors. Although Sparton was the best-known company producing mirrored radios, there were many other companies as well.

Green tuning eyes. Green tuning eyes were featured on radios from 1935 until World War II. The round eye was found on middle-and higher-priced radios; in fact, it was almost a standard feature on these radios. The more exactly the station was tuned in, the closer the green lights came to touching each other. For many people, this is the single feature they remember from the sets they grew up with.

CHAPTER

8

BUYING THAT SPECIAL RADIO

nyone hunting for a radio wants two things—the perfect radio and the lowest possible price.

Fortunately for collectors, not everyone considers the same radio as "perfect." One person wants a bread-board, whose price is already high, while another wants a console, which is still relatively low priced. Sometimes, however, everyone wants the same set. At present, this is happening to Catalin radios, and their prices have skyrock-eted. Several years ago, you could get them for $5 to $10; they were consid-ered cheap, plastic radios. Now they are hard to find at any price.

Everyone wants to find and pur-chase that special radio inexpensively. Here are some hints on where to look for radios and what sort of prices you may have to pay. (Remember, the prices in the price guide are based on radios in working condition sold in the retail market.)

WHERE TO LOOK

Your neighbor. Most often these radios will have come out of the attic or basement, and the owner considers

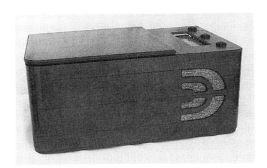

1946 Puritan radio-phonograph model 503.

1946 RCA model 65X1.

1946 Philco radio-phonograph model 46-1201. Record is placed in drawer in bottom.

1946 Westinghouse model H-130.

1946 Den Chum made by Wilmak, model W-446. Although it would appear that the top radio is the earlier model, this isn't true. The knobs on the bottom radio have detents and only tune the stations that are preset on the bottom of the radio.

1946 Arvin model 544 (Ed and Irene Ripley).

1946 Silvertone model 07025; brown Bakelite; Deco.

them surplus. Because you know the owner, there is a good chance that the price will be low. The condition of the cabinet may be only fair, but if it doesn't cost much, it may be a good deal anyway. Up to a point, the same goes for the electronics. If the insides look too terrible (extensive mouse nests or wires that don't go anywhere), it may not be a good buy at any price.

1946 General Electric model 321.

1946 Musicaire model 576. Some people claim it looks like a miniature console, others think it resembles a jukebox. Sold by Coast-to-Coast Stores, same model as the Detrola model 576-1-6A.

1946 Trav-Ler model 5066; brown plastic (Ed and Irene Ripley).

Garage Sales/Yard Sales. The biggest problem with trying to find things cheaply at garage sales is that there is a wide variety of sellers. They range from people who are trying to clean out things they don't want and just hope to pick up some extra cash to the person who is a professional dealer in everything but name. Some garage sales feature prices similar to those found in antiques shops.

It may take many visits to garage sales to find the right radio. Many won't have any radios; others will consider theirs almost priceless. Some people swear by shopping at these sales, while others swear at the time they've spent with few results.

One smart idea is to concentrate your garage sale trip into a logical route, through older neighborhoods. Most young couples won't have moved radios into an already-crowded starter home. Read the local newspaper ads to find out who's having garage sales and where. Spotting the most common days for sales saves time and gas. Near a city, driving around and watching for those cardboard signs nailed to light posts will lead you to many sales, even some you might have missed in the paper.

Auctions. There is no way to predict prices realized at an auction. The

1946 Artone model R-1046-U; white painted Bakelite with aqua dial; identical to an Olympic model.

1946 Crosley, cabinet marked 63TJWC; label missing—probably model 66TC; "Victory" model.

National Radio Institute model 7AN2. Kit was probably built as part of a home radio course. Cabinet is homemade (John Wilson).

1946 Motorola portable model HS7; cloth-covered.

prices depend on so many things: how many people come, whether there is another auction that is draining off many of the bidders, the weather, and how long it looks like it will take to get to the things you want.

At an auction, find out what guarantees are given by the auctioneer. If you can't talk to the auctioneer, ask the clerk. Some auctions guarantee an electrical item to be working. If you plug it in and it doesn't work, you can imme-diately bring it back to be resold. Before you do this, however, check the line cord. *If it's in bad condition, do not plug it in.* Assume that you're going to have to replace the cord before you do anything else. Auctioneers often say that the radio was working before the sale. "Working," in their parlance, means that there was sound coming

1946 Temple model F616; wood table.

1946 Monitor; no model number; almost a "generic" radio—no identifying characteristics; date approximate.

1946 Electromatic radio-phonograph; model 512; wood cabinet; one of two models the company made.

from the set. This does not mean that the radio actually picks up stations, or it may mean that it picks up only the strongest local station. Don't count on more than that.

Radio Swap Meets. If you live near a medium-size city, there is a good chance that there is a local radio club. These clubs run swap meets/ parking lot sales periodically. Because the members of the club are often tinkerers, you may find the radios are not working. The sellers will tell you this, and often give you hints for repairing

the radio. Many times the radios are duplicate sets, so the seller has little ego tied up in them. Therefore the prices are often reasonable.

There are two practical methods for finding a radio club. One is to contact the public library in your city. Libraries usually have a list of local organizations. With luck, a radio club will be listed. The other method is to write the Antique Wireless Association, Inc. (Holcomb, NY 14469) to find what clubs are nearby and a current address for you to contact.

Flea Markets. Flea markets can be a good source for radios. If there are many dealers, there's a good chance that someone will have brought along several old radios. Prices will generally be higher than garage sales, because the dealer has an idea of what his merchandise is worth. There is some leeway on prices, however. Attempting to get a better price is well worth trying. If the dealer says "no," you're no worse off then if you hadn't tried. If the price can be substantially lowered, you'll be happy. Flea market dealers like bargaining. A good idea is to make

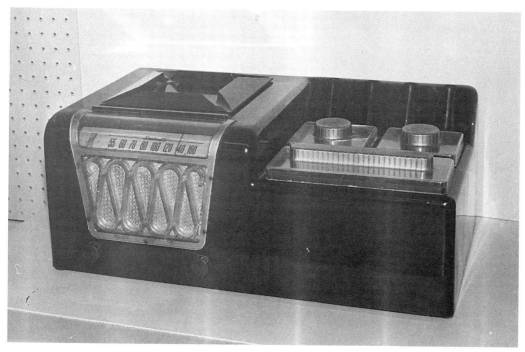

1947 Smokerette made by Porto Products; radio built into smoker's stand; includes ashtray, humidors, and pipe stand (John Wilson).

1947 RCA model X551.

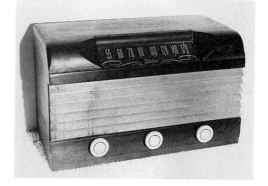

1947 Delco model R-1229; two-tone wood radio (John Wilson).

a fair offer. It may be accepted, or you may come to some compromise price.

Mail Order. Radio magazines contain information and addresses for mail-order radios. It seems that more and more radio collectors are advertis-ing their sets. It can be difficult to tell the real condition of the set by reading a classified ad. Some dealers print a list that tells what you'll find—scratches, repairs, tubes missing, etc. Others use one of the various grading systems. No

1947 Firestone model 4A27; black plastic (Ed and Irene Ripley).

Matching stand for 1947 Zenith radio-phonograph.

1947 Zenith model 6R886; blond wood table model radio-phonograph.

grading system has been universally accepted.

There have been numerous attempts to standardize grading of radios. The Antique Wireless Association tried on two different occasions. "Excellent" meant perfect both in 1979 and 1983. "Very Good" meant that the finish could have some scratches. But when they came to the poorer radios, the grading moved upwards during those four years. What had been "Poor" now became "Fair" (extensive repairs needed), and "Fair" became "Good" (refinished cabinet). A controversy developed when, in 1984, another suggestion was made. "Mint" meant perfect, "Excellent" meant the finish was scratched, "Very Good" included refinished cabinets, and "Good" meant extensive repairs would be necessary. Of course this led to still more suggestions. One system would

1947 Airline model 64BR-1808; push-button; 3-band.

have coded in virtually all electrical and cabinet flaws, which would have made the system too complicated. This is why one mail-order dealer prefers describing the radio in plain English. Here's an example from one of their sales lists: "PHILCO 1949 #49-602 hand bag-shaped 3-way portable, chocolate brown styrene with black leather carrying handle, horiz. louvered grille, slide rule dial, cracks bottom & back, clean." You have a good idea of what this radio looks like just from reading the description. This is the same information you want from any seller.

Beware of seller's claims. "Mint" should be exactly that: never used, absolutely perfect original finish, all parts original. Very few items fifty years old are mint. "Near Mint" is a better de-

scription. If you put two identical "mint" radios together, most likely one would look more "mint" than the other. Since it's virtually impossible to make this comparison, be cautious and believe that the radio is NM (Near Mint). If you've come across a set you want, the first thing to do is to call the dealer and find out what, precisely, is its condition. Is it original? refinished? restored? Does it have the correct knobs? Does it work? Can you return it (at your expense) if it isn't as you expect? Before you send a check, understand what you're getting. Ask lots of questions. Don't worry if you sound foolish; it's more foolish to send off the money trustingly.

If a picture would make you feel better about buying the set, ask the seller to send a Polaroid print. If

1947 Gilfillan portable model 66B, "The Overland;" leatherette covered with unusual copper grille.

1947 Emerson model 578A; wood, European styling (Ed and Irene Ripley)

1947 Regal portable model 747; metal case with plastic front and back; flip-up cover; AC/battery operation.

there's a charge for this, it's still a good investment. Certainly it's cheaper than sending a radio back.

Also find out how long it is before you can expect to receive the radio. Since the seller may want to have your check clear before he ships, a three-week wait is not unreasonable. If it's

1947 Pilot FM tuner model T-601; played through the phonograph input on a conventional AM radio.

going to be much longer than that, find out how long. Everyone has at some time ordered something and then waited for it to come through, all the time becoming angrier and angrier. Avoid the problem: know in advance.

If you're planning on spending a lot of money for your radios and you don't know the seller, consider having the order sent C.O.D. It avoids the problem of someone taking the money and disappearing.

Antiques Shops/Antiques Malls. You will find the highest prices at an antiques shop or mall. The dealer has the regular costs of any business (rent, utilities, salaries). These are not major expenses for any of the other sellers listed. The dealer is also concerned about his reputation and will not want

1947 General Electric model 202.

1947 Fada; wooden table, similar to series 652 Catalin radios.

1947 Sentinel model 309-I; ivory Bakelite (Ed and Irene Ripley)

to sell an unsafe item (unless it's clearly marked "not working" or "as is"). Many dealers have refinished poor cabinets so the radio looks fresh. This is the retail level reflected in this price guide.

As with flea marketers, there may be some flexibility in dealers' prices. Some antique dealers do not believe in dickering. They consider themselves professional retailers and believe that since local department stores don't make deals, they shouldn't either. There are some dealers who love to wheel and deal, and who consider a sale more enjoyable if this has gone on. Making an offer, instead of asking for the "best price," will allow any dealer to state his policy without anyone being insulted.

An article several years ago stated that dealers were buying items for 25 to 30 percent of the selling price. This would have allowed a good deal of bargaining room. Unfortunately, most dealers buying from individuals or at auctions today are paying closer to 50 percent of the selling price. Be reasonable when you make an offer.

EXAMING THE RADIO CHASSIS

When repairing either a radio cabinet or chassis, remember the rule of thumb: Don't do anything that can't be undone later if it's wrong.

Condition. The price guide assumes that the radio is in working order. That means the knobs should all be there and match. It doesn't guarantee that the knobs are the correct ones, but that's an assumption you'll have to make. If they don't match, there's obviously something wrong. All the tubes should be there. The cord should be in good condition. (If it isn't, do not, repeat, *do not* plug it in. Replace it immediately.) The dial should move and the knobs should work. If not, lower the price accordingly. When looking at the chassis from the back of the set, don't worry about dust. You may find a little rust or some oily looking spots. These are not problems.

Those are the simple, first steps in checking out a radio. Sometimes it's all you can do. You really don't have any idea of whether or not the set will be

Coradio coin-op radio; gray metal; from a hotel in Black River Falls, Wisconsin.

Unknown coin-op radio; gray metal.

1948 Fada model 790; white urea. The Deco style of this radio is misleading in that the radio appears to have been made in the late 1930s instead of 1948, when it actually was manufactured.

1948 Philco model 48-250.

good, or how expensive it will be to fix. If possible, check further.

Problems. If you see a good deal of greasy wax or black tar on the chassis, something is wrong. The radio likely has overheated at some time. It will take an evaluation by a repair per-

1948 Motorola portable model 67L11; simulated alligator. Note square knobs.

127

1948 General Electric model X-415. This multi-band set has both of the FM bands.

1948 Philco radio-phonograph model 48-1401; slide-in record player; black plastic top, wood bottom (David Tuttle).

1948 RCA model 75X16. The frame around the radio is brass.

1949 Philco Transitone model 49-506; wood cabinet.

1948 RCA portable model 8 BX 6; operates on both AC and batteries; aluminum and plastic.

1949 Sentinel model 332.

1949 Coronado model 43-8360A; brown plastic with aqua front.

son to know how serious the problem is. Unless you know about radio repairs, don't pay too much, and don't tinker yourself unless you know what you are doing.

If you have a chance, try the radio before you buy it. If you're only buying it for the cabinet, this is not necessary. Go on to the section about cabinet condition instead.

This is important! Before you plug it in, make sure the power cord is in safe condition. If you can see any copper wire or the insulation is badly broken, *do not plug it in!*

Look in the back at the chassis. If any tubes are missing from their sockets, don't bother to plug it in. It won't work anyway. Is the loudspeaker in there? This is a separate circular metal

1949 RCA model 9X571; brown plastic case with brown fake wood front.

frame with a paper cone. If it's missing, don't bother to try the set. If there are a bunch of wires that are not attached to anything, don't turn it on.

There may be, however, two wires

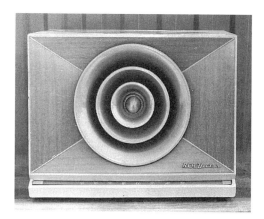

1949 RCA Victor model 9X572; blond plastic.

1949 Silvertone model 132.857; brown Bakelite (Ed and Irene Ripley).

1949 Silvertone model 7054; chassis number 101.808. Postwar styling with rounded cabinet corners.

coming through a hole in the back of the chassis. These are the antenna and ground wires. Normally, there will be nothing attached to their ends (which is not a problem). You may have to add a little wire to one of these to get many stations, though.

If nothing seems amiss, you can turn on the radio. Turn the volume control up about half way. Now watch the back of the radio. If there is a loud sputtering sound, any sparking, or any smoke, do not turn the set off.

Instead, pull the plug! You've got problems.

If all is still going well, continue to watch the back. The tubes should light up. Any black-painted metal tubes should get warm after a few minutes. Any small bulbs used to light up the dial most likely will be burned out. They aren't hard to replace.

After a couple of minutes, you should hear something. Is there a soft humming sound from the speaker? Good, that's fine. If it is dead silent, there is something wrong. If all is well, you will hear some soft crackling sounds and hiss, showing that most of the circuits are functioning.

Now try the switches on the front of the set. Band switches (AM/SW/PHONO) produce a noticeable pop in the speaker when they are moved. If they produce any other strange sounds, it shows that they are in need of cleaning (not a difficult task).

If there is a band switch, make sure it is set to the regular broadcast band. Turn the volume control almost all the

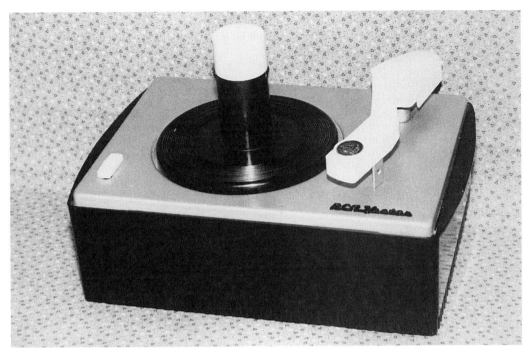

45-rpm phonograph attachment for radios. Usually these are found with the top of the changer in red rather than white. They were designed to plug into the phono jack on the back of many table radios; original price $12.95; c. 1948–49.

way up. If there is a loud scratching sound in the speaker when you move the knob, this control will need cleaning as well. Try tuning the dial from one end to the other. It should, of course, move. There should be some sort of sound from a local station. If you hear any station at all, the set is not in bad condition.

By now you have had the set operating for several minutes. It's time to check again. Does it smell hot or waxy? Is there any burned smell (even if there is no smoke)? If there is any strong smell from the set, some component is going bad and will need fixing.

If you do receive a local station, you may still have one or two problems needing attention. There may be a

*1949 Philco portable model 49-602; purse-shaped, brown plastic; slide rule dial (**Ed and Irene Ripley**).*

1950 Zenith model H-725.

1950 Capehart model 3T55E; brown plastic.

loud hum that makes it hard to hear the station. If so, filter capacitors will need replacing. The sound may be very disagreeable, distorted, and hard to listen to. If this is the case, you may have problems with your speaker or need replacement coupling capacitors.

These radios are not high fidelity, but they do sound good. A properly operating old tube-type radio will have a mellow, pleasant sound on local stations, with just barely noticeable background hum and a little hiss and crackle. Anything other than this shows a radio that is not as good as it could be. It still may be good enough for you. You are the judge.

The very small (and cheap) old radios, by the way, will not sound very mellow. They will sound very much like the cheap transistor sets which followed them.

WARNING! If the label on the bottom or on the inside of the radio says anything about "AC-DC" operation, use extreme caution when plugging it in. Some—not all—of these radios have a dangerous design fault which places 110 volts on the metal

1948 Setchell-Carlson portable model 447; AC/battery (Ed and Irene Ripley).

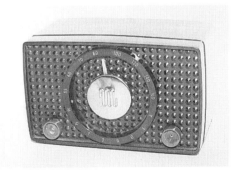

1950 Motorola model 5H11; brown plastic with red knobs.

1950 Policalarm model PR8; a police-band radio, made by Regency Electronics (Ed and Irene Ripley).

1950 Packard Bell model 5R1 (Ed and Irene Ripley).

1950 Silvertone model 2001; metal cabinet.

1950 Coronado model 05RA22-43-8515; AM/FM.

1950 General Electric clock radio model 65.

parts of the radio. If you touch a metal part and are standing on damp ground or touching a sink, *it could be fatal!*

If you want to test an AC-DC set before you buy, you can do all of the above checks, but be careful that you are not on anything damp or touching any metal on or off of the radio. You might prefer to test nothing at all until you know conditions are safe.

For further information on testing, evaluating, and repairing old radios, see our other book, *Antique Radio Restoration Guide, 2nd edition* (Wallace-Homestead Books).

Repairs. How do you decide how much to lower your offer if the radio has problems? Find a local radio repair person and ask about the cost of an average radio repair. Your radio won't be average, but this will give you a place to start. Once you have a figure in mind, subtract it from the suggested price to come up with what you can spend.

1950 Arvin model 451T; aqua plastic. Once painted plastic starts chipping, it looks just as bad as chipped metal.

1951 General Electric model 423; white plastic; original price $34.95.

1950 Setchell Carlson intercom-radio model 458R.

1951 Zenith model H-615 (Ed and Irene Ripley).

1951 General Electric model 422; marbleized maroon plastic.

To find someone who can repair radios, start with the local television service shops. They are unlikely to work on old radios, but they may know someone who does. Ask at the local antiques shops. Many dealers have a list of repair

1951 Sparton model 141XX; AM/SW.

places that they use. If there's a local radio amateurs' organization, someone in it may do the work. The best place to find people to work on old tube-type radios is a local radio club. A member is bound to know someone who works on old radios. Information about finding radio clubs is given in the section on buying at radio swap meets.

If you're seriously interested in collecting old radios, figure out how to handle the repairs before you get a garage full of nonworkers.

EXAMINING THE RADIO CABINET

Condition. This is the single most-important item to consider in looking at a radio cabinet. If the condition is good, you won't have any fur-

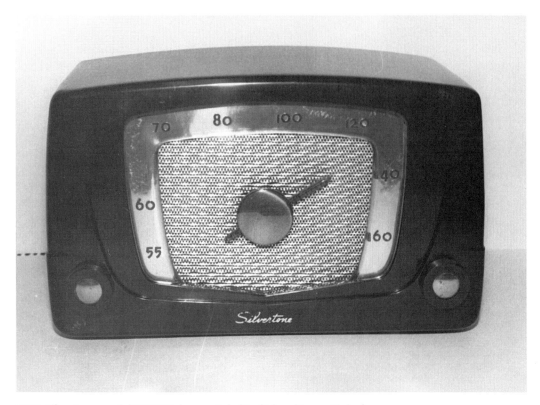

1951 Silvertone model 132.881; brown Bakelite (Ed and Irene Ripley).

1951 Admiral model 5S22A N; brown Bakelite.

1952 Sentinel model IU-343; black Bakelite.

ther expense in getting the set into your house. If it's not so good, then you have to lower your offer. After all, you're the one who's going to have to pay for those repairs.

If you're going to pay price guide prices, wood cabinets should be good enough to place in your living room without work. This doesn't mean that the finish must be great, but it certainly shouldn't require a complete

1952 RCA portable model 6BX63; gray plastic.

1952 Coronado model 15RA2-43-8230A; burgundy plastic with gold grille.

1952 Philco Transitone model 52-542.

1953 CBS Columbia model 515.

1952 RCA model 3-RF-91; AM/FM.

facelift. If cabinet repairs or refinishing will be necessary, lower your offer.

Problems. If you see that gluing will be necessary when you are considering a radio for purchase, or that major cabinet repairs are essential, the cost of the repairs is probably going to make the set worth very little. Unless you have the skills to do the job yourself and like doing it, make sure this is a radio you desperately need for your collection.

Veneer repair is costly. It's possible to get a replacement piece the right thickness and the right grain to go into a place where the original is missing, but it takes patience and careful work to do the job right. If the missing piece is on the side of the cabinet, it won't be too noticeable, even if the repair is not perfect. If the repair is on the top or the front of the radio, on the other hand, it needs to be extremely well

1953 Philco Transitone model 53-561; white plastic **(Ed and Irene Ripley).**

done. Think carefully about buying a cabinet with a piece missing.

Beware of painted grain. When it is new, it looks great—almost as good as the expensive veneer that it copies. Unfortunately, when it becomes badly scratched, the temptation is to have it stripped and refinished as any other wood. If you try this, you will find that the stripper removes the underlying paint (used to get the correct base color) and you will have a sludgy mess on your hands and nothing resembling fancy wood on your radio. If painted grain is in bad condition, avoid the radio. Paper veneer is even worse when in bad condition. Stripping this leaves you with a mess of stripper-soaked, soggy paper and a cabinet usually constructed of unmatched, cheap woods.

Missing trim can be more difficult to repair than poor cabinet finishes. If it's wood trim, you have to find someone to duplicate it, which can be a time-consuming, expensive project. Then you have to get it stained and finished to match the cabinet. If hardware is missing from the cabinet itself, you may be able to replace it with something similar.

If the plastic or glass dial cover is cracked or broken, do not buy the set unless you like it the way it is. If the plastic or metal dial surround is gone, do not buy the radio. You're unlikely to ever find replacements in either case.

At this time plastic cabinets are not repairable. There is no way to repair a cracked or broken Bakelite or Catalin set. It seems that you should be able to

1953 Crosley clock radio model D-25MN. A striking design, with gold bezels on burgundy plastic; definitely the 1950s look.

melt some scrap Bakelite to fill the crack. It won't work! Bakelite is a thermoset plastic. Instead of softening and melting, it burns like wood when the temperature gets hot enough. Currently there is no glue that works either. This leaves you with a decision. If the crack isn't going to bother you (on the bottom of the cabinet, for instance), you may want the radio anyway. But know that your chances of reselling it for close to book value are very low.

Repairs. Getting a rough idea of the cost of repairing or refinishing the cabinet is easier to do than determining the cost of fixing the chassis. Many professional firms do stripping and re-

finishing. You still have to find one who can handle old radios, however.

Most of the cabinets were veneered. The glues holding the veneers together are forty or fifty years old and are drying out and crumbling. Many of the cabinets were made of mixed woods. When the manufacturer finished them with colored varnish or lacquer, they looked like a single species. When the finish comes off, they may be completely unmatched and look nothing like the radio you bought.

That means you have to search for a good refinisher as carefully as you searched for a good radio shop. If you know someone who has had lots of luck with having old furniture refin-

1954 Packard Bell model 631; made by Teledyne (Ed and Irene Ripley).

1955 Motorola model 56R; red plastic.

Capehart portable model number 213; green metal-and-plastic case with interesting tartan grille; mid-1950s.

ished, start there. Do you like what you see? Find out if any of the furniture they had done had a veneer finish. How long ago was the work done and how well is it holding up?

Otherwise, check with local refinishers. No matter what stripping technique they use, find out if they have handled any old veneer. If they're not

Trav-Ler, mid-1950s; black plastic (Ed and Irene Ripley).

careful, the veneer can loosen and the job will become a major repair.

Subtract the price of estimated repairs from the figures in the price guide. If you can do either the chassis or cabinet repairs yourself, you have more flexibility. Remember, however, that your time is valuable, too.

WHAT TO PAY?

Condition. This is the single most unpredictable factor in deciding what to pay. The prices given are for working radios in good condition. Then you begin subtracting the things that need fixing. There are some fine-quality radios out there, but most of them aren't in very good condition.

Styles and fads. When something is in style, its price changes rapidly and unpredictably. This has happened with some (but certainly not all) plastic radios during the last few years. In the 1970s, collectors turned up their noses

Dahlberg coin-op radio model 430-D1; also known as 'Pillow Speaker.' The speaker, hanging on a hook on the left of the radio, goes under a pillow to keep from disturbing another sleeper, c. 1955.

1956 Motorola model 56H; dramatic gold tuning dial on a brown plastic radio.

1956 Silvertone radio-phonograph model 6057A; 3-speed phonograph; blond wood.

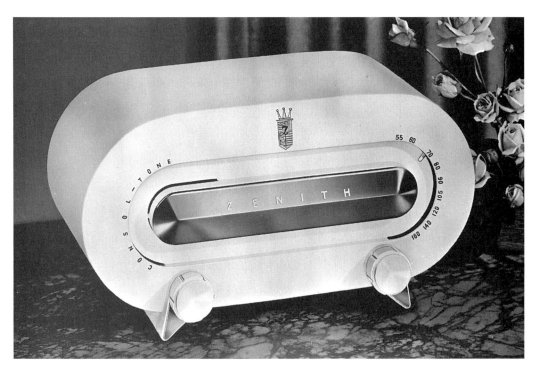

1954 Zenith model H511W; white plastic, also walnut or ebony (courtesy of Zenith Radio Corp.).

1957 Motorola model 66X.

1957 Silvertone model 7013; black plastic.

1958 Arvin model 1581; ivory plastic.

1958 Arvin model 950T2; one of the most striking designs for an inexpensive radio.

1959 Admiral model 566; transistor table radio; chartreuse and white plastic.

at these cheap sets. The popular area then was cathedral radios. Today, certain plastic sets have been discovered. Catalin, urea, and some Bakelite sets are immensely collectible; their prices have increased tenfold to one hundred-fold. Presumably they will settle down again, but no one knows when, or even if, that will happen. Who knows what other style will become the "in" radio? No price guide can predict these fads, and the prices can soon be badly out of date.

Regional preferences. Price guides reflect averages. If a particular style of radio is popular in one part of the country, the prices there will be higher than those listed. People from that area look at the guide and wonder why in the world they're paying so much. If local premium prices were included in the guide, people in the rest of the country would wonder how the authors could be so far off in their figures.

1959 Zenith model B-513V.

1959 Arvin model 2585; definitely a 1950s look, in coral and white plastic

If something is popular where you are and not elsewhere, you'll just have to expect to pay more for it than we suggest. It's the law of supply and demand.

Crossover buyers. These are the buyers who turn the whole pricing structure into a shambles. There is the Coca-Cola collector, for instance, who is bidding against you for that Coke cooler radio. Not because it's a radio, but because it's Coke. The Disney collector wants a Mickey Mouse radio, because it's Mickey. When two fields like this collide, prices usually become very high.

At an antiques shop, the price that goes on the radio depends on what customers the dealer expects. If there are few Disney collectors around, Mickey's price may remain comparatively low. The dealer will think of it as a "cute" radio, price it for a quick sale, and you'll have a chance of getting it at a moderate price. If there are a number of Disney collectors, the price will reflect that group of buyers and

1960 Motorola model C9G13; green plastic clock radio.

1961 Zenith model J506C; green plastic.

1964 Admiral model Y3523; white plastic with black dial.

may be higher than you are willing to pay.

Our general feelings about prices. Personally, we feel that there are certain guidelines to radio prices. If you're looking at radios as an investment, these might be useful. We consider buying radios (or any collectible, for that matter) as an investment particularly risky, however. No one can predict what people will want

These are two of the current replicas of the Philco 90B. Philco started it all with its own transistorized, smaller version in 1976. The larger one here is a Windsor, made in Hong Kong. It's AM/FM. The smaller one is a Greenland, made in Taiwan and only 5' high.

in ten years. If we could, we'd all be wealthy. So buy it because you like it. If the price goes up, that's great. If the price falls it doesn't matter, because you've got something you enjoy.

These are general statements about the current levels of radio prices.

High priced
Catalins
ureas
extremely colorful plastics
mirrored radios

Moderately high priced
Deco (whether wood or plastic)
cathedrals

Average
Upright wood table
metal table

Low priced
Horizontal wood table
console
portable
plain small wood radio
plain plastic

ALTERATIONS AND FAKES

With the surge of interest in Catalin and other early small sets, certain myths have started. Bakelite radios

Many products have used radio as a selling point. The 'microphone' is a glass Avon bottle. The 'Radio Bank' is plastic. The jigsaw puzzle is from the 1920s.

were often painted; now it's possible to find them in color schemes that the designers of the 1930s never thought of.

Also, the chrome plating of inexpensive Arvin and Silvertone metal sets from the late 1940s has begun. The sets originally were painted black or brown or white or ivory. (It's very difficult to imagine Sears Roebuck chrome-plating sets they were selling through the catalog.) Beware of these if someone is selling them as original.

Occasionally you will find a modern transistor radio lurking inside an old cabinet. This may become more common in the future. It can happen to anyone; it certainly happened to us. We bought a Radiola 60, sight unseen,

only to find someone had switched the insides. Although it had probably been done a number of years ago, that did not make us feel any better. If we had checked that radio out properly, we never would have bought it.

Many classic radios have been reproduced, but are no problem for the collector. They are solid state instead of tube radios and frequently come with a slot for playing cassettes. Neither transistors nor cassettes existed when the original sets were made. A careful look will easily identify these sets. They can be attractive additions to a collection and they generally do not cost much. You simply need to know what you have.

PART TWO

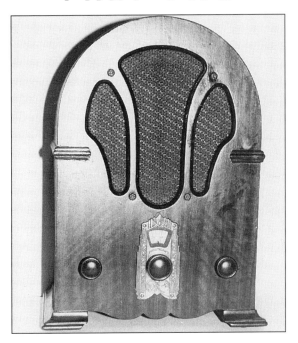

PRICE GUIDE

How to Get the Most Out of This Price Guide

Remember that this (or any other) price guide is simply that—a guide to prices. A price guide is subject to many variables. Use it for assistance only.

These prices come from many sources. Where possible, they include published prices realized at auctions, want ads in various radio journals, lists of radios sold through the mail, and radios actually seen in shops and at swap meets. Actual pictures of the radios had a lot to do with settling on prices.

Prices gathered from various sources don't tell the whole story. Auction prices don't tell you what sort of auction it was. Were there a lot of radio buyers (with the prices going higher) or were there just a few (and the radios were real bargains)? Classified ads include prices, but don't mention whether the seller would dicker or if the prices are firm. Flea markets post prices, but it's almost ex-

pected that no one will pay them. How much less will the seller take—10 percent, 25 percent, or a trade of some sort? Antiques shops, shows, and malls are more likely to be firm on their prices, but that still means there are many (certainly not all) who will accept 10 percent less than the marked price.

Realize also that prices are affected by many things. These prices are at least a year old by the time you use them. In the publishing process there is no way to avoid this.

Prices in one part of the country may not be the same as in another. Fads and fancies cause abrupt changes. The condition of the radio itself (working, sort of working, not working) affects the price. The condition of the cabinet is very important when pricing a radio. However, in the end it always comes down to the fact that a fair price is a price on which both a buyer and a seller agree.

In general, these prices are based on certain assumptions:

- The radio is in reasonable working condition.
- The cabinet looks good enough to put in your living room.
- The prices are those you would pay in a retail antiques shop setting.

Again: Take all prices with a grain of salt.

MODEL

There is no standard way to write model numbers. They come in all sorts of alphanumeric combinations, with or without dashes and sometimes they even come with periods. RCA and Zenith have been arbitrarily separated into alphabetical and numerical groups, simply to make their numbers easier to use. As for other companies, we tried to group the numbers as the manufacturer listed them. However, the manufacturers were not always consistent. Numbers that came from classified ads were even less useful. Everyone tends to break up long strings of characters into comfortable groups. These may not have a lot to do with how the manufacturer originally listed them. Be creative when you search. You might need to look under 7-501, 75-01, 750-1, or 7501.

Early manufacturers used the word "type" in much the same way we use "model." They're all listed as models.

Where a model name ("Bluebird" or "Pup") is used, it will usually follow the model number. If there is no model number, it will be found alphabetically.

Numbers are listed before letters.

PRICE

Most prices will include a range (20-40, 200-300, for example). There is no clear-cut formula for determining the width of this range; typically it's determined by selling prices, which sometimes are very far apart. If you buy a radio within the range (even if it seems like a widespread range), you will probably be doing well. If you get it lower than the bottom price (all things being equal), you are doing very well. If you pay higher than the top price, know that you are doing so. You may want the radio very badly, the prices may have climbed higher in your area, or another fad may be starting.

Occasionally a single price is listed. This happens when there are too few prices to come up with an average and no picture of the radio is available. A single price is a guide, but no great weight can be placed on it.

Some prices are in the 500+ or 2500+ categories. In these cases we have examples of extremely high prices actually being paid or advertised. There is no way to know if the prices will continue at this level, or if this is the result of a single "price-is-no-object" collector. Arbitrarily we lowered these prices (often 25 to 40 percent) and added the "+" to show that the sky may be the limit.

DESCRIPTIONS

Descriptions of radios (cabinet styles, colors, dials, etc.) are made to the best of our knowledge. Since these descriptions rely on many types of sources, they are not guaranteed. If something has been left out (for instance, "2 dials"), it does not mean that the radio absolutely won't have that detail. If it is listed, though, the radio should have it.

Cabinet. Radio cabinets are usually made of wood unless otherwise noted. In a few cases it was impossible to tell from the picture or description whether or not the cabinet was wood. These will have no further description. Odds are that a radio without a description of material will have a wood cabinet.

Where a radio is plastic, we have tried to identify the more common plastics, such as Bakelite, Catalin, urea, etc. If we were not sure, we continued to use "plastic."

Color. When cabinets are wood, they will be varnished or lacquered. If they are painted or covered with a fabric, we have tried to indicate that.

If the cabinet is any sort of plastic, it most likely will be brown or black unless something else is listed. However, there is always a possibility that a manufacturer used several colors without identifying this in its model information. Bakelite didn't come in white or very light colors. If the description says "Ivory Bakelite" it means that the Bakelite was painted ivory.

Style. The following descriptions should help. Don't rely on how manufacturers advertised their models. General Electric identified one model as a highboy and another as a lowboy, but from the illustrations there seems to be no difference in leg heights.

Box	Table radio where the tubes and knobs are on the top of the box. It may have a cover.
Breadboard	Early sets where there is no cabinet and the electronics are out in the open. Atwater Kent built many of these. Few other companies did. Most early sets were panel sets.
Cathedral	An upright table radio whose style supposedly reminds you of a church window. It ranges from the truly pointed top of a traditional arch to a rounded shape following the same general lines. Another group (Jackson-Bell, for instance) were radios defined as 'Moderne" when they were manufactured. These had the same proportions and the same single-piece wood front, but the curve was replaced by sharp angles. They are sometimes referred to in ads as Deco cathedral.
Chairside	A set built into the top of an end table. It allowed someone sitting in a chair to operate the controls without getting up. Do not confuse it with an end table.
Chassis	Radio without a cabinet. These were designed to be put into a custom cabinet. Sometimes called a panel set.

Chest	Looks like a chest. Sometimes it looks like a pirate chest, with a rounded cover instead of a flat one. It also may look like a jewelry box.

1946 Sparton model 7-46.

Console	Upright floor model radio, higher than it is wide, or one lacking a description. The sides go straight to the floor or the feet are 4 inches or less. The upright style is considered normal for floor models. If no better descriptions were given in ads, it can include highboys or lowboys as well.
Deco	A style that originated in the mid 1920s and was popular until 1950. It is characterized by one or more of the following: chrome trim, large geometric shapes, sharp angular forms, streamlined appearance. Deco, instead of the more purist Moderne, seems to be what radio collectors have settled on. Not everything we have listed as Deco may be; in some cases we're taking the word of a seller.
End table	The radio practically disappeared by being built into the end of a conventional end table.
Highboy	A 4- to 6-legged upright floor model. The legs are

	approximately one-half the height of the set.
Horizontal	Can apply to console, lowboy, or highboy. It means that the radio is wider than it is high.
Lowboy	A 4- to 6-legged upright floor model. The legs are more than 4 inches high and less than one-half the height of the radio. (Highboy and lowboy were used interchangeably by some manufacturers, most likely based on what they expected would sell.)
Panel	No cabinet. There is a front panel, which allowed the set to be built

	into a wood box if desired.
Portable	A battery-powered or AC/battery radio designed to be carried around by its built-in handle. A portable radio-phonograph will usually be AC-powered only but will have a handle.
Table	Either a horizontal table radio or one lacking a description. The horizontal style (wider than it is high) is considered usual for table radios.
Transistor	Refers to a small radio that uses transistors or integrated circuits in its operation.
Upright table	Higher than it is wide. It may have a flat or slightly rounded top. A variant of the upright table is the tombstone. This is generally considered to be a tall table radio with rounded top corners. Because it is a popular term, advertisers use this word to describe anything that could even conceivably be called a tombstone. We prefer upright table.
Vertical	Simply means higher than it is wide in referring to any radio.

Dates. Dates reflect the model year. All dates may be plus or minus one year. This is because *Rider's Manuals,* which we used as primary sources for dating, often overlap two calendar years. If the circuit diagrams are not dated, there is no easy, accurate way to narrow the range. Radios, like automobiles, were likely to start the next model year somewhere during the fall of the year. A 1940 Philco, for instance, may first have been advertised in 1939. Post-World War II radios are dated and identified using SAMS guides and are more accurate in dating.

Bands. What we call AM was known as the broadcast band in early radio and shortened to BC. Nowadays we're so used to referring to AM/FM that AM is a more understandable word for general broadcasting. If an ad refers to BC/SW, it's what we call AM/SW.

There are a few radios listed with "old" FM. This was a pre-war band that was changed by the end of the war to what we now think of as the FM band. Some radios had both FM bands.

Sources. To help identify radios we've included page references to photographs or ads found in some of the standard sources for radio information. For instance, FOS-120 means *Flick of the Switch,* page 120. Photographs from this book are not listed with page numbers.

ARR	*Antique Radios: Restoration and Price Guide,* by Johnson.
ARR2	*Antique Radio Restor-*

ation Guide, 2nd edition, by Johnson.

B1   *Antique Radios*, by Bunis.

B2   *Antique Radios*, 2nd edition, by Bunis.

FOS   *Flick of the Switch*, by McMahon.

GOR   *Guide to Old Radios* (this book, either edition).

RGA   *Radios: the Golden Age*, by Collins.

RR   *Radios Redux*, by Collins.

VR   *Vintage Radio*, by McMahon.

.

PRICE LISTING

R A D I O S

A-C DAYTON
It is just A-C in their ads, even though it's often written now either "AC" or "A.C." The company produced AC motors in 1901. They were advertising radios in 1922. Dayton was last heard of in 1930.

Model Name/Number	Price Range($)	Description
AC-98 "Navigator"	80-100	Table. Walnut wood. Inlay on lid. 1929. (GOR)
AC-9960 "Navigator"	90-120	Lowboy. Walnut. Matte finish. 1929. (GOR)
AC-9970 "Navigator"	90-120	Lowboy. Wood. Sliding doors. 1929. (ARR-45; GOR)
AC-9990 "Navigator"	100-150	Highboy with doors. Wood. 1929. (GOR)
XL 5 "Polydyne"	60-80	Table. Battery. 3 dial. 1925. (VR-135) (B1-7)
XL 10	60-100	Table. Battery. 3 dial. 1925. (B2-7)
XL 20	60-110	Table. Battery. 3 dial. 1926.
XL 25	90-125	Table. Battery. 2 dial. 1926. (VR-135)
XL 30	80-120	Table. Battery. 2 dial. 1926.
XL 71 "Navigator"	75-100	Table. Battery. 1929.

A.C. GILBERT
Experimenter's set	200-225	Kit.

ACE *(See both Crosley and Precision)*

ARR: *Antique Radios: Restoration and Price Guide* / ARR2: *Antique Radio Restoration Guide, Second Edition* /
B1: *Antique Radio Price Guide, First Edition* by Bunis / B2: *Antique Radio Price Guide, Second Edition* by Bunis /
FOS: *Flick of the Switch* / GOR: *Guide to Old Radios* / RGA: *Radios: The Golden Age* / RR: *Radios Redux* / VR: *Vintage Radio.*

ADDISON

Model Name/Number	Price Range($)	Description
5F	1200+	Table. Burgundy and butterscotch. Catalin. Deco. Columns in front of grille. AM/SW. c1940. (RGA-56,57)
	600-700	Yellow Catalin.
	600-800	Green and caramel Catalin.
6E	600-800	Yellow and green Catalin with maroon grille and knobs.
55	30-50	Brown Bakelite.
A2A	800-1100	Table. Green and caramel Catalin. 1940. (RGA-50,51)
	1000+	Caramel and red Catalin.
L2	150-200	Table. Brown with cream.
RSA-1	125-200	Deco table.

ADLER

Royal	150-200	Table. Battery. 1924. (GOR) (VR-142)

ADMIRAL

Admiral began as Continental Radio & Television Corporation before World War II.

4B21	25-35	Portable. AC/battery. Black. 1954.
4B22	25-35	Maroon plastic. Same as 4B21.
4B24	20-30	Beige plastic. Same as 4B21.
4B28	20-30	Green plastic. Same as 4B21.
4B29	15-25	Gray plastic. Same as 4B21.
4L20 / 4L20A	20-25	Table. Plastic. Gray. 1959.
4L21 / 4L21A	15-20	Black plastic. Same as 4L20.
4L24 / 4L24A	25-30	Pink plastic. Same as 4L20.
4L25 / 4L25A	25-30	Red plastic. Same as 4L20.
4L26 / 4L26A	25-30	Yellow plastic. Same as 4L20.
4L28 / 4L28A	20-25	Green plastic. Same as 4L20.
4M22	20-25	Clock radio. Brown plastic. 1959.
4M23	20-25	Ivory plastic. Same as 4M22.
4M25	30-40	Coral plastic. Same as 4M22.
4M28	30-40	Green plastic. Same as 4M22.
4P21	25-30	Transistor. 1957.
4V12	25-30	Portable. Brown plastic. AC/battery. 1952.
4V18	30-35	Green plastic. Same as 4V12.
4V19	40-45	Black plastic with red handle, knobs, and dial face. Same as 4V12.
4Y11	15-25	Portable. Black plastic. Metal grille. AC/battery. 1953.
4Y12	20-25	Maroon plastic. Same as 4Y11.
4Y18	20-25	Green plastic. Same as 4Y11.
4Y19	15-25	Gray plastic. Same as 4Y11.
4Z11	15-20	Portable. AC/battery. Black plastic. 1954.
4Z12	15-20	Maroon plastic. Same as 4Z11.
4Z14	15-20	Beige plastic. Same as 4Z11.
4Z19	15-20	Gray plastic. Same as 4Z11.
5A32	25-30	Clock radio. Brown plastic. Bright panel. 1952.
5A33	25-30	Ivory plastic. Same as 5A32.
5B1A	25-30	Table, wood. Radio-phono. 1947.
5D31	40-45	Table. Radio-phono. Black plastic. 1953.
5D32	45-50	Maroon plastic. Same as 5D31.
5D33	45-50	Ivory plastic. Same as 5D31.
5D38	50-55	Green plastic. Same as 5D31.
5E21	20-25	Table. Large dial. Black plastic. 1951.
5E22	20-25	Ivory plastic. Same as 5E21.
5E23	20-25	Brown plastic. Same as 5E21.
5E31	15-20	Clock radio. Black plastic. 1953.

ADMIRAL—*continued*

Model Name/Number	Price Range($)	Description
5E32	25-30	Maroon plastic. Same as 5E31.
5E33	20-25	Ivory plastic. Same as 5E31.
5E38	25-30	Green plastic. Same as 5E31.
5E39	15-20	Gray plastic. Same as 5E31.
5F1	15-20	Portable. Plastic. Flip-up lid. AC/battery. 1949.
5F31/5F31A/5F31B	25-30	Clock radio. Black plastic. 1954.
5F32/5F32A/5F32B	30-35	Maroon plastic. Same as 5F31A.
5F33/5F33A/5F33B	25-30	Ivory plastic. Same as 5F31A.
5F34B	20-25	Beige plastic. Same as 5F31A.
5F38/5F38A/5F38B	30-35	Green plastic. Same as 5F31A.
5G22	30-35	Clock Radio. Brown plastic. 1951.
5G31	25-30	Table. Black plastic. 1953.
5G32	25-30	Brown plastic. Same as 5G31.
5G33	25-30	Ivory plastic. Same as 5G31.
5J23	30-40	Table. 1951.
5J31	60-70	Desk set (pen, clock, radio in stand). Black plastic. 1953.
5J33	50-60	Ivory plastic. Same as 5J31.
5J38	60-75	Marbleized green plastic. Same as 5J31.
5K13	35-40	Table. Maroon with gold trim. 1948.
5K31	20-25	Portable. Black plastic. AC/bat. 1954.
5K32	20-25	Maroon plastic. Same as 5K31.
5K34	20-25	Beige plastic. Same as 5K31.
5K38	20-25	Green plastic. Same as 5K31.
5K39	20-25	Gray plastic. Same as 5K31.
5L2 (chassis)	20-25	Clock radio. 1952.
5M2 (chassis)	30-40	Table. Brown plastic. Radio-phono. 1947.
5R11	20-25	Table. Black plastic. 1949.
5R12	20-25	Table. Ivory plastic. 1949.
5R13	20-25	Table. Brown plastic. 1949.
5R33	20-25	Table. Plastic. 1955.
5RP41	70-90	Table. Radio-phono. Bakelite. 1958.
5S21 / 5S21AN	25-30	Table. Black plastic. 1952.
5S22 / 5S22AN	25-30	Table. Brown plastic. Same as 5S21.
5S23 / 5S23AN	25-30	Ivory plastic. Same as 5S21.
5S32	20-25	Clock radio. Maroon plastic. 1954.
5S33	20-25	Ivory plastic. Same as 5S32.
5S34	20-25	White plastic. Same as 5S32.
5S35	30-35	Red plastic. Same as 5S32.
5S36	25-30	Green plastic. Same as 5S32.
5T33N	25-30	Table. White plastic with gold. 1955.
5W32	25-30	Clock radio. Ivory plastic. Metal base. 1957.
5X12	20-25	Table. Brown plastic 1949.
5X13N	25-30	Tan plastic. Same as 5X12.
5X21	30-35	Clock radio. Black plastic. 1952.
5X22	30-35	Brown plastic. Same as 5X21.
5X23	30-35	Ivory plastic. Same as 5X21.
5Y22 / 5Y22A	50-70	Radio-phonograph. Brown Bakelite. 1952.
5Z22	25-30	Table. Brown plastic. Large dial. 1952.
5Z23	25-30	Ivory plastic. Same as 5Z22.

ARR: *Antique Radios: Restoration and Price Guide* / ARR2: *Antique Radio Restoration Guide, Second Edition* /
B1: *Antique Radio Price Guide, First Edition* by Bunis / B2: *Antique Radio Price Guide, Second Edition* by Bunis /
FOS: *Flick of the Switch* / GOR: *Guide to Old Radios* / RGA: *Radios: The Golden Age* / RR: *Radios Redux* / VR: *Vintage Radio.*

Model Name/Number	Price Range($)	Description
6A21	30-35	Table. Black plastic. 1950.
6A22	25-30	Brown plastic. Same as 6A21. (B1-9)
6A23	25-30	Ivory plastic. Same as 6A21.
6C11	25-35	Portable. Flip-up lid. AC/battery. 1949.
6C22 / 6C22A	30-35	Table. Brown plastic. 1952. (B2-8)
6C23 / 6C23A	30-35	Ivory plastic. Same as 6C22.
6C71	80-100	Console Radio-phonograph. Push-button. AM-3SW. 1946.
6J21	50-75	Radio-phonograph. Black Bakelite. 1949.
6J21N	50-75	Table. Radio-phono. 3 speed. Black 1950-51. (GOR)
6J22	50-75	Brown Bakelite. Same as 6J21.

1951 Admiral radio-phonograph model 6J21N; 3-speed; black Bakelite. Notice case variations.

6R11	50-75	Table. Radio-phono. Bakelite. AM/FM. 1949.
6V12	50-60	Table. Radio-phono. 1949.
7B1(chassis)	25-30	Table, wood. Radio-phono. 1947.
7C65W	50-70	Console (horizontal) Radio-phono. 1947.
7C73	60-80	Console (horizontal) Radio-phono. AM/FM. 1947. (FOS-50)
7C93B/7C93M/ 7C93W	60-80	Console (horizontal) Radio-phono. AM/FM. 1947.
7G11/7G12/7G14/ 7G15	60-80	Console (horizontal) Radio-phono. 1948.
7G16	60-80	Blond wood. Same as 7G11.
7RT41	40-50	Table, Radio-phono. Bakelite. 1947.
7RT43	40-50	Table. Radio-phono. Walnut wood. 1947.
7T10E-N	30-35	Table. Bakelite. 1948. (B2-9)
8D15	50-60	Console (horizontal) Radio-phono. FM/AM. 1949.
9E15	50-60	Console (horizontal) Radio-phono. FM/AM. 1949.
42-KR3	30-50	Table. White painted wood. 1942. (GOR)
237	15-20	Portable. battery. Beige plastic.
251 / 251A	25-30	Clock radio. Black. 1954.
566	25-35	Table. Early transistor. Chartreuse and white plastic. 1959. (GOR)

ADMIRAL—*continued*

Model Name/Number	Price Range($)	Description
935-11S	100-120	Console. AM/SW. 1937.
4203-B6	35-45	Table. Wood. 1942.
4204-B6	40-60	Table. Wood. AM/SW. 1941. (GOR)
AM786	90-120	Console. AM/LW/SW. 1936. (FOS-48)
Y1012	50-60	Console (horizontal). Radio-phono. Stereo. FM/AM. 1961.
Y2256	20-25	Transistor. 1963.
Y2993	20-30	Table. White plastic. Small. 1961.
Y2996	20-35	Table. Yellow plastic. Small. 1961.
Y2998	20-35	Table. Turquoise plastic. Small. 1961.
Y2999	20-30	Table. Gray plastic. Small. 1961.
Y3523	20-25	Table. White plastic with black dial. 1964. (GOR)
YH302-GP	20-25	Transistor. Red. 1966.

AERMOTIVE

181-AD	30-40	Table, wood. Clipper plane on dial. 1946.

AERO

Midget	100-150	Cathedral. 1931.

AETNA

Aetna radios were sold by Walgreen's Drug Stores.

	75-85	Upright table. Black Mt. Aetna dial. 1936.
	40-60	Horizontal wood table. Oval gold Mt. Aetna dial.

AIR CHIEF *(See Firestone)*

AIR KING

720	30-40	Table. 1937.
800	40-50	Console (horizontal) Radio-phono. FM/AM. 1949.
824	125-150	Wood table. AM/SW. 1937.
4603	20-35	Wood table. 1946.
4604-D	30-45	Wood Table. Reverse painting on dial. AM/SW. 1946. (GOR)
4608	20-30	Table, plastic. 1946.
4609	25-30	Table. Wood, simple design. 1946.
4625	20-25	Table. Wood. Radio-phono (single play). 1946.
4700	40-60	Console (horizontal) Radio-phono-wire recorder. 1948.
4704	25-30	Table. Wood. Radio-phono. 1947.
A-403 "Court Jester"	25-35	Table. Radio-phono. 1947.
A-410	125-150	Portable. Built-in camera. Battery. Snakeskin. 1948.
A-511	30-40	Table. 1947.
A-600	700+	Table. Green and yellow Catalin. 1947.

AIR KNIGHT

CA-500	25-30	Table. Wood. 1947.
N5-RD291	25-30	Table. Wood. Radio-phono. 1947.

AIRCASTLE

Aircastle's radios were available at Spiegel's in the 1940s.

7B	60-80	Table. Radio-phono. FM/AM. 1948.
211	20-25	Table, brown with white knobs. 1949.
212	20-25	Table. FM/AM. 1949.
568	40-50	Table. Metal. Gray hammertone. AM/SW. 1946.
572	45-60	Console (horizontal). Radio-phono. 1949.

ARR: *Antique Radios: Restoration and Price Guide* / ARR2: *Antique Radio Restoration Guide, Second Edition* /
B1: *Antique Radio Price Guide, First Edition* by Bunis / B2: *Antique Radio Price Guide, Second Edition* by Bunis /
FOS: *Flick of the Switch* / GOR: *Guide to Old Radios* / RGA: *Radios: The Golden Age* / RR: *Radios Redux* / VR: *Vintage Radio.*

Model Name/Number	Price Range($)	Description
603.880	35-40	Portable. Leatherette. Radio-phono-recorder. 1954.
651	25-30	Table. Brown or white plastic. 1947.
652.5C1M/ 652.5T1M	25-35	Table. Maroon plastic. 1954.
652.5C1V/ 652.5T1V	25-35	Table. Ivory plastic. 1954.
738.5400	20-25	Portable. Plastic. AC/battery. 1954.
1068	40-50	Table. White with curved end. 1946.
5000	25-30	Table. White with stepped top. 1947.
5002	40-50	Table. White plastic. 1948.
5003	30-40	Table. Plastic, white or brown. 1947.
5011	25-30	Table. Wood. AM/SW. 1947.
5020	20-25	Portable. AC/battery. Leatherette. 1947.
6042	20-25	Table. Wood. Radio-phono. 1949.
6053	25-30	Table. Wood. Radio-phono. 1950.
6514	20-25	Table. Wood. 1947.
6547	20-25	Table. Wood. Radio-phono. 1947.
6634	30-40	Portable. Radio-phono. AM/SW. Leatherette. 1947.
9008-I	30-35	Table. Ivory. 1950.
9008-W	30-35	Table. Brown. 1950.
10002	40-50	Table. Plastic. 1949.
10003-I	50-60	Table. Ivory plastic. Wrap-around speaker grille. 1949.
10005	30-35	Table. White. FM/AM. 1949.
108014	30-40	Table. Plastic. 1949.
121124	50-60	Console (horizontal). Radio-phono. FM/AM. 1949.
127084	40-50	Console (vertical). Radio-phono. 1949.
131504	20-25	Table. FM/AM. 1949.
132564	20-25	Table. Wood. Battery. 1949.
138104	40-50	Console (vertical). Radio-phono. 1949.
138124	40-50	Console (horizontal). Radio-phono. FM/AM. 1949.
147114	30-40	Portable. Metal. Flip-up lid. AC/battery. 1949.
G-521	40-50	Portable. Leatherette. Tambour top. AC/battery. 1949.
G-724	25-30	Table. Wood. AM/FM. 1948.
PC-8	25-30	Table. Radio-phono. Leatherette. 1950.
SC-448	20-25	Table. FM tuner. 1949.

AIRADIO
3100	25-30	Table. Wood. FM only. 1948.

AIRLINE

Sold by Montgomery Ward. The store was active in radio very early, advertising radio catalogs in 1922 radio magazines. Tri-City made their early sets.

—	160	Table. 1 tube. 1925.
04BR-514A	30-50	Table. Push-button. Bakelite. 1940.
05BR-1525B	25-35	Table. Brown Bakelite. 1950.
05GCB-1540A	700+	Table. Rudolph the red-nosed reindeer. 1951. (RGA-98)
05WG-2752	60-70	Console (horizontal). Radio-phono. FM/AM. 1950.
14BR-514B	80-100	Table. White plastic. Push-button. 1946. (B2-15)
14BR-522A	50-70	Table. White plastic. 1941. (GOR)
14BR-911A	395	Console. Fully restored. 1941.
14WG-624A	30-40	Table. 1941.
14WG-806A	50-70	Wood table. Push-button. Cabinet curves over grille. 1941. (GOR)
15GHM-1070A	15-25	Portable. AC/battery. 1952.
15WG-1545A	25-30	Table. Brown. FM/AM. 1952.
15WG-1546A	25-30	Table. Ivory. FM/AM. 1952.
15WG-2749F	75-100	Console (horizontal). Blond. Radio-phono. FM/AM. 1951.
25BR-1542A	40-50	Table. Plastic. 1953. (B2-16)

AIRLINE—*continued*

Model Name/Number	Price Range($)	Description
25WG-1570B	30-40	Table. Bakelite. FM/AM. 1952.
54BR-1503B	30-35	Table. 1946.
54BR-1506A	30-50	Table. Ivory plastic. Push-button. 1946. (GOR)
62-77	70-90	Cathedral. Battery. 1933.
62-123	50-70	Upright table. 1935.
62-131	100-140	Console. 1935.
62-151	50-70	Upright table. 32 volt. 1934.
62-229	50-100	Cathedral. Battery. Movie-dial drive. 1936.
62-230	20-30	Table. Battery. 1935.
62-267	150-200	Console. Movie-dial drive. 1936.
62-277	75-125	Table. Movie-dial drive. 1936.
62-288 "Miracle"	75-125	Table. Push-button. Leaf design. 1936. (B2-17)
62-306	40-60	Table, wood. 1937.
62-315	50-60	Table. Deco. 1937.
62-326W	80-100	Cathedral. Battery. 1936.
62-350	75-100	Table. Brown. Push-button. Side knob. 1938.
62-351	60-80	Table. Push-button. 1936.
62-370	45-65	Table. 1939.
62-376	30-50	Table. Wood. AM/SW. Battery. 1939. (GOR)

1939 Airline model 62-376; AM/SW; 6-volt battery.

62-425	40-60	Table. 1936.
62-437	50-100	Cathedral. Battery. Movie-dial drive. 1936.
62-475	40-50	Table. 1936.
62-476	50-70	Table. White or brown Bakelite. Telephone dial. 1941. (GOR)
62-502	100-125	Table. White Bakelite. Push-button. 1939.
62-636	100-150	Table. Deco. 1938.
64BR-1208A	30-35	Table. Wood. Battery. Push-button. 1947.
64BR-1514A	50-60	Table. White Bakelite. Push-button. 1947.
64BR-1808	30-50	Table. Wood. AM/2SW. Push-button. 1947. (GOR)
64WG-1207B	20-25	Table. Wood. Battery. 1947.
64WG-1804	30-40	Table. Wood. 1946.
64WG-2010B	25-30	Table. Wood. Radio-phono. 1947.
74BR-1053A	20-30	Portable. AC/battery. 1948.
74WG-2505A	75-100	Console (vertical). FM/AM/SW. Push-button. 1947.
74KR-2706B	40-50	Console (vertical). Radio-phono. 1948.
74WG-1057A	30-40	Portable. AC/battery. 1947.
84BR-1517A	50-60	Table. Brown Bakelite. Push-button. 1947.

ARR: *Antique Radios: Restoration and Price Guide* / ARR2: *Antique Radio Restoration Guide, Second Edition* /
B1: *Antique Radio Price Guide, First Edition* by Bunis / B2: *Antique Radio Price Guide, Second Edition* by Bunis /
FOS: *Flick of the Switch* / GOR: *Guide to Old Radios* / RGA: *Radios: The Golden Age* / RR: *Radios Redux* / VR: *Vintage Radio.*

Model Name/Number	Price Range($)	Description
84BR-1518B	50-60	Table. White painted Bakelite. Push-button. 1947.
84BR-1815B	40-50	Table. Wood. Unusual plastic dial and grille. 1949.
84GCB-1062A	30-40	Portable. Flip-up lid. Metallic plastic front. Battery. 1948.
84HA-1810C	25-30	Table. Wood. FM/AM. 1949.
84KR-1520A	30-50	Table. Metal. Available in ivory, red, green, yellow, and blue. 1948.
84KR-2511A	50-60	End table. Drop down front for dial. 1949.
84WG-1804	20-25	Table. 1948.
84WG-2015A	25-30	Table. Wood. Radio-phono. FM/AM. 1948.
84WG-2506B	75-100	Console (vertical). FM/AM. 1949.
84WG-2714A	60-90	Console. Radio-phono. AM/FM. 1948.
93BR-460A	40-45	Table. Wood. Battery. 1940.
93BR-720A	35-45	Table. Wood. 1938.
93WG-800B	30-50	Table. AM/SW. Push-button. 1946.
94BR-1535A	80-100	Table. Wood with plastic grille. FM/AM. 1949.
94HA-1527C	25-30	Table. Brown. Woven grille. 1949.
94HA-1528C	25-30	Table. Ivory. Woven grille. 1949.
94HA-1528B	20-30	Table. White painted Bakelite. 1949.
94WG-1811A	30-40	Table. Wood. FM/AM. 1950.
94WG-2748A	60-80	Console (horizontal) Radio-phono. FM/AM. 1947.
GAA-990A	20-30	Radio-phono. Portable. 1956.
GEN-1130A	15-20	Transistor. 1961.
GEN-1218A	30-35	Transistor. Black. 1962.
GEN-1667A	20-25	Table. Transistor. Pink. 1961.
GEN-1668A	20-25	Table. Transistor. Maroon and white. 1961.
GEN-1685A	20-25	Table. Transistor. Turquoise and white. 1961.
GEN-2030A	15-20	Table. Transistor. 1961.
GSE-1077A	20-25	Portable. Green plastic. AC/battery. Personal style. 1954.
GSE-1078A	20-25	Rust plastic. Same as GSE-1077A.
GSE-1622A	50-60	Table. Marbleized plastic. 1956.
GTM-1200A	25-30	Transistor. Portable. AM/SW. 1961.
WG-2680A	30-40	Console (horizontal). Radio-phono. FM/AM. 1961.
WG-2805A	30-40	Console (horizontal). Radio-phono. Stereo. FM/AM. 1961.

AIRWAY
F	200-250	Table. Battery. 2 dial. 1923.
G	250-275	Table. Battery. 1923.

AIWA
AR-111	20-30	Portable. Early Japanese transistor. FM/AM.

ALGENE
AR-406 "Middie"	30-50	Portable. Cosmetic case style. Fake alligator. Battery. 1948.

ALTEC-LANSING
Still in business today, Altec-Lansing has manufactured hi-fi equipment and loudspeakers for decades.
60	50-60	Preamplifier.

AMBASSADOR
A-880	25-30	Transistor. 1960s.

AMC
126	40-50	Table. Triple circle grille. 1947.
DM-1800	50-60	Console (horizontal). Radio-phono. FM/AM. 1961.

AMERICAN BOSCH

American Bosch originally was a sales agency for Robert Bosch (Stuttgart, Germany). In 1912, it became the Bosch Magneto Co. with a plant in Massachusetts. However, Robert Bosch returned to Germany at the start of World War I, and the plant was seized and its assets sold as enemy property. Bosch, meanwhile, had formed another company in Germany, again with an American sales agency. Court fights followed through much of the 1920s to decide who owned the "Bosch" name. This was settled in 1929. During 1930 the two companies combined and became United American Bosch Corp.

Model Name/Number	Price Range($)	Description
5A	60-70	Table. Wood. 1931.
16 "Amborola"	150-200	Table. Battery. 2 dial. 1925.
28	100-125	Table. Wood. 1928.
460	65-75	Upright table. AM/SW. 1934.
505	50-70	Table. Wood. AM/Police. 1936.
515	40-50	Table. AM/SW. 1936.
604	30-40	Table. Wood. 1935. (GOR)
660T	40-50	Table. Wood. AM/SW. 1936. (FOS-53)
?	1000+	Table. Wood. Swastikas on knobs. Backlit German eagle surmounting another swastika on dial. 1936. (GOR)

AMRAD

Financier J. P. Morgan developed the idea for American Radio and Research Corp. By the time the company started, the elder Morgan had died. The company stayed busy during World War I. Unfortunately, during the early 1920s, they took many more orders than they could ever fill. Lagging behind demand, they couldn't keep up with the new ideas. Powel Crosley wanted their Neutrodyne license and bought the company in 1925. The Amrad name continued, and there was a plan to produce higher-priced sets under this marquee. The Depression put an end to this idea, and Amrad closed in 1930.

2596 and 2634	450-550	Tuner-detector. 2 dial. Near mint. Includes original instructions. One of several Amrad sets referred to as "Double-Decker." 1924.
A	250-300	Crystal. 1924.
DT	200-250	Amplifier. 1922.
Neutrodyne	75-100	Table. 3 dial. 1924.
T 5	100-130	Table. 1925.
81	100-125	Console. Highboy. 1929.

ANDREA

CPR-A25	40-50	Console (horizontal). Radio-phono. FM/AM. 1961.
P-163	40-50	Portable. AC/battery. 3 band. Fake snakeskin. 1947.

ANDREWS

II	150-200	Table. Battery. 3 dial. 1925.

ANSLEY

41 Paneltone	40-50	In-the-wall model. 1940s.

APEX

7B5	20-30	Table. Plastic. 1948.
41	150-175	Lowboy. Wood. 1930s.

ARBORPHONE

27	100-150	Table. Battery. 1927.
45	70-90	Table. 1928.
	90-100	Console. 1928. Same as model 45, except this has been installed in a cabinet supplied by another manufacturer.
Arborphone	225-250	Highboy. Included 18" Metro cone speaker. Battery. 1925.

ARR: *Antique Radios: Restoration and Price Guide* / ARR2: *Antique Radio Restoration Guide, Second Edition* / B1: *Antique Radio Price Guide, First Edition* by Bunis / B2: *Antique Radio Price Guide, Second Edition* by Bunis / FOS: *Flick of the Switch* / GOR: *Guide to Old Radios* / RGA: *Radios: The Golden Age* / RR: *Radios Redux* / VR: *Vintage Radio*.

ARTONE

Model Name/Number	Price Range($)	Description
R-1046-U	40-50	Table. White Bakelite. Aqua dial. 1946. (GOR)

ARVIN

Arvin radios were made by Noblitt-Sparks Industries, Inc.

10R16	20-25	Table. Green. 1961.
10R18	20-25	Table. Beige. 1961.
10R22	25-30	Table. Knobs in slots. 1961.
10R32	20-25	Table. Ivory. Twin speakers. 1961.
58	75-100	Table. Black Bakelite. 1937.
60R63	15-20	Transistor. Red. 1961.
60R69	15-20	Transistor. Black. 1961.
61R48	30-40	Transistor. 1961.
61R58	15-20	Transistor. 1963.
61R16	30-50	Transistor. Mint green. 1962.
71G	30-50	Table. Wood. 1937.
78	50-60	Table. Push-button. AM/SW. 1938. (FOS-60)
151TC	30-40	Table. Wood. Radio-phono. 1948.
152T	30-35	Table. Plastic. 1948.
182TFM	30-40	Table. Wood. AM/FM. 1947.
242T	60-75	Table. Ivory metal. 1948. (RGA-100)
	60-75	Yellow metal.
243T	60-80	Green metal. Same as 242T.
	60-80	Red metal. Same as 242T.
250P	30-40	Portable. AC/battery. 1948.
255T	30-40	Table. Plastic. 1949.
264T	25-30	Table. Wood. 1949.
265T	30-35	Table. Blond wood. 1949.
350P	30-40	Portable. AC/battery. Blue-green. Large center grille. 1949.
350PB	30-40	Portable. AC/battery. Maroon. 1950.
350PL	25-30	Portable. AC/battery. Beige. 1950.
358T	30-45	Table. Beige Bakelite. 1948. (GOR)
402	60-75	Table. Metal. 1940.
405	20-30	Table. Aqua plastic. 1950. (GOR)
440T	80-100	Table. Metal. Yellow. 1950.
441T	300-500	Table. Metal with foil front panel. "Hopalong Cassidy," Red or black. Foil must be in good condition. The aerial (called a Lariatenna) was designed to coil up when it wasn't in use and be hooked on the "pommel" of a saddle on the back of the set. 1950. (FOS-61; RGA-90, 91)
442	60-70	Table. Metal. 1948. (FOS-60)
444	60-80	Table. Metal. 1946.
450	20-25	Table. Bakelite. 1950.
451T	70-90	Table. Brown and gold Bakelite. Green and gold dial. 1950.
502	60-70	Table. White metal. 1939. (GOR)
522A	60-75	Table. White metal. 1941. (B2-26) (RR-49)
532A	1000+	Table. Butterscotch Catalin. 1941.
540T	70-80	Table. Red metal. 1951.
542T	50-70	Table. Metal. 1950.
544	50-60	Table. Bakelite. 1946. (GOR)
551T	25-30	Table. Wood. Large dial. 1951.
553	25-30	Table. Large dial covers grille. 1952.
554CCB	50-60	Console (vertical). Blond wood. Radio-phono. 1952.
554CCM	50-60	Console (vertical). Mahogany wood. Radio-phono. 1952.

ARVIN—*continued*

Model Name/Number	Price Range($)	Description
555	25-30	Table. Brown Bakelite. Push-button. 1946.
581TFM	30-40	Table. Plastic. Brown, rosewood, or black. AM/FM. 1953.
582CFB	50-60	Console (vertical). Brown wood. Radio-phono. 1952.
590TFM	25-30	Table. White. FM/AM. 1951.
664	20-40	Table. Brown Bakelite with handle. 1947.
665	60-70	Console (horizontal). Radio-phono. 1947.
950T2	25-35	Table. Black plastic. Ivory knobs. 1958. (GOR)
954P	20-30	Portable. Green plastic. 1955. (GOR)
1237 "Phantom Prince"	90-150	Console. Wood. Telephone dial. 1937. (FOS-59; GOR)
1581	20-25	Table. Ivory plastic. 1958. (GOR)

1955 Arvin model 954P; green plastic portable.

2572	30-40	Table. Unusual grained front. 1958.
2585	30-40	Table. Coral with white plastic. 1959. (GOR)
3510P	30-40	Portable. AC/battery. Jade-green. Large center grille. 1949.
5571	25-30	Clock radio. Ivory or green. Woven front. 1958.
5572	25-30	Clock radio. Red or charcoal. Woven front. 1958.
8571	20-25	Portable. AC/battery. Gray plastic. 1958.
8572	20-25	Portable. AC/battery. Green or tan plastic. 1958.
8573	20-25	Portable. AC/battery. Red or turquoise plastic. 1958.

ATLAS

AB-45	25-30	Table. Wood. AM/SW. 1947.

ATWATER KENT

Atwater Kent had been producing automobile parts for a number of years. A recession after the war led Kent to look for another product that would use the production techniques he knew. Deciding that radio was the coming thing, the company started making radio components. Soon they were being wired together at the factory. Eventually Atwater Kent radios became a household word. The radios were available in table models, but, until the end of the 1920s, other companies produced the highboys, lowboys, and tables to house them. Later on Atwater Kent made a full line of radio cabinets. Kent closed his business in 1936.

5	5000+	Breadboard. Battery. 1921. (VR-73)
9	600-900	Breadboard. Battery. 2 dial. 1924. (VR-75)
10	600-900	Breadboard. Battery. 3 dial. 1923.
10A	700-1000	Breadboard. Battery. 3 dial. 1924. (VR-75)
10B	500-700	Breadboard. Battery. 3 dial. 1924.
10C	500-700	Breadboard. Battery. 3 dial. 1924. (VR-75)
12	700-1000	Breadboard. Battery. 3 dial. 1924.

ARR: *Antique Radios: Restoration and Price Guide* / ARR2: *Antique Radio Restoration Guide, Second Edition* /
B1: *Antique Radio Price Guide, First Edition* by Bunis / B2: *Antique Radio Price Guide, Second Edition* by Bunis /
FOS: *Flick of the Switch* / GOR: *Guide to Old Radios* / RGA: *Radios: The Golden Age* / RR: *Radios Redux* / VR: *Vintage Radio.*

Model Name/Number	Price Range($)	Description
19	300-400	Table. Battery. 2 dial. 1924. (VR-76)
20	100-125	Table. Battery. 3 dial. Often called the "Big Box." 1924. (AR-9)
20C	75-125	Table. Battery. 3 dial. May be known as the "20 Compact." 1925. (VR-76)
20 DeLuxe	75-150	Table. 1925.
21	150-250	Table. 3 dial. Dry cell set. 1925.
24 DeLuxe	225-275	Table. Battery. 3 dial. 1925.
30	75-100	Table. Battery. 1926. (VR-76; ARR-21)
	175-225	Console. Same as 30, except this has been installed in a cabinet supplied by a different manufacturer. (ARR-11 has one example of a console cabinet. There were many others.)
32	75-100	Table. Battery. 1926. (VR-76)
33	90-120	Table. Battery. 1927. (VR-76)
35	30-70	Table. Metal. Battery. 1926. (VR-77; ARR-22)
	100-150	Console. Made by other companies.
36	75-100	Table. Metal. 1927. (VR-77)
37	50-100	Table. Metal. 1927.
40	50-80	Table. Metal. AC. 1928. (VR-77)
	100-150	Console. Same as 40, except this has been installed in a cabinet supplied by a different manufacturer.
42	50-80	Table. Metal. AC. 1928.
43	40-60	Table. Metal. AC. 1928.
	150	Console. Red Lion wood cabinet.
44	60-90	Table. Metal. AC. 1928. (VR-77)
45	50-80	Table. Metal. AC. 1929.
46	35-60	Table. Metal. AC. 1929.
	125-175	Console (various cabinets).
47	60-80	Table. Metal. AC. 1929.
48	60-80	Table. Wood. Battery. 1928. (VR-77)
49	60-80	Table. Metal. Battery. 1928.
50	60-80	Table. Battery. 1928. (VR-77)
52	90-120	Console. Metal. 1928. (ARR-40)
55	80-100	Table. Metal. 1929. (VR-77)
	125	Table. Red and black metal.
55C	125-175	Highboy and lowboys. Same as 55 but installed in various cabinets supplied by different manufacturers. (ARR-40,42 show examples of different cabinets.)
	200-300	Kiel table. Same as 55, except this is installed in a Kiel table, where the chassis is in the drawer and the speaker faces down underneath the table and bounces the sound from the floor.
55C	100-150	Lowboy. Wood. 1929. (ARR-40—picture identified as model 55 is really a 55C; AR-41—chassis.)
60	60-90	Table. Metal. AC. 1929.
60C	150-200	Lowboy. 1929. (FOS-63)
	200-300	Kiel table. Same as model 60 except installed in Kiel table. See model 55 for description.
70	125-150	Lowboy. 1929.
75	150-200	Lowboy. Radio-phono. 1930.
80	350-450	Cathedral. 1931. (B2-29)
82Q	175-225	Upright table. Battery. 1932.
84	350-450	Cathedral. 1931. (VR-263; FOS-64)
	400	Grandfather clock.
84Q	175-225	Upright table. Battery. 1932.
89	100-150	Lowboy. 1931.

Model Name/Number	Price Range($)	Description
90	350-450	Cathedral. 1931.
145	75-125	Upright table. AM/SW. 1934. (FOS-68)
165	150-250	Cathedral. AM/SW. 1933. (FOS-66)
184	200-240	Upright table. Wood. 1935.
185A	150-200	Upright table. Wood. 1934.
206	150-250	Upright table. Round top. AM/SW. 1934. (FOS-66)
217	250-350	Table. Round top. AM/SW. 1933. (FOS-66)
	450	Fully restored.
318K	175-225	Console. AM/SW. 1934. (ARR-59; FOS-68)
425	100-150	Console. AM/SW. 1934.
545	100-150	Upright table. Wood. 1936.
555	250-350	Chest. Inlaid walnut. 1933. (B2-31)
627	300-400	Cathedral. 1932. (B2-32)
700	1000+	Console. Oriental style.
708	250-300	Cathedral AM/SW. 1933. (FOS-66)
735	150-250	Table. 1935.
856	100-125	Upright table. AM/SW. 1935.
944	250-300	Cathedral. 1934. (FOS-68)

AUDIOSOUND

JB1939C	80	Novelty, juke box. FM/AM cassette.

AUTOMATIC

601	25-30	Table. Brown Bakelite. Louvered grille. 1946.
620	25-30	Table. Wood. Waterfall front. 1946.
B-44 Tom Thumb	50-60	Portable (Bike Radio). Metal. Battery. 1949.
TT 600	50-75	Portable. 1955.
Tom Thumb Buddy	30-50	Portable. Metal and plastic. AC/battery. 1949.

AVIOLA

601	30-40	Table. White. Eggcrate grille. 1947.
608	25-30	Table. Wood. Radio-phono. 1947.
612	25-30	Table. White. 1947.

AZTEC

Aztec radios were made by the Fred W. Stein Co.

130C	125-150	Cathedral. 1930.

BEARDSKY

Radios with the Beardsky moniker were made by the Beardsky Radio Shop.

	200-225	2-tube radio.

BELL

2255	50-75	Hi-fi. Tuner. FM/AM. 1955.
2440	30-40	Hi-fi. Stereo Amplifier.

BELMONT

Belmont Radio Corp. also made radios for several other companies, including Airline, Truetone, and Wings.

4B115	60-80	Table. Battery. Plastic. Large dial surrounding speaker. 1948.

ARR: *Antique Radios: Restoration and Price Guide* / ARR2: *Antique Radio Restoration Guide, Second Edition* /
B1: *Antique Radio Price Guide, First Edition* by Bunis / B2: *Antique Radio Price Guide, Second Edition* by Bunis /
FOS: *Flick of the Switch* / GOR: *Guide to Old Radios* / RGA: *Radios: The Golden Age* / RR: *Radios Redux* / VR: *Vintage Radio*.

Model Name/Number	Price Range($)	Description
5D128	100-125	Table. Black or White Bakelite. Push-button. 1946.
6D111	100-200	Table. Brown or ivory Bakelite. 1946. (RGA-69)
401	150-200	Cathedral. 1935.
534	100-200	Table. Push-button. Brown Bakelite. 1940.
602 "Scotty"	70-100	Table. Bakelite. 1937. (GOR)
635	75-100	Table. Ivory. 1940.
636	70-100	Table. Brown Bakelite. Push-button. 1939. (GOR)
840	100-150	Console. Wood. AM/2SW. 1937. (GOR)

BENDIX

A division of Bendix Aviation, they began making radios after World War II.

0526A	50-70	Table. Brown Bakelite. 1946.
0526B	50-70	Table. White Bakelite. 1946.
0526C	400-600	Table. Green and black Catalin. 1946.
0526D	400-600	Table. Tan and brown Catalin. 1946.
0526E	30-50	Table. Wood. 1946.
55X4	20-25	Portable. AC/battery. 1948.
65P4	30-40	Table. Plastic. Built-in handle. Metal grille. 1948.
69M9	50-60	Console (horizontal). Radio-phono. FM/AM. 1949.
75M8	50-60	Console (vertical). Open bottom. Radio-phono. FM/AM. 1949.
75P6U	40-50	Table. Brown plastic. AM/FM. 1949. (GOR)

1949 Bendix model 75P6U; AM/FM; brown plastic.

79M7	40-50	Console (horizontal). Radio-phono. FM/AM. 1949.
95M3	40-50	Console (horizontal). Radio-phono. FM/AM. 1949.
114	150-350	Table. Tan and brown polystyrene. Like 0526C/0526D. 1947.
115	150-350	Table. Ivory and burgundy polystyrene. Like 0526C/0526D. 1947. (RGA-70)
301	30-40	Table. Wood. 1948.
416A5	30-40	Table. Wood. 1948.
613	25-35	Table. Radio-phono. 1948.
626A	30-40	Table. White painted Bakelite. 1947.
636A	30-40	Table. Wood. Dark woven grille. 1947.
	30-40	Table. Wood. Light woven grille. 1947.
	30-40	Table. Plastic, brown. White knobs. 1947.
687A	25-30	Portable. AC/battery. Leatherette. 1949.
1524	60-90	Console (horizontal). Radio-phono. AM/FM. 1948.
PAR-80	30-35	Portable. Leatherette. AC/battery. AM/LW/SW. 1948.

BEVERLY

Warwick Manufacturing Co., Beverly radio's manufacturer, produced radios under at least 40 trade names, including Clarion and Steinite.

Model Name/Number	Price Range($)	Description
?	175-225	Cathedral. Made by Warwick Manufacturing Co.

BLAUPUNKT

20003 "Ballet"	50-60	Table. AM/FM/SW. Ivory Bakelite. 1961.

BOGEN

PR100A	20-25	Hi-fi Monaural preamp. 1957.
R602	20-25	Hi-fi Tuner (chassis only) FM/AM. 1949.
R775	25-30	Hi-fi Tuner. FM/AM. 1957.

BRANDES

B-15	125-175	Highboy. 1929.

BREMER TULLY

This was a company known for the quality of its workmanship. For more information about them, see Brunswick.

?	75-100	Kit. Nameless parts only. Battery. 1925. (VR-149)
Counterphase 5	75-100	Kit. Battery. 2 dial. 1925.
Counterphase 6	75-100	Kit or Table. Battery. 2 dial. 1926.
Counterphase 8	100-150	Table. Battery. 1926.
81	100-150	Console. 1929.

BRISTOL

?	100	Amplifier. 1 tube.

BROWNING-DRAKE

After several years of producing a kit radio which not only had innovative circuitry but also worked, Browning-Drake began business in 1927 to make complete receivers under its own name. By 1930 they were in financial trouble, and the company folded in 1937.

5R	100-150	Table. Battery. 2 dial. 1926-27. (VR-130)
6A	75-100	Table. Battery. 1927.
7A	75-100	Table. Battery. 1927.
	175-200	Same as one above, but installed in a cabinet supplied by a different manufacturer.
B-D	150-175	Kit. Battery. 1925. (VR-149)

BRUNSWICK

The Radiola name is found on Brunswick as well as RCA. They bought the Radiola chassis from RCA, then put their own name plate on it. Brunswick-Balke-Collendar had been making bowling and billiard supplies since 1845 (and still are). After using RCA radios in the 1920s, they bought Bremer-Tully and Farrand Loudspeaker Co. and made their own complete sets. In 1930, due to poor business, they sold the radio, phonograph, and recording business to Warner Brothers. Warner's kept the record end, but closed the radio business in 1932. (There was a 1933 line of Brunswicks brought out by Brunswick Engineers Inc., New York City).

D-1000	100-125	Console (horizontal). Radio-phono. FM/AM. 1949.
T-4400	60-90	Console (horizontal). Radio-phono. FM/AM. 1949.

BRYANT

?	300	Table. Wood. Battery. 1922.

ARR: *Antique Radios: Restoration and Price Guide* / ARR2: *Antique Radio Restoration Guide, Second Edition* /
B1: *Antique Radio Price Guide, First Edition* by Bunis / B2: *Antique Radio Price Guide, Second Edition* by Bunis /
FOS: *Flick of the Switch* / GOR: *Guide to Old Radios* / RGA: *Radios: The Golden Age* / RR: *Radios Redux* / VR: *Vintage Radio*.

BUCKINGHAM

Model Name/Number	Price Range($)	Description
2	100-125	Console. 1928.

BULOVA

Bulova made radios at two different times in its history—once in the early 1930s and again in the late 1950s.

100	40-60	Table. Blue plastic. 1957.
200	20-25	Portable. AC/battery. Leather case. 1957.
300	20-30	Table. 1957.
310	35-40	Table. Bright blue plastic. 1957.
600 series	200-250	Clock radio. Cathedral. 1933.

C

CANDLE

PTR-85C	30-40	Transistor with case. Black. 1963.

CAPEHART

The company was eventually purchased by Farnsworth.

1P55	15-20	Portable. AC/battery. Maroon and gold trim. 1955.
2C56	25-30	Clock radio. Ivory plastic. 1956.
3T55E	15-25	Table. Brown plastic. 1950. (GOR)
29P4	60-70	Console (horizontal) Radio-phono. FM/AM. 1949.
33P9	60-80	Console (horizontal) Radio-phono. FM/AM. 1949.
41P3	200-300	Console (horizontal) Radio-phono. FM/AM/SW. 28 tube. 1949.
406D	750	Console. Radio-phono. Flip-over changer. 1935.
P-213	30-45	Portable. Plastic. AC/battery. Available in green, gray-blue, black. Tartan grille. 1954. (GOR)
TC-100	20-30	Clock radio. Brown or ivory plastic. 1953.
TC-101	25-35	Clock radio. Gray plastic. 1953. (ARR2-5)

CBS-COLUMBIA

515	25-35	Table. Plastic. 1953. (GOR)

CHANNEL MASTER

6475	15-20	Transistor. 1965.
6508	15-20	Transistor. Black. 1961.
6509	25-30	Transistor. With case. Black. 1961.
6509	25-30	Transistor. Red. 1961.
6511	20-25	Table. Transistor. Battery. Green. 1961.
6512	20-25	Transistor. 1960.
6515A	30-40	Transistor. With case. 1961.
6610	25-30	Hi-fi. Tuner. FM/AM. 1960.

CISCO

1A5	30-40	Table. 1948.
9A5	30-40	Table. Contrasting grille and knobs. 1947.

CLAPP-EASTHAM

HR Radak	250-350	Table. Receiver. 1 tube. 2 dial. Battery. 1922.
HZV	100-200	Box. Detector-amplifier. Battery. 1922.
R4	250-300	Box. Receiver. 1 tube. Battery. 1924.
Radak DD	100-125	Table. Receiver. Battery. 1925.
RZ Radak	500-700	Table. Receiver. Battery. 2 dial. 1922.
ZRA	200	Box. Detector. Battery. 1920.

CLARION

Clarion radios were Gamble's house brand. Clarion radios were produced by the Transformer Corp. of America. Up until 1930, when they began making radios, TCA had been making radio parts. The company was sold in 1933, although the name stayed around until at least 1946. Current models with this name are being produced in Japan.

Model Name/Number	Price Range($)	Description
80	150-175	Upright table. Wood. 1931.
220	100-125	Upright table. Wood. 1931.
320	75-125	Upright table. Wood. 1933. (ARR2-92)
470	150-200	Cathedral. 1933.
510	75-100	Upright table. Wood. 1934.
691	50-75	Table. Wood. Telephone dial. 1937. (GOR)
770	30-50	Table. Wood. AM/SW. 1937. (GOR)
11011	20-25	Portable. AC/battery. Plastic grille. 1947.
11305	25-30	Table. Wood. Radio-phono. 1947.
12708	40-50	Console (small). Radio-phono. 1948.
12801	25-35	Table. Ivory, red, black, or green. 1949.
12110M	40-50	Console (horizontal). Radio-phono. AM/FM. 1949.
12801-N	30-40	Table. Plastic. 1948.
13201	20-25	Table. Ivory or brown. 1949.
13203	20-25	Table. Wood. 1949.
14601	20-25	Table. White or brown. 1949.
14965	25-30	Table. FM/AM. 1949.
AC40	150-200	Cathedral. 1931.
AC60 "Junior"	150-200	Cathedral. 1932.

CLEARFIELD

Made by Sherman Radio Corp., New York City.

TRF 6 RC	2000+	Table. Plate glass case. 1925.

CLEARSONIC

5C66	25-30	Table. Wood. 1947.

CLEARTONE

110 "Standard"	150-200	Table. Available in both a 1 dial and 2 dial version. Wood. 1926.

COLONIAL

32 "Cavalier"	100-150	Highboy with doors. Wood. 1929. AC. (GOR)
New World	1400-1700	Globe on stand. Black with Gold plated trim. 1933. (RGA-15)

COLUMBIA PHONOGRAPH

When radio came in, phonograph and record sales dropped disastrously. Columbia Phonograph Co. decided to move into the new broadcasting market and also began producing radios. In 1927, it became the Columbia Phonograph Broadcasting Co. and began network broadcasting. A few years later it was sold and became Columbia Broadcasting System.

C-4	125-175	Highboy. 1928.

COLUMBIA RECORDS

530	25-35	Table. Plastic. 1953. (GOR)
600BX	15-20	Transistor. Shiny round grille. Black. 1960.
600G	15-20	Transistor. Shiny round grille. Green. 1960.

ARR: *Antique Radios: Restoration and Price Guide* / ARR2: *Antique Radio Restoration Guide, Second Edition* /

B1: *Antique Radio Price Guide, First Edition* by Bunis / B2: *Antique Radio Price Guide, Second Edition* by Bunis /

FOS: *Flick of the Switch* / GOR: *Guide to Old Radios* / RGA: *Radios: The Golden Age* / RR: *Radios Redux* / VR: *Vintage Radio.*

CONCORD

Concord radios were distributed through Chicago and Atlanta mail-order houses.

Model Name/Number	Price Range($)	Description
1-504	25-30	Table. AM/SW (2 bands). Plastic. 1949.
6C51B	50-70	Table. Deco. Plastic. 1947.
6D61P	25-30	Table. Radio-phono. 1947.
6E51B	20-25	Table. Handle. 1947.
6F26W	30-40	Table. Wood. AM/SW. 1947.
CD61P	25-30	Table. Wood. Radio-phono. 1947.

CONTINENTAL

44	35-40	Table. Plastic. Bullet shape. (RR-75)
1000	80-100	Table. Plastic. Deco. About World War II. (GOR)
TR-801	10-15	Transistor. 1961.

J.K. COOR

	45-55	Crystal.

CORONADO

Coronado radios were sold by Gambles.

Note: Although Coronado used the entire model number on its radios, it isn't always found when looking at a set. In the Sams circuit diagrams, the first group of numbers is omitted. Therefore, if you don't find your set using the first numbers, check all of the numbers, starting with 43-.

05RA1-43-7755A	40-50	Radio-phonograph. Console. AM/FM. 1950.
05RA1-43-7901A	50-70	Radio-phonograph. Horizontal console. AM/FM. 1950.
05RA2-43-8515A	30-40	Table. Plastic. AM/FM. 1950. (GOR)
05RA4-43-9876A	20-30	Portable. Plastic, Metallic grille. AC/battery. 1950.
05RA33-43-8120A	40-50	Table. Plastic. 1950.
05RA33-43-8136A/ 8137A	15-20	Table. Walnut or ivory plastic 1950.
05RA37-43-8360A	40-60	Table. Plastic. Aqua front panel. 1950. (GOR)
15RA1-43-7654A	40-50	Console. Radio-phono. AM/FM. 1950.
15RA1-43-7902A	50-70	Console (horizontal). Radio-phono. AM/FM. 1950.
15RA2-43-8230A	25-35	Table. Burgundy plastic. Gold metallic grille. 1952. (GOR)
15RA33-43-8245A	40-50	Table. Red plastic. 1951.
15RA33-43-8246A	25-30	Table. Ivory plastic with green dial. 1951.
15RA33-43-8365A	25-30	Table. Plastic. AM/FM. 1951.
15RA37-43-9230A	30-40	Table. Radio-phono. Wood. 1951.
15RA38-43-8235A/ 8236A	20-25	Clock radio. Walnut or ivory plastic. 1950.
15RA38-43-8238A/ 8239A	20-25	Clock radio. Brown or ivory plastic. 1952.
35RA33-43-8125A "Chatterbox"	25-30	Table. Plastic. 1953.
35RA33-43-8145 "Ranger"	25-30	Table. Black with white plastic. 1953.
	30-35	Same as above. Red with white plastic.
35RA33-43-8225 "Moderne"	30-35	Table. Plastic. 1953.
35RA33-43-8375	25-30	Table. Brown with tan plastic. 1953.
35RA37-43-8355	25-30	Table. Plastic. 1953.
35RA40-43-8247A	20-25	Clock radio. Plastic. 1953.
43-37I-1	30-40	Table. Brown plastic. 1948.
43-37I-2	35-45	Same as above. Ivory plastic.
43-852	25-30	Table. White. Push-button. 1947.
43-6301	30-40	Table. Wood. Battery. 1946.

Model Name/Number	Price Range($)	Description
43-6730	60-70	End table. 1949.
43-6927	50-75	Console. 1948.
43-6951	50-75	Console. AM/FM. 1948.
43-7601/7601A/ 7601B	70-90	Console. Radio-phono. 1946.
43-7602	70-90	Console. Radio-phono. 1947.
43-7603	70-90	Radio-phonograph. Console. 1948.
43-7851	60-75	Radio-phonograph. Horizontal console. AM/FM. 1948.
43-8130	25-30	Table. Plastic. 1946.
43-8160	40-50	Table. Brown. Unusual center dial. 1947.
43-8177	25-30	Table. Plastic. 1947.
43-8180	30-40	Table. Plastic. 1947.
43-8190	150-200	Table. Plastic. Contrasting handle, knobs, dial. 1947. (RGA-77)
43-8201	40-50	Table. White painted Bakelite. Red grille. 1947.
43-8213	20-25	Table. Wood. 1946.
43-8240	30-40	Table. Brown Bakelite. 1946.
43-8305	40-50	Table. Plastic. 1947.
43-8312	40-50	Table. Plastic. 1946.
43-8330	35-45	Table. Square shape. 1947.
43-8351/8351A/ 8351B	40-50	Table. Plastic. Push-button. 1946.
43-8354	30-40	Table. Plastic. Push-button. 1947.
43-8360	40-50	Table. Brown Bakelite. Teal front.
43-8420	30-35	Table. Blond wood. 1947.
43-8437	30-40	Table. Wood. 1946.
43-8470/8471	25-35	Table. Wood. 1946.
43-8515	50-60	Table. Brown Bakelite. FM/AM.
43-8576	25-35	Table. Wood. AM/SW. 1946.
43-8685	25-35	Table. Wood. 1947.
43-9196	50-70	Table. Radio-phono. 1947.
43-9201	25-35	Table. Radio-phono. 1947.
43-9235A	25-35	Console. Radio-phono. 1954.
43-9751	20-25	Portable. AC/battery. Leatherette. 1947.
45RA1-43-7666A	50-60	Console (horizontal). Radio-phono. 1953.
45RA1-43-7910A	60-75	Console (horizontal). Radio-phono. AM/FM. 1953.
45RA33-43-8147A/ 8148A	30-40	Table. Black or maroon plastic with contrasting front. 1953.
45RA37-43-9235A	30-40	Radio-phonograph. Table. Wood. 1954.
94RA1-43-6945A	50-60	Console (vertical). FM/AM. 1948.
94RA1-43-6945B	50-60	Console (vertical). FM/AM. 1948.
94RA1-43-7605A	60-70	Console (vertical). Radio-phono. AM/SW. 1949.
94RA1-43-7656A	60-80	Console (horizontal). Radio-phono. AM/FM. 1949.
94RA1-43-7853A	60-70	Console (horizontal). Radio-phono. 1949.
94RA1-43-8510A/ 8511A	35-45	Table. Brown or ivory plastic. AM/FM. 1948.
94RA31-43-8115A/ 8115B	30-40	Table. Plastic. 1949.
94RA31-43-9841A	25-35	Portable. AC/battery. 1949.

ARR: *Antique Radios: Restoration and Price Guide* / ARR2: *Antique Radio Restoration Guide, Second Edition* /
B1: *Antique Radio Price Guide, First Edition* by Bunis / B2: *Antique Radio Price Guide, Second Edition* by Bunis /
FOS: *Flick of the Switch* / GOR: *Guide to Old Radios* / RGA: *Radios: The Golden Age* / RR: *Radios Redux* / VR: *Vintage Radio.*

Model Name/Number	Price Range($)	Description
94RA33-43-8130C/ 8131C	25-35	Table. Brown or ivory plastic. 1949.
94RA4-43-6945A	60-80	Console. AM/FM. 1948.
94RA4-43-8129A/ 8129B/8130A/ 8130B/8131A/ 8131B	25-30	Table. Plastic. Brown, white or black. 1949.
516	300	Lowboy. 2 speaker. 1935.
550	20-30	Table. Wood. 1933.
675	100-125	Upright table. AM/SW. 1934.
686	60-80	Table. Wood. AM/2SW. 1935. (GOR)
813	40-50	Table. Wood. Farm battery. 1938.
907	50-60	Table. Wood. 1939.
908	50-75	Upright table. 1939.
990B	100-125	Console. 1941.
RA12-8121A	20-25	Table. Plastic. 1957.
RA33-8115A "Pal"	20-25	Table. Plastic. 1955.
RA37-43-9240A	25-30	Table. Radio-phono. Wood. 1955.
RA37-43-9855	25-35	Portable. Plastic. AC/battery. 1954.
RA44-8140A/8141A	25-30	Table. Rosewood or coral plastic. 1955.
RA44-8340A/8341A	25-30	Table. Green or ivory plastic. 1955.
RA48-8182	20-25	Clock radio. 1960.
RA48-8257	20-25	Table. Plastic. 1958.
RA48-8342A	25-30	Table. Brown plastic. 1956.
RA48-8351A	40-50	Table. Ivory plastic. Striking "V" and crown grille. 1956.
RA48-8357	20-25	Table. Plastic. 1958.
TV2-9245A/9246A/ 9246B	50-70	Console. 1955.

CRAFTSMAN

900	100	Hi-fi. Tuner, FM. Chrome. 1954.

CROSLEY

In 1921, Powel Crosley developed an inexpensive radio design when he found that it would cost $130 to buy a set for his son. A talented engineer, he found ways to produce better, cheaper parts for radios. Station WLW (Cincinnati) was started to promote radio sales. In 1929, Crosley acquired Amrad. He was always interested in making good quality, inexpensive appliances. Crosley produced refrigerators in the 1930s, including one with a radio built into the front of the cabinet. He also tried to produce a cheap car, both before and after World War II. **Note:** Roman numerals are listed as numbers, not letters of the alphabet.

3R3 "Trirdyn"	50-80	Table. 2 dial. Battery. 1924.
IV	150-200	Table. 2 dial. Battery. 1922.
4-29	150-175	Table. Battery. 1926.
V	150-175	Table. Battery. 1923.
5-38	80-100	Table. Sloped panel. 3 dial. Battery. 1926. (VR-81)
5-50	75-100	Table. Slope-front. Battery. Wood. 1926.
5M3	100-125	Upright table. Small. 1934.
VI	150-200	Table. 2 dials. Battery. 1923. (VR-78)
	250	Same as above with rare mahogany case.
6-60	85-125	Table. Battery. Wood. 1927.
6H2	80-100	Upright table. 1933.
7H3	70-80	Table. Wood. 1934.
7V2	90-100	Upright table. Deco. 1934.
VIII	150-200	Table. 2 dial. Battery. 1923.
9-101	30-40	Table. Brown. Arched grille. 1948.
9-105	20-25	Table. AM/SW. 1949.

Model Name/Number	Price Range($)	Description
9-113	30-40	Table. Plastic. Metal grille. 1949.
9-121	30-40	Table. Plastic. 1949.
9-202M	60-70	Console (horizontal). Radio-phono. FM/AM. 1948.
9-205M	60-70	Console (horizontal). Radio-phono. FM/AM. 1949.
9-207M	60-80	Console (horizontal). Radio-phono. AM/FM/SW. 1949.
9-212M	60-75	Console (horizontal). Radio-phono. 1949.
9-214M	60-70	Console (horizontal). Radio-phono. FM/AM. 1949.
9-302	25-35	Portable. AC/battery. 1948.
X	150-200	Table. Battery. 2 dials. 1922. (GOR) (VR-78,81)
10-135	75-100	Table. White plastic. chrome grille. 1950.
10-139	90-110	Table. Lime green and chrome. 1950. (B1-45)
11-100U "Coloradio"	75-100	Table. 1951. (AR2-11)
11-102U	75-100	Table. 1950.
11-103U	80-100	Table. Orange plastic. Bullseye grille. 1949.
11-106U	25-40	Table. Black. Square center dial. 1952.
11-107U	25-40	Table. Beige. Square center dial. 1952.
11-108U	25-40	Table. Burgundy. Square center dial. 1952.
11-109U	25-40	Table. Green. Square center dial. 1952.
11-117U	75-100	Table. Plastic. 1951.
11-119	80-100	Table. Blue plastic. Bullseye grille. 1950.
11-123U	60-90	Clock radio. Maroon plastic. Deco.
XV	200-250	Table. Battery. Same as model X with speaker. 2 dials. 1922.
24AU	40-60	Table.
24AW	50-60	Table. AM/2SW. Push-button. 1941. (AR2-92)
25W	30-40	Table. 1941.
31-S	100-150	Table radio with legs. Metal. Deco. Speaker has design of electric bolts. 1929. (GOR)
33-S	80-100	Lowboy. Wood. 1929. (GOR)
34-S	100-125	Lowboy with doors. Wood. 1929. (GOR)
46FB	25-30	Wood. Table. Battery. AM/SW. 1946.
50	100-125	Table. Battery. 1 tube. 1924. (VR-79)
50A	100-125	Box. Amplifier. 2 tubes. 1924.
50P	225-300	Portable. Leatherette. Battery. 1924.
51	65-100	Table. Wood. Battery. 1924.
51A	100-125	Box. Amplifier. 2 tubes. 1924.
51P	75-125	Portable. Leatherette. Battery. 1924. (VR-79,80)
51S	80-110	Table. Sloped front panel. Battery. 1924. (VR-79)
51SD "Special Deluxe"	80-110	Table. Battery. 1924.
52	100-125	Table. Battery. 1924. (VR-81)
52S "Special"	100-125	Table. Battery. 1924.
52SD "Special DeLuxe"	100-125	Table. Battery. 1924.
52-TG	30-40	Table. Wood. 1941. (GOR)
54G "New Buddy"	175-250	Upright table. Molded wood. 1930. (GOR)
56TN-L	30-40	Table. Wood. AM/SW. 1947.
56TP-L	30-45	Table. 1948.
56TS	30-35	Table. Wood. Radio-phono. 1947.
56TZ	40-50	Table. Radio-phono. 1948.
58TA	40-50	Table. Burl grain paint. 1948.
58TK	30-40	Table. Plastic. 1948.

ARR: *Antique Radios: Restoration and Price Guide* / ARR2: *Antique Radio Restoration Guide, Second Edition* /
B1: *Antique Radio Price Guide, First Edition* by Bunis / B2: *Antique Radio Price Guide, Second Edition* by Bunis /
FOS: *Flick of the Switch* / GOR: *Guide to Old Radios* / RGA: *Radios: The Golden Age* / RR: *Radios Redux* / VR: *Vintage Radio.*

Model Name/Number	Price Range($)	Description
58TL	30-40	Table. Ivory plastic. Clear handle 1948.
58TW	40-50	Table. Plastic. Handle. 1948.
61	50-75	Table. Metal. DC. 1929.

Note: There was a model Sixty-One, an upright table radio, made in 1934.

Model Name/Number	Price Range($)	Description
63TA "Victory"	90-110	Table. Wood. The word "Victory" is decorated in red, white, and blue. 1946. (GOR)
66CS	60-90	Console (horizontal). Radio-phono. AM/SW. 1947.
66TA	50-75	Table. Brown Bakelite. AM/SW. 1946.
66TC	50-75	Table. Wood. AM/SW. 1946.
68TW	40-50	Table. White Bakelite. 1948.
82-S	100-130	Highboy with doors. Wood. 1929. (GOR)
86CR	60-90	Console (vertical). Radio-phono. FM/AM/SW. 1947.
87CQ	80-100	Console. Radio-phono. AM/FM/SW. 1948.
88TC	30-40	Table. AM/FM. 1948.
124H	200-250	Cathedral. 1931.
125	150-200	Cathedral. 1932. (GOR)
126-1	200-300	Grandfather-clock style. 1932.
141	300-350	Designed to look like a stack of books. 1932.
148 "Fiver D"	60-75	Table. Wood. 1933.
	150-200	Cathedral.
154	100-150	Cathedral. 1933.
158	150-200	Cathedral. 1932.
167	100-150	Console. AM/SW. 1936.
	150-200	Cathedral. (GOR)
169	150-200	Cathedral. 1934. (FOS-75)
181	75-100	Upright table. Wood. 1934.
515	75-100	Upright table. Wood. AM/SW. 1934.
516	50-60	Upright table. 1935.
517 "Fiver"	75-100	Upright table. Wood. 1934.
555	100-125	Upright table. AM/SW. Wood. 1935. (GOR)
566	35-50	Table. Wood. Battery. 1937. (GOR)
567 "Fiver"	30-40	Table. Metal. 1941.

1937 Crosley model 566; farm set. The impressive grille and the very small dial make this an interesting set.

Model Name/Number	Price Range($)	Description
587	60-80	Upright table. Wood. Six volt and AC. 1939. (AR2-9)
601 "Bandbox"	60-80	Table. Metal. Battery. 1927.
608 "Gembox"	75-100	Table. Metal. 1928. (VR-81) (ARR-32)
635-C "Buccaneer."	60-80	Table. AM/SW. 1935.
635-M "Buccaneer"	100-125	Console. Same as 635-C.
704 "Jewelbox"	60-80	Table. Metal. 1929.

CROSLEY—*continued*

Model Name/Number	Price Range($)	Description
706 "Showbox"	75-100	Table. Metal. 1928.
716	50-75	Upright table. 1941.
817	50-75	Table. AM/SW. 1937.
5628B	40-50	Table. Plastic. Push-button. 1937.
7739	100-125	Console. Push-button. AM/SW. 1939.
AC 7	60-80	Table. Slope-front. 1927.
Ace	100-125	Table. 1 tube. 1922.
Ace 3B	150-200	Table. Battery. 1923.
Ace 5	150-200	Table. Battery. 1923.
Bandbox		Applies to both models 601 and 602.
Bandbox Jr.	50-75	Table. Metal. Battery. 1928.
Buddy Boy	175-250	Table. Battery. Molded front. 1930.
Coca-Cola bottle	1500+	Bakelite. 1934?
D10CE	90-110	Table. Pale blue plastic. 1950.
D10TN	100-150	Table. Green plastic. 1950.
D25MN	90-110	Clock radio. Plastic. Various colors. 1953. (GOR)
E10BE/CE/RD/WE	60-80	Table. Various color Plastic. 1953.
E15	50-75	Table. White with chrome. 1951.
E20MN	75-85	Table. Square. Large center dial.
E75GN	40-50	Clock radio. Plastic. 1953.
F5TWE	40-50	Table. Radio-timer. "Musical Chef." 1959.
Fiver		Applies to various models, all with five tubes.
Harko	250-450	Crystal. 1921.
Harko Sr.	200-300	Table. Battery. 1922.
Harko Sr. V	250-350	Table. Battery. 1922.
Oracle	300-400	Clock radio. Grandfather clock style. 1931.
Pup	200-300	Box. Metal. 1 tube. Battery. 1925. (VR-79)
RFL 60	100-150	Table. Wood. Battery. Picturesque front panel. (ARR-22)
RFL 75	150-200	Table. 3 dials. Battery. 1926.
RFL 90	150-200	Table. Wood. Battery. 1926. Showbox. Applies to both model 705 and 706.
Super 11	50-75	Console. AM/SW. 1937.
Super XJ	175-225	Table. Battery. 2 dials. 1924.
Super Trirdyn	100-125	Table. Battery. 2 dials. 1925.
Super Trirdyn Special	100-125	Table. Battery. 2 dials. 1925.
Trirdyn		See model 3R3.
XJ	150-200	Table. 2 dials. Battery. 1923. (GOR) (VR-81)
XL	175-225	Table. 2 dials. Battery. 1923.

CROWN

TR-750	10-15	Transistor. 1961.
TR-999	25-30	Transistor. 1961.

CRUSADER

?	100-125	Cathedral.

CUTTING AND WASHINGTON

11A	300-350	Table. Battery. 2 dial. 1922.

CYART

	2000+	Table. Lucite.

ARR: *Antique Radios: Restoration and Price Guide* / ARR2: *Antique Radio Restoration Guide, Second Edition* /
B1: *Antique Radio Price Guide, First Edition* by Bunis / B2: *Antique Radio Price Guide, Second Edition* by Bunis /
FOS: *Flick of the Switch* / GOR: *Guide to Old Radios* / RGA: *Radios: The Golden Age* / RR: *Radios Redux* / VR: *Vintage Radio*.

D

DAHLBERG

Based in Minnesota, the Dahlberg Co. now makes hearing aids.

Model Name/Number	Price Range($)	Description
430-D1	100-200	Pillow speaker radio for hotels. (RGA-101)

DAY-FAN

The Dayton Fan and Motor Co. began in 1889 and made all sorts of heavy-duty fans for large buildings. In 1922 they came out with their first radios, which could be mounted on panels or breadboards. In 1926 the company changed its name to the Day-Fan Electric Co. After continuing to lose money (reported to be $200,000 a year), it was finally sold to General Motors and RCA in 1929. The government brought an anti-trust suit, and the company was finally liquidated in 1931.

5 (5114)	60-80	Table. Battery. 1925. (VR-128)
Dayola (5112)	80-100	Table. Battery. 4 dial. 1925.
OEM 7	80-100	Table. Battery. OEM 7 includes both model 5106 (1924) and model 5111. 3 dial. (1925).
OEM 11 (5105)	75-100	Table. Battery. 3 dial. 1924.

DE FOREST

When Lee De Forest invented the Audion tube, one that actually amplified, he created a major break-through in radio broadcasting. Unfortunately, his business mind wasn't as sharp as his scientific one. When he sold his patents to AT&T, however, he kept the right to produce amateur equipment. Always interested in broadcasting, he returned to the air in 1916 on a regular schedule. This helped create a market for his equipment. He also broadcast the election returns in 1916. Using a special line from the New York American, he announced to his audience that the winner was—Charles Evans Hughes.

15 panel	1500+	Panel. 2 dial. Battery. 1919. (VR-83)
D7	600-700	Table. Battery. 2 dial. 1922.
D10	500-600	Table. 2 dial. Loop antenna. Battery. 1923. (VR-84)
D12	400-500	Table. Battery. Loop antenna. 2 dial. 1924. (GOR)
D17	300-500	Table. 2 dial. Loop antenna. Battery. 1925.
DT600 "Everyman"	300-500	Crystal. 1922. (VR-84)
DT900 "Radiohome"	300-400	Box. 1 tube. 2 dial. Battery. 1922. (VR-84)
F-5 M	150-200	Table. Wood. 3 dial Battery. Enclosed speaker. 1925. (ARR-10; GOR)
F-5 AW	150-200	Table. Wood. Battery. 3 dial. 1925. (GOR)

DE FOREST CROSLEY

51	100-150	Table. Battery. 1924.

DEARBORN

100	120	Chairside. Radio-phono. 1947.

DELCO

We think of Delco as a division of General Motors. However, the division was really the United Motor Service, which produced GM parts. Delco was simply the trade name.

R-1116	30-40	Table. Wood. 1938.
R-1119	50-60	Console. AM/2SW/LW. 1937.
R-1128	65-75	Table. Wood. AM/SW. 1938.
R-1229	30-40	Table. 2-tone wood, white knobs. 1947. (GOR)
R-1230	50-70	Table.
R-1231A	30-40	Table. Plastic. 1947. (AR2-10)
R-1235	30-40	Table. Bakelite. 1946.
R-1238	50-60	Table. 2-tone plastic. 1948.
R-1241	30-40	Table. Wood. Radio-phono. 1949.
R-1243	25-35	Table. Plastic. 1947.

DELCO—*continued*

Model Name/Number	Price Range($)	Description
R-1249	40-50	Console (horizontal). Radio-phono. FM/AM. 1949.
R-1409	25-30	Portable. AC/battery. Striking style. 1947.
R-1430A	40-50	Table. White. Unusual grille. 1947.

DENCHUM

Denchum radios were made by Wilmak.

???	35-50	Table. Wood. Plastic handle. Wood louvers. Small. 1946. (GOR)
WW-446	50-75	Same as above, except stations are preset. Thumb knob is preset using screws on the bottom. 1946. (GOR)

DETROLA

100	50-75	Table. 1934.
302	200-300	Clock radio. Cathedral shape. 1938.
436	30-40	Table.
568-1	60-80	Table. Metal. AM/SW. 1946. (RR-57)
580	125-150	Chairside. Radio-phono. 1947.
582	60-90	Chairside. Radio-phono. AM/SW. 1947.
610-A	30-40	Table. Wood. Battery. 1949.
7270	25-30	Table. Wood. Radio-phono. 1947.

DEWALD

Dewald radios originally were produced by the Pierce Airo Co.

562	750-1000	Catalin. 1941.
802	100-150	Upright table. AM/3SW. 1934.
A501 / B501	250-850	Table. Catalin. Harp grille. Price depends on colors. 1946. (RGA-86,87)
A502	700-1000	Table. Catalin. 1946. (RGA-74)
A505	30-40	Table. Wood. AM/SW. 1947.
A605	25-30	Table. Wood. Radio-phono. 1947.
B400	25-30	Portable. Leatherette. Battery. 1948.
B401	50-60	Table. Ivory plastic. 1948.
	50-60	Table. Brown plastic. 1948.
B403	500-800	Clock radio. Catalin. Harp grille. 1948. (RGA-86,87)
B506	30-40	Table. White plastic. 1948.
B510	25-35	Table. Plastic. 1948.
B512	500-700	Clock radio. Catalin. 1948.
B515	30-40	Portable. AC/battery. 1949.
B614	35-45	Portable. Radio-phono. Alligator. 1949.
C516	25-30	Table. AM/SW. 1949.
C800	30-40	Table. FM/AM. 1949.
D518	25-30	Table. White. 1950.
H528	25-30	Clock radio. Plastic. 1954.
P705	30-40	Table. White. FM only. 1961.

DOTSON

E 7	75-100	Table. Battery.

DRAY

599	60-75	Table. Battery. 1925.

ARR: *Antique Radios: Restoration and Price Guide* / ARR2: *Antique Radio Restoration Guide, Second Edition* /
B1: *Antique Radio Price Guide, First Edition* by Bunis / B2: *Antique Radio Price Guide, Second Edition* by Bunis /
FOS: *Flick of the Switch* / GOR: *Guide to Old Radios* / RGA: *Radios: The Golden Age* / RR: *Radios Redux* / VR: *Vintage Radio*.

DUMONT

Model Name/Number	Price Range($)	Description
RA-346	75-125	Clock radio. Red lacquer with gold trim. Controls on side of the cabinet. 1956. (GOR) Also available without clock with same stock number.

1956 Dumont clock radio model RA-346; painted red with gold accents. The label on the bottom of the set identifies this number as a clock radio; however, it shows the tube layout for a similar-looking radio with the same model number.

DYNACO

FM3	30-40	Hi-fi. Tuner (stereo). FM.

DYNAVOX

3-P-801	20-25	Portable. AC/battery. Leatherette. 1948.

E

EAGLE

Neutrodyne	50-100	Table. Battery. 1923. (VR-133)
Neutrodyne, type B	50-100	Table. Battery. 1926.

ECA

102	30-40	Table. Brown Bakelite. Unusual grille. 1947.
104	25-30	Table. Wood. Radio-phono. 1946.
105	20-25	Portable. Radio-phono (single play). 1947.
121	75-100	Chairside. Radio-phono. Side changer. 1946.
131	25-35	Portable. Radio-phono Leatherette. 1947.
201	25-30	Table. Wood (two toned). 1947.

ECHOPHONE

Radio Shop (which consisted of three different companies) produced the earlier radios. Echophone was the sales organization. In the 1930s, they were produced by the Echophone Radio Manufacturing Co.

3	200-300	Table. 2 dial. Battery. 1923.
80	200-300	Cathedral. 1931.
A	150-200	Table. 2 dial. Battery. 1923. (VR-126)
EC-1A	75-100	Table. Communications receiver. 1AM/2SW. 1940.
EC-306	20-25	Table. Wood. Radio-phono. 1947.
EC 600	40-50	Table. Battery. 1946.
EX-102	25-30	Table. AM/SW. Unusual center dial. 1949.
R-3	50-75	Table. Sloped panel. Battery. 1925.
R-5	50-75	Table. Sloped panel. 2 dial. Battery. 1925.
S-3	200-300	Slant front. Exposed tubes.
S-4	100-150	Cathedral. 1931.
S-5	200-250	Cathedral. 1931.

EDISON

For many years Edison did not approve of radio. When he heard his Edison phonograph being used to play records over WJZ (Newark), he phoned to ask them to stop using the machine. "If the phonograph sounded like that in any room, nobody would ever buy it." But when he decided to build a radio himself, he built it in typically Edison fashion—a substantial, solid piece of furniture that was well engineered and built to last.

Model Name/Number	Price Range($)	Description
C4	600-750	Console. Radio-phono. 1929.
R2	100-150	Console. 1929.
R5	150-200	Console. 1929.

EICO

2715	60-70	Hi-fi. Tuner. FM (monaural).
HF-12	25-30	Hi-fi. Amplifier. 1959.
HF-65	25-30	Hi-fi. Preamplifier.
HF-81	60-75	Hi-fi. Power amplifier. 1959.
HFT-90	30-40	Hi-fi. FM tuner. 1960.

EISEMANN *(See also Freed-Eisemann)*

6-D	100-125	Table. Wood. 3 dial. Battery. 1925. (GOR)

EKCO (British)

AD 65	150-250	Table. Bakelite. Deco. 1934.

ELECTONE

T5T53	20-25	Table. 1946.

ELECTRO

B-20	20-25	Table. Wood. 1946.

ELECTROMATIC

512	75-100	Table. Wood. Radio Phono. 1946. (GOR)

ELECTRONIC LABORATORIES

710W	30-40	Table. Two speakers. 1947.

ELECTRO-TONE

555	25-30	Table. Wood. Radio-phono. 1946.

ELECTROVOICE

3304	40-50	Hi-fi. Tuner. FM/AM. Round dials. 1958.

EMERSON

31P56	20-25	Transistor. 1967.
32	75-100	Table. AM/SW. 1935.
38	75-100	Table. 1934. (FOS-82, identified as U6D)
107	100-125	Table. Deco. AM/SW. 1936.
149	60-75	Table. Bakelite.
238	200-250	Chest. Looks like jewelry box. 1939.
375	600-750	Table. Catalin. 5 slats left, 1 slat right. 1941.
400	500-700	Table. Catalin. Various colors. 1940. (RGA-53)
400 "Patriot"	750-1000	Red, white and blue.
410 "Mickey Mouse"	1000+	Table. Wood with metal trim. Black with chrome or ivory with cream. 1933. (FOS-82; RGA-13)
411 "Mickey Mouse"	1200+	Table. Molded wood. 1933. (RGA-12)
501	225	Table. Clear grille. 1946.
506B	60-80	Table. 1946.

ARR: *Antique Radios: Restoration and Price Guide* / ARR2: *Antique Radio Restoration Guide, Second Edition* /
B1: *Antique Radio Price Guide, First Edition* by Bunis / B2: *Antique Radio Price Guide, Second Edition* by Bunis /
FOS: *Flick of the Switch* / GOR: *Guide to Old Radios* / RGA: *Radios: The Golden Age* / RR: *Radios Redux* / VR: *Vintage Radio.*

Model Name/Number	Price Range($)	Description
507	30-40	Table. Brown or ivory plastic. 1946.
508	40-50	Portable. Black. 1946.
509	40-50	Table. Brown Bakelite. 1946.
511	50-60	Table. 1946.
515	30-40	Table. Brown Bakelite. 1947.
517	80-100	Table. Black Bakelite. 1947.
519	40-50	Table. Wood. 1947.
520	200-250	Table. Swirled brown Catalin, white front. Aqua dial. 1946. (GOR)
522	50-75	Table. Ivory Bakelite. 1946.

1946 Emerson model 520; swirled brown plastic, white front; aqua dial; knobs not original.

524	30-40	Table. 4 band. 1947.
530	30-40	Table. AM/SW. 1947.
532	30-40	Table. Battery. 1947.
535	30-40	Table. Wood. Perforated metal grille. 1947.
536	30-40	Portable. AC/battery. Leatherette. 1948.
539	30-40	Table. 1946.
540A	60-80	Table. Small. 1947. (ARR2-111)
541	40-50	Table. Wood. 1948. (GOR)
543	40-50	Table. Plastic. Metal grille. Deco. 1947.
544	40-50	Table. Plastic. 1947.
547	100-150	Table. Marbled green. 1947.
547A	30-40	Table. White or red plastic. 1947. (GOR)
552	25-30	Table. Wood. Radio-phono. 1947.
553A	30-40	Portable. New in box. 1947.
558	30-40	Portable. 1947.
559A	30-40	Portable. Swirled maroon plastic front. Molded alligator grain case. 1948. (ARR-67)
560	60-70	Portable. Red. 1947.
561	50-60	Table. Setback gold grille. 1949.
564	800+	Midget table. Green, red, or black Catalin. 1940.
568A	20-25	Portable. AC/battery. 1949.
569	25-30	Portable. White. 1949.
570 "Jewel Box"	50-75	Table. Battery. Cover opens. Picture in lid. 1950.
572	80-100	Table. Large gold grille looks like clock. 1940.
576A	60-80	Console (horizontal). Radio-phono. 1948.
578A	40-50	Table. Wood. European styling. 1946. (GOR)
579A	25-30	Table. Bakelite. Radio-phono (open top). 1949.
581	30-40	Table. Ivory. Handle. 1949.

EMERSON—*continued*

Model Name/Number	Price Range($)	Description
587	25-30	Table. White plastic. 1949.
591	20-25	Table. Walnut or Ivory. 1949.
597	40-45	Table. Plastic. AM/2SW. 1950.
599	20-25	Table. Large. 1949.
602C	50-60	Table. Plastic. Side controls. FM only. 1949.
605	40-50	Console (vertical) Radio-phono. FM/AM. Dial under phonograph. 1949.
610A	50-70	Table. Plastic. Side controls. 1949.
635	30-40	Table. Plastic. Radio-phono (45 RPM only). 1950.
636A	40-50	Table. Plastic. Eggcrate grille. 1950.
641B	30-40	Table. Brown plastic. 1953.
645	30-40	Portable. Battery. 1949.
652	30-40	Table. White plastic. 1950.
653B	40-50	Table. White urea. 1952.
659	30-40	Table. AM/FM. 1949.
671B	20-40	Clock radio. Plastic. 1950.
688	20-40	Table. Wood. AM/FM. 1951.
691B	20-25	Table. Brown or ivory. AM/SW. 1952.
702B	25-30	Table. Wood. 1952.
703B	30-40	Table. Wood. Radio-phono. 1952.
707	80-90	Transistor. Red or black with case and box. 1962.
729B	30-40	Table. Ivory plastic. Metallic grille. 1953.
	30-40	Red plastic.
	30-40	Blue or green plastic.
745B	30-40	Portable. AC/battery. Tartan grille. 1954.
747	30-40	Portable. Plastic. Battery. 1954.
754D	25-30	Portable. Leatherette. Black or brown. AC/battery. 1954.
756B	20-30	Table. Black or brown plastic. 1953.
	30-40	Red plastic.
778B	35-50	Table. Black or ivory plastic. 1953.
	40-50	Red or green plastic.
779B	30-40	Table. 1953.
783B	30-40	Table. Radio-phono. 1953.
788B	50-60	Clock radio. Brown, black or ivory plastic. 1953.
801	50-30	Portable. Battery. Green, maroon, black or gray. 1954.
805B	20-30	Table. Brown or ivory plastic. 1954.
808B	25-30	Table. Black, ivory or gray plastic. 1954.
	30-40	Red, green, yellow or maroon plastic.
809A	60-75	Radio-phonograph. Horizontal console. 1954.
810	25-35	Table. Black plastic. 1954.
810B	25-35	Table. Brown, black, or ivory plastic. 1954.
	25-35	Green or maroon plastic.
811B	25-35	Table. Black, brown, ivory, green, or gray plastic. 1954.
812B	20-30	Table. Black. green, gray, or ivory plastic. 1954.
813B	25-35	Table. Black, brown, ivory, green, or gray plastic. 1954.
814B	25-30	Table. Radio-phono. 1954.
823B	20-25	Table. Brown or ivory plastic. 1955.
	20-25	Black plastic.
	25-30	Green plastic.

ARR: *Antique Radios: Restoration and Price Guide* / ARR2: *Antique Radio Restoration Guide, Second Edition* /
B1: *Antique Radio Price Guide, First Edition* by Bunis / B2: *Antique Radio Price Guide, Second Edition* by Bunis /
FOS: *Flick of the Switch* / GOR: *Guide to Old Radios* / RGA: *Radios: The Golden Age* / RR: *Radios Redux* / VR: *Vintage Radio*.

Model Name/Number	Price Range($)	Description
825B	20-25	Clock radio. Black, ivory, brown, green, or gray plastic. 1955.
826B	25-30	Clock radio. Black, ivory, brown, green, or gray plastic. 1955.
	30-35	Red or pink plastic.
830B	20-25	Portable. Plastic. AC/battery. 1955.
832B	20-25	Table. Brown, gray, ivory plastic. Side control. 1955.
	25-30	Green plastic.
833B	25-30	Portable. AC/battery. Tuning knob on top. 1957.
835A	35-40	Console (small). Radio-phono. 1955.
837A	25-30	Portable. Leather. 1955.
883B	30-40	Clock radio. 1947.
888	40-50	Transistor. White. "Pioneer." 1964.
888	50-60	Transistor. Red. "Vanguard." 1964.
888	125-150	Transistor. Black "Atlas." 1960.
888	150-200	Transistor. White. "Vanguard." 1960.
1002	25-30	Table. Bakelite. Earphone output. 1947.
AR-180	580	Console. Fully restored. 1937.
AU-190	2000+	Table. Catalin, Butterscotch, green. 1938. (RGA-40,41)
AX-235	750-1000	Table. Catalin. 1938. (FOS-83) (RGA-29)
BA-199	75-100	Table. Brown Bakelite. 1938. (FOS-82; GOR; RGA-31)
BD-197	300-350	Table. Wood. AM/SW. Deco. Known (for self-evident reasons) as the "Dolly Parton" set. 1941-1942.
BL-200	50-60	Table. Brown Bakelite, AM/SW. 1938. (B2-70)
BM-206	30-50	Table. Bakelite. 1938.
BT-245	3000+	Table. Catalin. Yellow. 1939. (RGA-40)
CG-268	30-40	Table. 1939.
CH-256	300-400	Table. Wood. Violin-shaped case. 1939.
CJ-211	75-100	Table. 1938.
CQ-273	50-75	Table. Wood. AM/SW. 1939.
EC-301	30-40	Table. 1940.
FP-421	30-40	Table. 1941.
FU-427	25-35	Portable. Cloth covered. 1941. (GOR)
J-106	50-60	
K-40	75-100	
L-559 "Radio chest"	200-250	Chest. 1932.
Mickey Mouse	See models 410 and 411.	
Patriot	See model 400.	
Q-236 "Snow White"	1000+	Table. Molded wood. Characters hand-painted by Disney artists.
R-156	50-100	Upright table. Wood. 1936.
U-5A	250-350	Table. Urea. 1935. (FOS-82; RGA-18)

EMUD (German)

915	60-70	Console (vertical). Stereo radio-phono. FM/AM/SW. 1961.
Rekord 196 "Junior"	75-100	Table. 1960. (AR-68)
Rekord Senior	50-60	1950s.

ERLA

22P	300-400	Cathedral with clock.
DeLuxe 5	100-150	Table. Battery. 3 dial. 1925.
Pearson 5	80-90	Table. Battery. 3 dial. 1925.
Single 6	80-90	Table. Battery. 1927.

ESPY

18B	25-30	Table. Wood. Square. 1950.
581	60-70	Table. Metal. AC/battery. 3 band. Portable. 1947.
6613	25-30	Table. Wood. AM/SW. 1946.
RR-13	30-40	Table. Wood. AM/SW. 1946.

ESQUIRE

Model Name/Number	Price Range($)	Description
551	20-25	Clock radio. 1952.
60-10	30-40	Table. White. Contrasting grille. 1947.

EVEREADY

1	150-200	Table. Battery. 1927.
2	75-100	Table. Battery. 1928.
3	75-100	Table. Battery. 1928.

FADA

Frank A. d'Andrea changed his company's name to Frank A.D. Andrea, F.A.D. Andrea, and finally to Fada. Even though the corporate name might change, the sets were always Fada. As with so many companies, F.A.D. Andrea failed during the Depression. In 1932, the company was sold and its new name was the Fada Radio and Electric Corp. Andrea had meanwhile formed the Andrea Radio Corporation and was still running it when he died in 1965. In spite of current usage, Fada was not spelled in upper-case letters.

35-B	100-150	Highboy with doors. Wood. 1929. (GOR)
115	800+	Table. Catalin. This was the prewar version of the famous bullet. Price depends much on color. 1941. (RGA 64,65)
136	2000+	Table. Catalin. Blue. 1941.
160	100-150	Console. Wood. AM/SW. 1935.
160-T	75-100	Table. Wood. AM/SW. 1935.
170-A	75-100	Console. AM/SW. 1935.
175	60-75	Console. Radio-phono. AM/SW. 1941. **Note:** Fada also made the 175A, a 3 dial set in 1924.
185	75-100	Radio-phonograph. Console. AM/SW. 1941.
185/90A "Neutrola Grand"	150-250	Lowboy. Slant front panel. Drop front. Base has doors. Enclosed speaker above radio panel. 1925. (GOR)
192-A	100-150	Table. Battery. 1924. This model number was also used with different suffixes in 1935.
195	75-100	Console. Radio-phono. 1940.
252	200-250	Table. Wood. Similar to series 652 Catalin radio. 1947. (GOR)
254	150-200	Table. Black Bakelite. 1937. (RGA-27)
260B	100-200	Table. Black. 1935.
390T	150-200	Table. Wood. 1938.
454	300-400	Table. White plaskon with gold trim. 1937.
602	25-30	Table. Wood. Radio-phono. 1947.
637	20-25	Portable. Radio-phono. Leatherette. 1947.
652	700+	Table. Catalin. 1946. (RGA-67)
700	700+	Table. Catalin. Handle. 1947.
790	75-100	Table. White urea. FM/AM. Deco. 1949. (GOR)
795	40-50	Table. Plastic. FM only. 1948.
830	50-60	Table. Brown Bakelite. 1950.
845	150-200	Table. White plastic. Red handle and knobs. 1950.
855	40-50	Table. Swirled plastic. 1950.
1000	650-2000	Table. Catalin. Variety of colors. 1946. (GOR; RGA-64)
1001	25-30	Table. Wood. 1947.

ARR: *Antique Radios: Restoration and Price Guide* / ARR2: *Antique Radio Restoration Guide, Second Edition* / B1: *Antique Radio Price Guide, First Edition* by Bunis / B2: *Antique Radio Price Guide, Second Edition* by Bunis / FOS: *Flick of the Switch* / GOR: *Guide to Old Radios* / RGA: *Radios: The Golden Age* / RR: *Radios Redux* / VR: *Vintage Radio*.

1946 Fada model 1000. This Catalin radio has become highly collectible in the last few years.

Model Name/Number	Price Range($)	Description
Bullet		Refers to both model 115 and model 1000.
Streamliner		Refers to both model 115 and model 1000.

FAIRBANKS MORSE

9AC-4	125-175	Console. Wood. Telephone dial. 1937. (GOR)
68	20-30	Table. Wood. 1936.

FARNSWORTH

Farnsworth also made Capehart after World War II.

AT-50	50-75	Upright table. AM/SW. Push-button. 1939.
BT-54	40-50	Table. 1940.
CK-111	100-150	Console (Horizontal). Radio-phono. FM/AM. 1949.
DT-64	20-30	Table. 1946.
ET-066	40-60	Table. Wood. 1946.
ET-061	50-60	Table. Wood finish plastic. 1946.
ET-067	40-50	Table. Wood. 1946. (GOR)
GT-050	60-80	Table. Plastic. Deco. 1948.
GT-051	60-90	Table. Plastic. 1948.
GT-064	40-50	Table. Plastic. 1948.
GT-065	40-50	Table. Ivory plastic. 1948.

FEDERAL

57	400-500	Table. Metal. Battery. 1922. (VR-86)
58-DX "Orthosonic"	500-600	Table. Wood or metal. Battery. 1922. (VR-86)
59	700-1000	Table. Wood or metal. Battery. 3 dial. 1923. (VR-86)
61	700-900	Table. Wood or metal. Battery. 3 dial. 1924. (VR-86)
102	300-450	Portable. Battery. 2 dial. 1924.
110	600-1000	Table. Wood or metal. Battery. 2 dial. 1924.
141	300-400	Table. Battery. 2 dial. 1925.
161	750-1000	Highboy. Battery. 3 dial. 1925.
200	75-100	Panel. 3 dial. 1925.
A10 "Orthosonic"	100-150	Table. Battery. 3 dial. 1925.
Orthosonic		Refers to many models during 1925 and 1926 besides the A10.

FERGUSON

TRF (several models)	75-100	Portable. Battery. 1925.

FERRAR

T61-B	25-35	Table. AM/SW. 1948.
C-81-R	50-60	Console (vertical). AM/SW. 1947.

FIRESTONE

4-A-1	40-50	Table. Plastic. 1948.
4-A-2	20-25	Table. White. 1947.

Model Name/Number	Price Range($)	Description
4-A-3	50-60	Table. Plastic. 1948.
4-A-10	50-60	Table. Plastic. 1948.
4-A-15	75-100	Console (horizontal) Radio-phono. Large. AM/FM/SW. 1948.
4-A-17	30-40	Table. Radio-phono. 1948.
4-A-20	30-40	Table. Wood. AM/SW. 1947.
4-A-21	60-75	Table. AM/SW. Push-button. 1946.
4-A-25	25-30	Table. White. Knobs on top front. 1946.
4-A-26	40-50	Table. White plastic. 1948.
4-A-27	40-50	Table. Black plastic. 1947. (GOR)
4-A-31	50-60	Console (horizontal). Radio-phono. 1947.
4-A-37	60-75	Console (vertical). AM/SW. 1947.
4-A-41	40-50	Table. White plastic. 1948.
4-A-60	75-100	Console (horizontal). Radio-phono. FM/AM. 1948.
4-A-62	50-60	Console (horizontal). Radio-phono. FM/AM. 1947.
4-A-64	40-50	Console (horizontal). Radio-phono. FM/AM. 1949.
4-A-68	40-50	Table. Plastic. 1949.
4-A-69	30-40	Clock radio. Clock in center of grille. 1949.
4-A-71	25-30	Table. Wood. Radio-phono. 1949.
4-A-84	20-30	Table. Brown plastic with flocked front. 1950.
4-A-92	20-25	Clock radio. 1951.
4-A-143	20-30	Table. Aqua. 1956.
4-A-160	20-30	Clock radio. Plastic. 1957.
4-A-187	20-25	Table. Coral and Ivory.
4-C-3	30-40	Portable. AC/battery. Leatherette. 1947.
4-C-5	40-50	Portable. AC/battery. 1948.
4-C-13	20-25	Portable. AC/battery. 1949.
4-C-24	25-35	Portable. Cloth. AC/battery. 1954.
R-1313A	30-40	Table. Wood.
R-3051	40-60	Table. Wood. AM/SW. 1939. (GOR)
S-7403-4	40-60	Table. Wood. Small. Angled grille. 1939. (GOR)
S-7403-8	100-150	Upright table. Wood. Push-button. AM/2SW. 1939. (GOR)

FISHER

TX50	25-30	Hi-fi. Stereo amplifier.
KX100	40-50	Hi-fi. Amplifier.

FREED-EISEMANN *(See also Eisemann)*

They made both Freed and Freed-Eisemann. Later the company became the Freed Radio and Television Corp.

10	75-100	Table. Battery. 1926.
30	100-150	Table. Battery. 1926.
46	50-60	Console. FM/AM/2SW. Top opening. 1946.
50	80-125	Table. Battery. 1926.
FE-15	100-150	Table. Battery. 3 dial. 1925. (VR-88)
FE-28	30-50	Table. Wood. AM/SW. 1937. (GOR)
NR5	80-125	Table. Battery. 3 dial. 1923. (VR-88)
NR6	100-150	Table. Battery. 3 dial. 1924.
NR7	75-100	Table. Battery. 3 dial. 1925. (VR-88)
NR20	150-200	Table. Battery. 3 dial. 1924.
NR45	150-200	Table. Battery. 3 dial. 1925.

ARR: *Antique Radios: Restoration and Price Guide* / ARR2: *Antique Radio Restoration Guide, Second Edition* /

B1: *Antique Radio Price Guide, First Edition* by Bunis / B2: *Antique Radio Price Guide, Second Edition* by Bunis /

FOS: *Flick of the Switch* / GOR: *Guide to Old Radios* / RGA: *Radios: The Golden Age* / RR: *Radios Redux* / VR: *Vintage Radio.*

FRESHMAN

Freshman radios of the 1920s were made by the Charles Freshman Co. It's worth noting, however, that B.R.C. Co. made cathedrals with this name in the 1930s.

Model Name/Number	Price Range($)	Description
Masterpiece	100-200	Table. 3 dial. Battery. 1924-1925. (ARR-8) (VR-89)

G

GAROD

4A-1	40-50	Portable (Miniature). Front closes. Battery. 1947.
4B-1	20-30	Portable. Plastic. Battery. 1948.
V	75-100	Table. Battery. 3 dial. 1924. (VR-132)
5A-1 "Ensign"	40-50	Table. Plastic. 1947.
5A-2	100-150	Table. Green and dark green. 1946.
5A-4	30-40	Table. Plastic. 1948.
5AP-1Y	25-30	Table. Plastic. Radio-phono (single play). Open top. 1947.
5D	25-30	Portable (small). AC/battery. 1947.
5D-55	25-30	Portable. AC/battery. Metal and plastic. 1948.
6AU-1 "Commander"	750+	Table. Catalin. 1941. (RGA-58)
6BU-1A	25-30	Table. Bakelite. 1946.
6DPS	75-80	Console (horizontal). Radio-phono. 1947.
11FMP	75-90	Console (horizontal). Blond wood. Radio-phono. 1948.
126	1500+	Table. Catalin. 1940.
769	90-120	Table. Wood. Push-button. AM/SW. Mid-1930s. (GOR)
RAF	150-200	Table. Battery. 3 dials. 1924-1926.

GEC

GEC is the British General Electric Co.

8336	40-60	Upright table. European styling. About 1936. (GOR)

GELOSO

G307	200	Portable. 4 band. Italian.

GENERAL

R85 737	30-40	Table. Blue and gray plastic. AM/SW/Japanese FM. Made in Japan. Dials in English, chassis markings in Japanese. Ca. 1960. (GOR)

GENERAL ELECTRIC

General Electric was one of the originators of RCA in an effort to keep transoceanic communication out of the hands of the English. Under the original agreements, RCA wouldn't be allowed to make radios, but it would market them under its own name. Ironically, in 1986 the RCA consumer electronics division was re-absorbed by G.E. Then, as a final step, this combined consumer electronics division was bought by the giant Thompson S.A., a French electronics company.

Note: The earliest General Electric sets were made for and sold under the RCA name. Look for them there.

42 "Musaphonic"	150-200	Console (horizontal). Radio-phono. AM/2FM/3SW. Large. 1947.
60	35-45	Clock radio. Plastic. 1948. (FOS-95)
65	30-40	Clock radio. White plastic. 1950. (GOR)
107	20-30	Table. Brown Bakelite. 1946.
113	20-30	Table. Plastic. 1948.
114W	50-70	Table. White. 1948.
119W	50-60	Console (horizontal). Radio-phono. 1948.
123	20-25	Table. Large dial. 1950.
145	30-40	Portable (personal). Lays flat with flip up lid. 1949.
160	20-30	Portable. Plastic. AC/battery. 1949.
180	20-25	Table. Wood. Battery. 1947.

Model Name/Number	Price Range($)	Description
202	30-40	Table. White plastic. 1948. (GOR)
203	30-40	Table. Wood. 1946. (FOS-93)
210/ 211/ 212	40-50	Table. Plastic. Cloth front. FM/AM. 1948.
218	30-40	Table. Brown Bakelite. White dial. 1951.
220	25-35	Table. Brown plastic. Large dial. Gold trim. 1946.
250	50-60	Portable. Cast aluminum. Rechargeable battery. 1946.
254	25-30	Portable. AC/battery. 1947.
260	50-60	Portable. Cast aluminum. Rechargeable battery. 1947.
303	25-30	Table. Wood. Radio-phono. 1947.
304	30-35	Table. Radio-phono. 1947.
321	30-40	Table. Wood. Push-button. 1946. (GOR)
324	50-60	Console (horizontal). Radio-phono. FM/AM. 1949.
354	60-75	Console (horizontal). Radio-phono. 1948.
356	30-40	Table. Plastic. FM/AM. 1948.
357	20-30	Table. Plastic. 1948.
400	125-175	Console. AM/2SW. Push-buttons. 1941. (GOR)
402	25-30	Table. Plastic. 1950.
408	40-50	Table. Plastic. 1949.
409	40-50	Table. Brown plastic. FM/AM. 1952.
410	60-80	Table. Wood. 1952.
414	35-45	Table. Dark red swirled plastic. 1950.
	25-35	Brown plastic.
417	80-100	Console (horizontal). Radio-phono. AM/2SW/2FM. 1947.
422	40-50	Table. Marbleized maroon plastic. 1951. (GOR)
431	20-30	Table. Brown plastic with gold trim. 1954.
440	40-50	Table. Plastic. AM/FM. 1954.
502	100-125	Console (horizontal). Radio-phono. AM/2FM/3SW. Big. 1948.
511	35-45	Clock radio. 1949.
517	35-45	Clock radio. Red plastic. 1949.
522	25-30	Clock radio. 1950.
535	20-25	Clock radio. 1951.
555	25-35	Clock radio. Ivory plastic with brown knob and dial. 1954.
555G	25-35	Same as 555. Gray, with brown knob and dial.
	30-40	Red, with ivory knob and dial.
556	25-30	Clock radio. Maroon plastic. 1951.
581	25-30	Clock radio. White plastic. Gold grille. 1955.
606	20-25	Portable. Green plastic. AC/battery. 1950.
670	25-30	Portable. AC/battery. Black. 1957.
671	25-30	Portable. AC/battery. Black and white. 1957.
672	25-30	Portable. AC/battery. Rust and white. 1957.
673	25-30	Portable. AC/battery. Light blue and blue green. 1957.
675	60-80	Transistor. Black. 1956. GE's first.
741	60-70	Console (vertical). Radio-phono. 1951.
850	20-25	Table. 1956.
913	30-35	Clock radio. Pink plastic.
955 "Musaphonic"	25-30	Table. Brown plastic. Large speaker. 1955.
A-53	100-150	Upright table. 1934.
A-63	100-150	Upright table. AM/SW. 1935. This same model number was available as AM only in 1936.

Model Name/Number	Price Range($)	Description
A-70	100-150	Upright table. 1934.
A-82	150-175	Console. Deco. AM/3SW. 1936.
B-52	50-60	Car radio. Metal. Crackle brown paint. Dual voltage (6v and 110v). 1934. (FOS-91; GOR)
C-415A	25-30	Clock radio. White plastic. Black clock. 1957. (ARR2-61)
C-420B	25-30	Clock radio. Plastic. 1958.
C-433B	25-30	Clock radio. White plastic. 1960.
C-434B	25-30	Clock radio. Beige plastic. 1960.
C-436A	40-50	Table. 1959.
C-453	20-30	Table. Plastic. 1960.
C-480	25-30	Clock radio. White plastic. 1960.
C-517	30-40	Table. Red with white plastic. 1961.
Coca-Cola	40-60	Coca-Cola logo on usual transistor FM/AM radio. 1970s.
E-50	60-90	Table. Red with black trim. 1937.
E-52	40-50	Table. Wood. 1936. (GOR)
E-61	125-150	Upright table. AM/SW. 1936.
E-71	100-125	Upright table. AM/SW. 1936.
E-81	100-125	Upright table. AM/SW. 1936.
E-101	90-120	Upright table. Colorama tuning. 1937.
F-63	75-100	Table. AM/SW. Strong curve on side. Louvered grille. 1937. (GOR)
F-65	75-100	Console. AM/SW. 1936.
F-70	60-75	Table. AM/SW. 1937. (B2-87)
F-74	50-75	Table. 1937.

1937 General Electric model G-50; wood table radio with teledial tuning.

Model Name/Number	Price Range($)	Description
G-50	60-75	Table. Wood. Telephone dial. 1937. (GOR)
H-51	250-400	Lowboy. Push-button. Made by RCA. Same as Radiola 82. 1931.
H-77	200-250	Console. Radio-phono. Push-button. AM/SW. 1939. (FOS-92)
H-530	75-100	Upright table. 1939. (B2-87)
H-600	250-300	Table. Brown marble on white. 1939. (RGA-43)
H-623	35-45	Table. Wood. AM/SW. 1940.
H-634	30-50	Table. Wood. AM/2SW. 1940.
H-7101Y	800	Lowboy. Push-button. Remote control. Made by RCA. Same as RCA Radiola 86. 1931.

GENERAL ELECTRIC—*continued*

Model Name/Number	Price Range($)	Description
HJ-624	50-75	Table. Wood. Push-buttons. Curved side. 1939. (GOR)
J-62	50-75	Table. Wood. AM/SW. (B2-88) 1941.
J-805	75-125	Console. Push-button. AM/SW. 1940. (B2-88) A fully restored example sells for about $700.
JCP-562	25-40	Table. Wood. 1942. (GOR)
K-40A	60-90	Table. Wood. 1933. (FOS-88)
K-43	125-175	Upright table. Wood. 1934. (AR-53) (B2-88)
K-48	75-100	Table. Radio-phono. AM/SW. 1933.
K-53	75-100	Table. Wood. Deco. 1933.
K-63	250-300	Upright table. AM/SW. 1933. (FOS-89)
K-80	200-250	Upright table. 1933.
L-630	40-50	Table. 2-tone wood. 1940. (B2-89)
L-631	40-50	Table. AM/SW. 1941.
L-641	40-50	Table. Wood. AM/SW. 1942. (GOR)
L-660	40-50	Table. Wood. Chrome grille. Push-button. (AR2-9)
L-740	50-75	Table. Wood. 3 band. 1941. (FOS-93)
L-916	100-125	Console. AM/2SW. Push-button. 1941. (GOR)
LB530X	45-50	Portable. AC/DC/battery. Self-charging wet battery. 1940.
LF-115	150-200	Table. AM/2SW/old FM. 1941.
Lowboy	125-150	Lowboy. Wood. Plain cabinet, fancy grille. 1930. (FOS- 86; GOR)
M-50	100-125	Upright table. (Made by RCA) 1934.
M-51A	100-125	Upright table. 1935.
M-62	60-90	Upright table. Wood. Made by RCA. Similar to RCA model 125. 1934.
M-63	40-50	Upright table. Deco. 1933.
M-81	125-150	Upright table. AM/SW. 1934.
P-780B	15-20	Transistor. 1958.
P-800A	30-40	Transistor. Case. 1960.
P-807E	20-25	Transistor. 1962.
P-815A	15-20	Transistor. 1961.
P-940C	10-15	Transistor. FM/AM Brown with gold grille. 1965.
P-968B	10-15	Transistor. 1965.
RC-1252A	40-50	Console (horizontal). Radio-phono. Stereo. FM/AM. 1961.
S-22A	50-60	Upright table. Made by RCA. 1931.
T-129C	20-25	Table. Turquoise. 1959. (B2-92)
T-142D	20-30	Table. White plastic. 1966.
T-155B	20-25	Table. Coca plastic. 1960. (AR2-46)
X-415	60-80	Table. Wood. AM/2FM/2SW. 1948. (GOR)
YRB-60-12	20-25	Table. White plastic. 1948.

GENERAL IMPLEMENT

9A5	50-75	Table. Plastic. 1948.

GENERAL MOTORS *(See also Dayfan and Delco)*

250 "Little General"	150-250	Cathedral. 1931.
252	125-150	Console (vertical). Pull-up door covers dial. Speaker faces the floor. 1932. (GOR)

ARR: *Antique Radios: Restoration and Price Guide* / ARR2: *Antique Radio Restoration Guide, Second Edition* /

B1: *Antique Radio Price Guide, First Edition* by Bunis / B2: *Antique Radio Price Guide, Second Edition* by Bunis /

FOS: *Flick of the Switch* / GOR: *Guide to Old Radios* / RGA: *Radios: The Golden Age* / RR: *Radios Redux* / VR: *Vintage Radio.*

GENERAL TELEVISION

Model Name/Number	Price Range($)	Description
3A5	30-40	Table. Plastic. 1946.
5B5Y	800+	Table. Yellow Catalin. Handle. 1947.
5B5G	1000+	Table. Yellow Catalin with green grille, knobs, handle. 1947.
9A5	300-400	Table. Bright yellow and green plastic. 1948.
9B6P	35-40	Table. Plastic. Metallic face. 1948.
19A5	30-40	Table. Plastic
21A4	20-25	Portable. Leatherette. 1947.
22A5C	25-30	Table. Wood. Radio-phono (single play). 1946.
23A6	20-24	Portable. Linen. AC/battery. 1947.
24B6	40-50	Table. Plastic. 1948.
27C5	40-50	Table. Plastic. 1948.
534	250-300	Table. Wood, piano shape. (B2-93)

GILFILLAN

Gilfillan began as a smelting and refining company in 1912. By 1915, it was producing parts for auto ignitions. Moving into early radio, it became a member of the Independent Radio Manufacturers, Inc., a group of 14 companies fighting RCA over its patents. In 1927, Gilfillan got the West Coast rights to the RCA patents.

66B "Overland"	40-50	Portable. Leatherette. Swing-out doors. Copper grille. 1947. (FOS-98; GOR)
68-48	75-100	Console (horizontal). Radio-wire recorder-phono. 1949.
68F	40-50	Table. Wood. 1947.
108-48	100-150	Console (horizontal). Radio-wire recorder-phono. FM/AM. 1949.

GLOBAL

GR-711	40-50	Transistor.

GLOBE

5BP1	20-25	Portable. Leatherette. AC/battery. 1947.
6P1	25-30	Table. Wood. Radio-phono (single play). 1947.
6U1	20-25	Table. Wood. 1947.
51	60-90	Table. Marbleized plastic. 2-tone. 1947.
62C	30-35	Table. Wood. Radio-phono. AM/SW. 1947.
457	50-75	Table. Plastic. 1948.
770	50-60	Portable. Battery. 2 dial. 1923.
830 "Duodyne"	125-150	Table. Battery. 3 dial. 1925.
900 "Duodyne"	175-200	Table. Battery. 3 dial. 1925.
Duodyne		Applies to at least 10 models from 1924 through 1926.

GLORITONE

Gloritone radios were made by U.S. Radio and Television Corp., which manufactured eight different small brands.

26	150-200	Cathedral. 1929.
26P	150-200	Cathedral. 1929.
27	150-200	Cathedral. Deco style. Dial is on right side, not centered. 1930. (GOR)
99P	150-200	Cathedral. 1931.

GRANCO

T-270	25-30	Table. Tuner. FM/AM. 1958.

GRANTLINE

W. T. Grant Co. sold Grantline radios.

501-7	40-50	Table. White plastic. 1948.
508-7	40-50	Portable. AC/battery. 1948.

GRANTLINE—*continued*

Model Name/Number	Price Range($)	Description
651	25-30	Table. Bakelite. 1947.
5610	100-125	End table. 1948.
6547	25-30	Table. Wood. Radio-phono. 1947.

GRAYBAR

Graybar was begun in 1925, and sold to its employees in 1928.

330	75-100	Table. Basically a Radiola 60 with a RCA 106 speaker. 1929.

GREBE

820	100-200	Highboy with doors. Back panel goes to floor. 1928. (GOR)
CR-5	300-450	Tuner-detector. Battery. 1921. (VR-93)
CR-8	300-450	Table. Battery. 3 dial. SW. 1922. (ARR-7; VR-93)
CR-9	400-500	Table. Battery. 2 dial. 1922. (VR-93)
CR-12	350-450	Table. Battery. 2 dial. 1923.
CR-13	500-650	Table. Battery. 3 dial. 1923.
CR-14	450-550	Table. Battery. 2 dial. 1924.
CR-18	500-700	Table. Battery. SW. 2 dial. 1926. (VR-94)
MU-1 "Synchrophase"	150-250	Table. Battery. 1925. (ARR-12)
RORK	250-300	Box. Amplifier. 2 tube. 1922.
Synchrophase Five	50-75	Table. Mahogany wood with mahogany Bakelite panel. 1928. (GOR; VR-94)
Synchrophase A-C Six	60-90	Table. Mahogany wood with burled walnut panel. 1928. (GOR)
Synchrophase Seven	150-175	Table. Battery. 1927.
"Synchrophase"		Model identification. Combined with model numbers on various models during the 1920s.

DAVID GRIMES

5 B "Baby Grand Duplex"	150-200	Table. 3 dial. Battery. 1925. (VR-127)
Baby Grand	75-150	Table. 2 dial. Battery. 1925.

GROMMES

10PG	30-35	Hi-fi. Monaural amplifier with controls. 1957.

GRUNDIG

87	30-50	Table. Ivory plastic. FM/AM. 1962.
97	40-60	Table. Maroon plastic. FM/AM/SW. 1958. (AR2-97)
200	70-90	Transistor. "Mini-boy" 1964.

GRUNOW

Grigsby-Grunow made the early Majestic radios. It folded during the Depression, and General Household Utilities got the Grunow name.

116	100-150	Console. 1932.
470	100-125	Upright table. 1934.
500	125-175	Upright table. Chrome grille. 1933.
501	100-150	Table. Wood with chrome grille. 1933.
502	40-70	Upright table. Battery. Deco. 1934.
620	30-50	Upright table. Battery. 1935.
680	50-75	Upright table. 1935.
750	100-125	Upright table. AM/3SW. 1934. (GOR)
850	60-75	Upright table. Wood. 1934.
1183	90-150	Console. Wood. Telephone dial. 1937. (GOR)

ARR: *Antique Radios: Restoration and Price Guide* / ARR2: *Antique Radio Restoration Guide, Second Edition* /
B1: *Antique Radio Price Guide, First Edition* by Bunis / B2: *Antique Radio Price Guide, Second Edition* by Bunis /
FOS: *Flick of the Switch* / GOR: *Guide to Old Radios* / RGA: *Radios: The Golden Age* / RR: *Radios Redux* / VR: *Vintage Radio*.

Model Name/Number	Price Range($)	Description
1291	250-300	Console. Wood. Telephone dial AM/3SW. Chassis 12B. 12 tube. 1936. (GOR)
1291 "Teledial 12"	200-300	Console. AM/2SW. 1936. (FOS-97)

GUILD

Guild sold a wide variety of novelty radios, tubes and transistors. These usually had a nostalgia theme to their styling.

Country bell wall phone	30-40	Old style wood phone.
American spice chest.	50-60	This was produced in several variations. (AR2-30)

HALLICRAFTERS

Hallicrafters originally specialized in amateur radio and communications equipment.

5R10A	25-30	Table. Metal. 4 band shortwave listeners radio. 1952.
5R230	25-30	Table. Maroon plastic. AM/SW. 1954.
5R231	20-25	Same as 5R230. White plastic.
5R232	25-30	Same as 5R230. Blue plastic.
406	60-90	Console (horizontal). Radio-phono. AM/FM/SW. 1948.
611	25-30	Table. Brown plastic, beige knobs. 1954.
612	30-35	Same as 611. Green plastic.
S-20R	40-60	Table. Multi-band. Metal. 1939.
S-22R	40-50	Table. Multi-band. Metal. 1940.
S-36A	40-50	Table. Multi-band. Metal. 1946.
S-38 A-E	30-60	Table. Multi-band. Metal. 1950s.
S-40	25-50	Table. Multi-band. Metal. 1946.
S-40B	50-60	Table. Multi-band. Metal. 1950.
S-41G	25-50	Table. Multi-band. Metal. 1946.
S-53	40-60	Table. Multi-band. Metal. 1948.
S-53A	40-50	Table. Multi-band. Metal. 1952.
S-55	40-50	Table. Metal. AM/FM. No built-in speaker. 1949.
S-58	40-60	Table. Metal. AM/FM. 1949.
S-72	30-40	Table. Multi-band. Metal. 1950.
Sky Buddy	25-50	Table. Multi-band. 1936.
SX-9 "Super Skyrider"	45-50	Table. Multi-band. 1936.
SX-24	80-100	Table. Multi-band. 1938.
SX-42	100-150	Table. Multi-band. 1948.
SX-43	75-125	Table. Multi-band. 1948.
SX-62	45-50	Table. Metal. Multi-band and FM. 1949.
TW 500	60-80	Portable. 3 band. AC/battery. 1954. (B2-98)
TW 2000 "World Wide"	75-100	Portable. 8 band. AC/battery. 1955.

HALTON

92-1	30-40	Table. Wood. Two tone.

HAMMARLUND

Hammarlund was a major manufacturer of Ham and communications receivers and transmitters.

HQ-129X	50-75	Table. Multi-band. Metal.

HARMON-KARDON

A-300	30-40	Hi-fi. Stereo amplifier.
A-400	20-25	Hi-fi. Monaural tuner.
Citation IIIX	150-200	Hi-fi. FM/AM tuner. 1962.
T-1040	30-40	Hi-fi. FM/AM stereo tuner.

HEATHKIT

Model Name/Number	Price Range($)	Description
AA-13	40-50	Hi-fi. Amplifier.
AJ-12	20-25	Hi-fi. Tuner. Stereo. FM/AM .
AR-3	20-30	Table. Multi-band.

Heathkit crystal set model CR1; the styling is the same as many of the other Heathkit products of the early 1950s (John Wilson).

3A	25-35	Hi-fi. Tuner. FM. (AR2-86)
GC 1-A "Mohican"	55-75	Table. AM/4SW.
GR-1085	25-300	Table. AM/SW.
SP-2A	30-40	Stereo preamplifier for hi-fi system. (AR2-108)
W-4B	30-40	Hi-fi. Amplifier. (AR2-108)
W-5M	40-50	Hi-fi. Amplifier. (AR2-108)
WA-2P	30-40	Hi-fi. Preamplifier. 1957. (AR2-86)

HI-DELITY

AM 51	20-25	Table. White plastic. Late 1950s.

HITACHI

TH-627R	50-60	Transistor. In box. 1961.
TH-848	20-30	Transistor. In box with accessories. 1964.

HOFFMAN

A-300	50-60	Table. Wood. 1946.
A-301	40-50	Table. Wood. 1946.
A-309	30-40	Table. Wood. Blond. Trapezoidal shape. 1947.
A-401	25-30	Table. Wood. Radio-phono. 1946.
A-700	25-30	Portable. AC\battery. 1947.
B-1000	80-100	Console (horizontal). Radio-phono. Blond wood. AM/2SW. 1947.
C-502	75-100	Console (horizontal). Radio-phono. Blond wood. AM/FM. 1948.
C-518	60-75	Console (horizontal). Radio-phono-wire recorder. FM/AM. 1949.
C1007	175-200	Console (horizontal). Radio-phono-wire recorder. Blond wood. AM/FM. 1949.
P-410	50-60	Transistor. Large (early) dial. 1957.
TP-706 "Trans Solar"	150-200	Transistor. Turquoise. 1959.

HOWARD

10	75-100	Upright table. Wood. 1931.
260	30-40	Table. 1937.
368	50-65	Table. Wood. 1938. (GOR)

ARR: *Antique Radios: Restoration and Price Guide* / ARR2: *Antique Radio Restoration Guide, Second Edition* / B1: *Antique Radio Price Guide, First Edition* by Bunis / B2: *Antique Radio Price Guide, Second Edition* by Bunis / FOS: *Flick of the Switch* / GOR: *Guide to Old Radios* / RGA: *Radios: The Golden Age* / RR: *Radios Redux* / VR: *Vintage Radio*.

Model Name/Number	Price Range($)	Description
435	50-75	Table. 1940.
474	40-50	Table. Plastic. AM/FM. 1947.
901A	40-50	Table. 1946.
906	50-75	Table. Wood. 1947. (GOR)
906C	100-150	Chairside. Radio-phono. 1947.

1947 Howard model 906; wood table radio.

HUDSON ELECTRONICS

RPM71	20-25	Portable. Radio-phonograph. Leatherette. 1952.

INTERNATIONAL (KADETTE)

The International Kadette was the first mass-produced plastic radio, back in 1932.

36	25-50	Table. Wood. AM/SW. 1937. (FOS-101)
40 "Jewel"	75-125	Table. Plastic. Contrasting grille. 1936.
66	40-50	Table. Wood.
77	60-80	Upright table. Wood. AM/SW. 1936.
B-2 "Kadette"	150-200	Table. AM/SW. 1933.
Classic	700+	Table. Striking horizontal grille. 1936.
K-25 "Clockette"	1000+	Clock shaped. Catalin. 1937.
K-28 "Clockette"	100-150	Clock shaped. Urea. 1937.

INTERSTATE

This company was based in Minneapolis, Minnesota.

130		Table. 3 dial. Neutradyne, battery. 1929. (AR2-10)

JACKSON

J-200 / J-400	20-25	Portable. Radio-phonograph. Leatherette. 1952.

JACKSON-BELL

Jackson (primarily a silent partner) and Herb Bell started this company in 1926. One of the Los Angeles companies that began making midget sets in 1929, they were well situated when the Depression hit. Because of poor order management, they were forced into receivership in 1933. Selling off the assets, the company paid off virtually all the money it owed.

60	100-150	Upright table. 1929. (FOS-102)

JACKSON-BELL—*continued*

Model Name/Number	Price Range($)	Description
62	200-300	Cathedral. Deco. 1930. (FOS-102; the top two models on the page are both 62.) **Note:** There were two distinctly different models known as 62. The one is an angular, Deco-appearing one with a sunburst grille. The other is a conventional rounded-top cathedral with a swan motif on the grille.
JP-50	20-25	Portable. Radio-phono (single play). Leatherette. 1952.

JEFFERSON-TRAVIS

Jefferson-Travis was an Emerson radio subsidiary.

JT-E212	15-20	Transistor. 1961.
JT-F211	20-25	Transistor. 1961.
JT-H105	20-25	Transistor. AM/2SW. 1961.
JT-H204	15-20	Transistor. 1961.

JETCO

PI-12	160	Bed table. Coin operated. Formica top.

JEWEL

300	30-45	Table. 1948.
304	40-50	Portable. Alligator. Battery. 1948.
502	20-25	Table. Plastic. 1947.
504	20-25	Table. Wood. 1947.
505	50-60	Clock radio (small). "Pinup." 1947.
814	30-40	Portable. Plastic. Strap over arm. 1948.
920	30-40	Clock radio. Brown plastic. 1949. (GOR)
935	30-40	Table. 1949.

1950 Jewel clock radio model 920; telechron clock; brown Bakelite **(Ed and Irene Ripley).**

960	40-50	Table. Large center dial on grille. 1950.
5040	20-25	Clock radio. Ivory. 1952.
5100E	20-25	Table. 1952.

JUBILEE

	85-100	Crystal.

JULIETTE MICRO

TR-73	40-50	Transistor. NIB.

KADETTE *(See International)*

KAPPLER
102T   35-40   Panel. Professional rack mount. 1949.

KELLER FULLER
14 "Radiette"   100-150   Cathedral. 1930.

KELLOGG
Wavemaster 500   100-150   Table. Wood. Battery. 1925. (VR-138)

KENMAN
5   50-100   Table. Battery. 3 dial. 1925.

KENNEDY
V   300-400   Table. Battery. Sloped front panel. 2 dial. 1923. (GOR; VR-96)
VI   300-400   Table. Battery. Sloped front panel. 2 dial. 1925.
X   400-500   Table. Battery. Sloped panel. 2 dial. 1923.
XV   300-400   Table. Battery. Wood. 2 dial. 1924. (VR-96)
20   150-250   Table. Battery. Wood. 1925.
63   100-150   Console (large). 1932.
110   600-900   Table. Battery. 4 dial. Wood. 1922. (VR-96)
220   500-600   Console (small). 1929. (ARR-4; VR-96)
281   600-800   Table. Battery. 3 dial. 1921. (VR-96)

KING
80   75-125   Table. Battery. Wood. 1927.
81A   80-100   Table. Battery. Wood. 1927.

KLITZEN
525   75-100   Table. Battery. 1924.

KNIGHT
Knight radios were the Allied Radio of Chicago house brand.
4D-450   25-30   Portable. 1948.
5A-152   25-30   Table. White painted. 1947.
5A-190   25-30   Table. White. Stepped top. 1947.
5B-160   20-25   Table. Radio-phono. (single play open top). Leatherette. 1947.
5B-175   25-30   Table. Plastic. 1947.
5D-250   30-40   Table. Plastic. 1949.
5D-455   20-30   Portable. AC/battery. 1948.
5F-525   30-40   Table. Plastic. 1949.

1941 Knight model B10517; sold by Allied Radio. This radio had no identification, since the decal under the push buttons had disappeared sometime in the past. It was only by chance that it was identified.

KNIGHT—*continued*

Model Name/Number	Price Range($)	Description
5F-565	30-40	Portable. Leatherette. AC/battery. 1949.
6A-195	20-25	Table. White painted Bakelite. 1947.
6B-210	20-25	Table. Wood. Radio-phono. 1947.
6D-235	50-70	Table. 1949.
6D-360	75-100	Console. Radio-phono. AM/SW. 1948.
7D-405	20-30	Table. Radio-phono. 1948.
11D-302	70-90	Console (horizontal). Radio-phono. AM/FM. 1949.
B10517	50-60	Table. Wood. Push-button. 1941. (GOR)

KODEL

C-13	150-250	Table. Battery. 2 dial. Wood. 1924. (AR-131; GOR)
C-14	80-100	Table. Wood. Battery. 2 dial. 1925. (AR-131; GOR)

KOLSTER

6D	60-90	Table. Wood. Battery. 1926. (AR-10)
6J	75-100	Table. Wood. 1927.
K-20	75-100	Table. 1928.
K-80	60-80	Console.

KORTING

1070	80-100	Table. Plastic, white front. 3 band\FM. 1962.

L

LAFAYETTE

E-77	20-30	Table. Plastic.
FA-15W	20-25	Table. Wood. 1947.
FS-204	10-15	Transistor. 1961.
J-62C	25-30	Table. Radio-phono. AM/SW. 1947.
MC-10B	20-25	Table. Brown Bakelite. 1947.
MC-13	25-30	Table. Wood. Radio-phono. 1947.

LAMCO

1000	40-50	Table. Mottled plastic. 1947.

LEADER

YT-98	20-25	Transistor. Black.

LEARRADIO

6617-PC	30-35	Table. Wood. Radio-phono. 1947.
RM-402C	30-40	Portable. AM/SW/LW. AC/battery.

LEUTZ

Pliodyne 6	275-350	Table. Battery. 1924.

LEXINGTON

6545	20-25	Table. Wood. Radio-phono. Open top. 1946.

LIBERTY

507-A	20-25	Table. Plastic. 1947.
A-6P	20-25	Table. Plastic. 1947.

LLOYDS

TR-10K	10-15	Transistor, with box. 1965.

ARR: *Antique Radios: Restoration and Price Guide* / ARR2: *Antique Radio Restoration Guide, Second Edition* /
B1: *Antique Radio Price Guide, First Edition* by Bunis / B2: *Antique Radio Price Guide, Second Edition* by Bunis /
FOS: *Flick of the Switch* / GOR: *Guide to Old Radios* / RGA: *Radios: The Golden Age* / RR: *Radios Redux* / VR: *Vintage Radio*.

MAGIC TONE

Model Name/Number	Price Range($)	Description
508	200-250	Keg novelty. 1948.
510	40-50	Portable. Fake snakeskin. Strap for overarm use. 1948.
900	250-300	Keg-lamp novelty. 1948.

MAGNAVOX

Magnavox entered the radio field by producing speakers ("Magnavox" = "Great voice"). They introduced the first one-dial receiver in 1924. Located in California, they had difficulty being competitive with more centrally located companies. The Depression forced them into a merger with a division of Amrad. The company continues to make consumer electronics, although since 1981 it's been as a part of North America Phillips.

2AM-70	10-15	Transistor. Portable. 1963.
2AM-80	30-35	Transistor. Case. 1964.
154B	100-125	Console (horizontal). Radio-phono. AM/SW. 1947.
155B	100-125	Console (horizontal). Radio-phono. AM/SW. 1947.
AM-22	20-25	Transistor. 1960.
AM-62	10-20	Transistor. Portable. 1962.
AM-80	25-35	Transistor. Portable. Aqua. 1965.
AM-89	10-15	Transistor. Portable (blue, beige, or white). 1965.
AMP-111A	75-100	Hi-fi. Receiver chassis. FM/AM/SW. 19 tube. 1949.
AT-61	20-25	Transistor. Table. (black, light green, beige) 1960.
FM-90	25-30	Transistor. Portable. FM/AM. 1961.
FM-96	25-30	Transistor. Portable. FM/2AM. 1961.
Imperial	1000+	Classic breakfront. Radio-phono. FM/AM. 1946. (FOS-105)
TRF-5	100-150	Table with doors. Large. Battery. 1924. (VR-128)
TRF 50	150-200	Upright table with doors Battery. 1924. (GOR; VR-100)

MAGUIRE

661	30-35	Table. Plastic. Round left dial. 1947.
700-E	25-30	Table. Wood with plastic front. Radio-phono. 1947.

MAJESTIC

Majestic was the name used by Grigsby Grunow until the company failed in 1934. After that, it continued as the Majestic Radio and Television Corp. while the Grunow name became associated with General Household Utilities.

1 "Charlie McCarthy"	500-1000	Table. 3-dimensional seated figure. 1938. (FOS-108; RGA-35)
1A-50	50-75	Table. Wood. Deco. 1939.
1A-59	40-50	Table. Wood. 1939. (GOR)
5A-410	30-40	Table. Wood. 1946.
6FM-773	40-50	Console. Radio-phono. Blond wood. 1949.
7C-432	25-30	Table. Wood. Square plastic grille. 1947.
7FM-888	50-75	Console (horizontal) Radio-phono. Leatherette door panels. AM/FM. 1949.
7JL-866	50-60	Chairside. Radio-phono. 1949.
7P-420	30-40	Portable. Leatherette. AC/battery. 1947.
8FM-889	60-80	Console (horizontal) Radio-phono. Leatherette inserts on doors. AM/FM. 1949.
10FM-891	60-70	Console (horizontal). Radio-phono. FM/AM. 1949.
12FM-895	80-100	Console (horizontal). Radio-phono. FM/AM/SW. 1949.
15	75-100	Cathedral. Deco. 1932.
	300-400	Grandfather clock. 1932.
20	100-150	Upright table. 1932.

Model Name/Number	Price Range($)	Description
50	150-200	Upright table. 1931. (FOS-107)
52	100-125	Table radio with legs attached. 1932.
	50-60	Table. Plastic. 1938. **Note:** Majestic used this model number for two very different models, one in 1932 and the other in 1938.
55	150-200	Cathedral. 1938.
75	100-150	Console (lowboy). 1936.
90	325	Highboy. Refinished. Restored. 1932.
92	100-150	Highboy. 1929.
101	75-100	Console (lowboy). Radio-phono. 1939.
103	100-150	Console (lowboy). Radio-phono. 1930.
130	60-80	Portable. Leatherette. Battery. Shaped like a purse. 1939. (FOS-107) **Note:** Another example of Majestic using the same number for two different years. There was also a model 130 console in 1930.
151	100-125	Upright table. 1931.
381	200-250	Treasure chest. 1933. (FOS-107)
461	100-150	Table. Deco. Chrome grille. 1933.
463	70-100	Table. Chrome grille. Deco. 1933.
511	300-350	Table. White Bakelite. Blue Catalin grille. 1938.
906 "Riviera"	200-300	Bookshelf radio. Deco. 1933.
921 "Melody Cruiser"	300-400	Ship with metal sails. 1946. (RGA-73)
T101	150-200	Radio-phono. 1941.

MALONE LEMON

Neutrodyne	50-75	Table. Battery. 1924-1925.

MANTOLA

Mantola radios were sold by B. F. Goodrich.

92-521	20-25	Table. Ivory. 1949.
92-522	20-25	Table. Brown. 1949.
R-654-PM	25-40	Table. Brown Bakelite. 1946.
R-7543	40-50	Table. Contrasting grille, handle. 1947.
R-75143	25-40	Table. 1948.
R-75152	25-35	Table. Radio-phono. 1948.
R-76162	50-60	Console. Radio-phono. 1948.
R-76262	100-125	Chairside. Radio-phono. Radio in drawer. 1948.

MARWOL

This company appears to have been in business only in 1925, but they listed thirteen different models for that year.

Console Grand	50-60	Lowboy. Battery. 1925.
Jewel	50-60	Table. Battery. 1925.

MASON

45-1A	25-30	Table. Brown Bakelite. 1947.

MCINTOSH

C-26	300-400	Hi-fi. Preamplifier.
C-8	150-200	Hi-fi. Preamplifier. 1956.
MC-30	575	Hi-fi. Pair of tube-type power amplifiers.
MC-60	995	Hi-fi. Pair of tube-type power amplifiers.
MX-113	400	Hi-fi. Tuner. FM/AM. 1968

MECK

Model Name/Number	Price Range($)	Description
4C7	30-40	Table. Ivory plastic. 1948.
6A6-W4	30-35	Table. Two-toned wood. 1947.
CD-500	20-30	Table. Radio-phono. 1948.
CE-500	30-50	Table. Plastic. 1948.
CM-500	25-35	Portable. Leatherette. AC/battery. 1948.
CR-500	30-40	Table. AM/FM. 1948.
CW-500	30-40	Table. Plastic. 1948.
PM-5C5-PW10 "Plymouth"	20-25	Table. Radio-phono. 1947.

MELODYNE

This Melodyne was made by the Melodyne Radio Co. of New York City. The four models listed in the Radio Collector's Guide were all made during 1926. Another company using the Melodyne name was the Radio Sales and Manufacturing Co. "Mellodyne" (with two "l"s) is a different company.

11	80-100	Console. 1926.

METRODYNE

Metrodyne radios were made by the Metro Electric Co., but Metro used its own name for the crystal radios it produced during 1923 and 1924. When they began building TRF sets, they used this more glamorous name.

Super 5	50-100	Table. Battery. Wood. 1926.
Super 6	100-125	Table. Battery. 1926.
Super 7	150-200	Table. Battery. Elaborate front panel. 1926. (ARR-23; VR-141)

MICHIGAN

It appears that Michigan made their radios during a four-year period, from 1922 to 1925.

Junior	100-150	Table. 2 dial. 1 tube. Battery. 1924.
Midget	200-250	Table. 2 dial. 2 tube. Battery. 1923.
MRC-3	250-300	Table. Battery. 1923. (VR-129)

MIDWEST *(See also Miraco)*

Note: Before World War II, Midwest appeared to have one of the finest model-numbering systems around. The first number shows how many tubes there are, the second is the model year.

18-37	200-300	Console. 18 tubes. 1937. (FOS-109)
P-6	25-30	Portable. AC/battery. AM/SW. Large. 1947.
TM-8	30-35	Table. Wood. 5 band. 1947.

MINERVA

L-728	35-40	Table. Wood, curved. 1947.
W-117-3	30-40	Table. Wood. AM/SW. 1947.
W-119	30-35	Table. Wood. 1946.
W-702B	25-30	Table. Plastic. 1947.

MIRACO *(See also Midwest)*

Miraco radios were made by the Midwest Radio Co.

MW	100-175	Table. Battery. 2 dial. 1924.
Ultra 5	200-300	Table. Battery. 3 dial. 1924. (GOR)

MIRRORTONE (Monarch)

850	50-60	Deco. c1935.

MITCHELL

1250	50-75	Bedlamp-radio. 1948.
1251	50-75	Bedlamp-radio. Ivory plastic. 1948.
1252	20-25	Table. Brown plastic. Woven grille. 1952.
1254 "Madrigal"	30-40	Table. Brown plastic. Large center dial. 1951.
1256	20-25	Portable. AC/battery. 1951.
1257	30-35	Clock radio. Ivory. Clock above radio. 1952.

MITCHELL—*continued*

Model Name/Number	Price Range($)	Description
1260	150-200	Lamp-radio. Rocket shape. 1949. (RGA-55)
1274	30-40	Table. Brown plastic. 1954.
1275	30-40	Same as 1274. White plastic.
1276	20-30	Portable. Plastic. AC/battery. 1954.
1287	25-30	Portable. Cloth. AC/battery. 1955.
Lullaby		Model name used to identify models 1250, 1251, 1260, and 1261.
Lumitone	100-125	Lamp-radio. 1940.

MOHAWK

After a merger with the All-American Radio Corp. in 1927, they became known as All-American Mohawk.

110 "Consolette"	150-200	Upright table. Interesting curved top piece. Battery. 1925. (GOR)
115 "Console"	150-200	Lowboy. Same radio as 110, with the addition of a base to make it into a floor model. Battery. 1925. (GOR)
A5	75-100	Table. Slant front panel. Wood. Battery. 1925. (GOR; VR-131)

MOHICAN

GC-1A	40-50	Portable.

MONITOR

TA56M	30-40	Table. Plastic. 1946. (ARR2-29)

MORSE

M-170	75-80	Transistor. Desk set.

MOTOROLA

Paul Galvin began building power supplies in 1928. By 1930 he was building automobile radios (hence "Motorola"). From car radios, it was an easy step into home radios.

3A5	30-40	Portable. AC/battery. 1941.
5A1	25-40	Portable. 1946.
5A5	30-40	Portable. AC/battery. Flip up cover. 1946. (FOS-113)
5A7A	40-50	Portable. AC/battery. 1948.
5A9B	20-30	Portable. Metal. 1949.
5C5	20-25	Clock radio, white.
5H11	20-30	Table. Brown plastic with red knobs. 1950. (GOR)
5J1	60-70	Portable. AC/battery. Lid, Oriental grille. 1950.
5J11R	30-40	Table. Red Bakelite. 1950.
5L1	20-25	Portable. AC/battery. 1950.
5M2U	40-50	Portable. AC/battery. Maroon. 1950.
5P21R	40-50	Portable. AC/battery. 1959.
5P32C	30-40	Portable. AC/battery. Light blue. 1957.
5P32R	40-50	Portable. AC/battery. Red and black swirl. 1957.
5P33W	25-30	Portable. AC/battery. White. 1957.
5R1	30-40	Table. Ivory Bakelite. 1951.
5T	75-100	Upright table. 1937.
5T22R1	40-50	Table. Orange plastic. 1958.
5T22Y	40-50	Table. Yellow plastic. 1958.
5X11U	40-50	Table. Brown, red knobs. Chrome grille. 1950. (RR-85)
5X12U	40-50	Table. Cream. Chrome grille. 1950. (RR-85)
5X13U	40-50	Table. Black. Chrome grille. 1950. (RR-85)
10Y	50-90	Console. Wood. 1937. (GOR)
41A	60-80	Table. Brown Bakelite. 1940. (GOR)

ARR: *Antique Radios: Restoration and Price Guide* / ARR2: *Antique Radio Restoration Guide, Second Edition* /
B1: *Antique Radio Price Guide, First Edition* by Bunis / B2: *Antique Radio Price Guide, Second Edition* by Bunis /
FOS: *Flick of the Switch* / GOR: *Guide to Old Radios* / RGA: *Radios: The Golden Age* / RR: *Radios Redux* / VR: *Vintage Radio.*

Model Name/Number	Price Range($)	Description
47B11	30-40	Table. Wood. Battery. 1947.
51A	50-75	Table. 1939.
51C	50-75	Table. Brown plastic. 1939.
51X11	30-40	Table. Brown Bakelite. 1941.
52B1U	20-30	Portable. Plastic. AC/battery. 1953.
52L1(A)	25-30	Portable. Green plastic with green knobs. AC/battery. 1953.
52L2(A)	25-30	Same as 52L1. Maroon plastic with maroon knobs.
52L3 (A)	20-25	Same as 52L1. Gray plastic with green knobs.
52M2U	40-45	Portable. AC/battery. 1952.
52M3U	20-25	Table. 1952.
52R11A	25-30	Table. Unusual grille. 1952.
52X13U	40-50	Table. Maroon. 1951.
53F2	30-40	Radio-phonograph. Bakelite. Table. 1954.
53H1	50-60	Table. Black plastic. 1954.
53H2	40-50	Same as 53H1. Gray plastic.
53H3	40-50	Same as 53H1. Green plastic.
53H4	50-60	Same as 53H1. Red plastic.
53R1(U)	25-30	Table. Brown plastic. 1954.
53R2(U)	25-30	Same as 53R1. Ivory plastic.
53R3(U)	30-35	Same as 53R1. Yellow plastic.
53R4(U)	25-30	Same as 53R1. Gray plastic.
53R5(U)	25-30	Same as 53R1. Green plastic.
53R6(U)	30-35	Same as 53R1. Red plastic.
56H	40-60	Table. Brown plastic. Large domed tuning knob. 1956. (GOR)
56R	40-60	Table. Red plastic. 1955. (GOR)
56X11	25-35	Table. Plastic. 1947.
57X1	25-30	Table. Aqua. 1957.
58A11	25-35	Table. Plastic. 1948.
58G11	25-30	Table. Brown. 1949.
58G12	25-30	Table. White. 1949.
58R11A	20-25	Table. 1949.
59F11	30-40	Portable. Radio-phono (45 RPM). Leatherette. 1949.
59H11	20-25	Table. 1950.
59H11U	25-30	Table. Large letters on dial. 1950.
59X11	20-25	Table. 1950.
62X11U	20-30	Table. Brown. Gold grille. 1954.
62X12U	20-30	Table. White. Gold grille. 1954.
62X13U	25-35	Table. Green. Gold grille. 1954.
65F12	20-25	Table. 1946.
65T21	60-75	Table. 1946.
65X1	20-25	Table. 1946.
66X2	30-40	Table. White plastic. 1956. (GOR)
67F12	30-40	Table. Radio-phono. Plastic. 1948.
67F14	60-90	Console. Radio-phono. 1949.
67L11	30-50	Portable. Simulated alligator. Flip-up lid. 1948. (GOR)
67X	40-50	Table. Dark wood. 1957.
67X2	30-40	Table. White. 1957.
67XM21	30-50	Table. Plastic. AM/FM. 1947.
68F11	40-50	Radio-phono. 1949.
68F14	30-40	Console (open bottom). Radio-phono. 1949.
68T11	30-40	Table. Plastic. 1949.
68X11	40-50	Table. Plastic. 1949.
69L11	50-70	Portable. AC/battery. Dial is a moving tape inside a clear handle. 1949.

MOTOROLA—*continued*

Model Name/Number	Price Range($)	Description
72XM22	25-30	Table. Green. FM/AM. 1952.
75F21	75-100	Console (vertical). Radio-phono. AM/SW. 1947.
77FM21	75-100	Console (vertical). Radio-phono. Setback top. AM/FM. 1948.
77XM21	40-50	Table. 2-tone plastic. AM/FM. 1948.
77XM22	30-40	Table. Wood. Walnut. Wrap-around grille. AM/FM. 1948.
77XM22B	30-40	Same as 77XM22. Blond wood.
78X11	60-80	Console. Radio-phonograph. 1949.
78X12	60-80	Console (horizontal). Radio-phono. 1949.
88FM21	50-60	Console (horizontal). Radio-phono. AM/FM. 1949.
95F31	60-75	Console (horizontal). Radio-phono. AM/FM/SW. 1947.
107F31	60-75	Console (horizontal). Radio-phono. AM/FM/SW. 1948.
A15J42	30-50	Table. Aqua plastic. 1960.
C2P6	60-75	Clock radio. Bright pink. 1960.
C4B1	25-30	Clock radio. Blue, gold trim. 1960. (AR2-60)
C9G13	20-25	Clock radio. Green plastic. 1960. (GOR)
C10P	20-25	Clock radio. 1961.
HS7	25-30	Portable. Cloth covered. 1946. (GOR)
X11B	40-50	Transistor. NIB. 1960.
X11E	10-15	Transistor. 1960.
X15A	15-20	Transistor. Gray-blue. 1961.
X15E	15-20	Transistor. Black. 1961.
X15N	15-20	Transistor. Brown. 1961.
X16B	10-15	Transistor. Blue. 1961.
X16G	10-15	Transistor. Blue or green. 1961.
X16N	10-15	Transistor. Tan. 1961.
X17B	20-25	Transistor. Blue, large speaker grille. 1961.
X17N	20-25	Transistor. Brown, large speaker grille. 1961.
X17R	20-25	Transistor. Red, large speaker grille. 1961.
X19A	15-20	Transistor. Gray with gold front. 1961.
X19E	15-20	Transistor. Black with gold front. 1961.
XT18B	15-20	Transistor. Blue. 1961.
XT18S	15-20	Transistor. Tan. 1961.

MUNTZ

820	75-100	Console (horizontal). Radio-phono. FM/AM. 1961.

MURDOCK

Murdock was bought out by Philco in 1929.

5-Tube Neutrodyne	100-150	Table. Battery. Wood. 1924.
CS-32	150-200	Table. Battery. 3 dial. 1925. (VR-122)

MUSIC MASTER

100	100-125	Table. Slant front panel. 3 dials.
215	300	Horizontal highboy. Spinet desk legs. Slant front panel. Enclosed speaker beneath radio panel. Battery. 2 dial. 1925. (GOR)

MUSICAIRE

Musicaire radios were sold by Coast-to-Coast stores.

576	75-100	Upright table. Wood. Resembles console. 1946. (GOR)
942T	25-30	Table. Wood. 1942. (GOR)

ARR: *Antique Radios: Restoration and Price Guide* / ARR2: *Antique Radio Restoration Guide, Second Edition* /
B1: *Antique Radio Price Guide, First Edition* by Bunis / B2: *Antique Radio Price Guide, Second Edition* by Bunis /
FOS: *Flick of the Switch* / GOR: *Guide to Old Radios* / RGA: *Radios: The Golden Age* / RR: *Radios Redux* / VR: *Vintage Radio.*

1942 Musicaire model 942T; wood table; Coast-to-Coast Stores brand.

N

NATIONAL

Model Name/Number	Price Range($)	Description
HF5	60-70	Table. Metal. Communications receiver. 5 band. 1949.

NATIONAL AIRPHONE *(See also Somerset)*

Monodyne	250-300	1-tube. 1923. (GOR)

NATIONAL UNION

571	25-30	Table. Wood. Metal grille. 1947.
G-613	25-30	Portable. AC/battery. Leatherette. 1947.
G-619	20-40	Table. Wood. 1947. (GOR)

1947 National Union model G619.

NEUTROWOUND

Neutrowound radios were made by Advance Automobile Accessories Corp.

	250-300	Table. Metal. Battery. 1926.
	300-350	Table. Metal. Blue. Battery. 1927.

NORDEN HAUCK

Admiralty	450-500	Amateur. 1933.
C-10	1000-1250	Table. Battery. AM/SW. 2 dial. 1925. (VR-144)
Super 10	800-1000	Table. Professional. 2 dial. 1926.

NORELCO

B2X98A/70R	30-40	Table. White front. FM/AM/SW. 1960.
B3X88U/70	30-40	Table. Creme plastic. AM/FM/2SW. 1961.
B4X87A	40-50	Table. White front. FM/AM/SW. Push-button. 1961.
L3X76T-01	20-25	Transistor. 1961.

NUMECHRON

Model Name/Number	Price Range($)	Description
	30-35	Clock radio. 1954.

OLSON

Model Name/Number	Price Range($)	Description
RA-340	20-25	Table. Ivory. FM only. 1961.
RA-341	25-30	Table. With intercom. 1961.
RA-347	10-15	Transistor. 1961.
RA-355	10-15	Transistor. 1961.

OLYMPIC

Model Name/Number	Price Range($)	Description
5-720W	30-40	Table. Plastic. Ivory grille. FM/AM. 1958.
6-606A	20-25	Portable. AC/battery. Linen and leatherette. 1947.
7-421W	45-60	Table. Plastic. 1949.
7-435V	50-75	Table. Plastic. FM/AM. 1948.
7-532W	30-45	Table. Plastic. 1947.
7-537	50-70	Table. Plastic. FM/AM. 1948.
7-622	30-40	Table. Radio-phono. 1948.
8-533W	30-40	Table. Plastic. FM/AM. 1949.
8-618	25-35	Table. Radio-phono. 1948.
9-435V	30-40	Table. Round sloped dial. AM/SW. 1951.
51-421W	40-50	Table. Round sloped dial. 1951.
402	20-30	Table. Blue with Gold dial. 1955.
466	20-25	Clock radio. 1961.
489	35-40	Portable (personal). Jewel box. 1951.
572B	40-50	Console. Radio-phono. FM/AM Front completely covered with grille cloth. 1954.
731	30-40	Console (horizontal). Radio-phono. FM/AM. 1961.
780	75-100	Transistor. NIB. Beige. 1961.
GBS-384	40-50	Console. Radio-phono. FM/AM.
GBS-386	40-50	Console (horizontal). Radio-phono. FM/AM/SW. 1961.
RP-10	30-40	Portable. Radio-phono. Stereo. Leatherette. 1960.

ORION

Model Name/Number	Price Range($)	Description
TR-714 "Micro"	50-60	Transistor. NIB. 1964.

P

PACIFIC ELECTRONICS

Model Name/Number	Price Range($)	Description
???	125	Coin-operated radio built into end table. Blond wood. Hard top. For a hotel or motel.

PACKARD-BELL

The "Bell" in Packard-Bell was the same man (Herb Bell) as the Bell in Jackson-Bell. After J-B folded in 1933, he looked around for a new partner, found one, and began a successful new company that same year. It was sold to Teledyne in 1971. Today it is best known for its line of low-priced computers.

Model Name/Number	Price Range($)	Description
5DA	30-40	Table. Bakelite. Handle. 1947.
5R1	30-40	Table. Plastic. 1950. (GOR)
5RC8	25-30	Clock radio. 1961.

ARR: *Antique Radios: Restoration and Price Guide* / ARR2: *Antique Radio Restoration Guide, Second Edition* /
B1: *Antique Radio Price Guide, First Edition* by Bunis / B2: *Antique Radio Price Guide, Second Edition* by Bunis /
FOS: *Flick of the Switch* / GOR: *Guide to Old Radios* / RGA: *Radios: The Golden Age* / RR: *Radios Redux* / VR: *Vintage Radio*.

Model Name/Number	Price Range($)	Description
100	30-40	Table. Plastic. 1949.
501	25-30	Table. Bakelite.
541	50-60	Console. Blond. Radio-phono. 1955.
542	40-50	Console. Blond. 1955.
568	25-30	Portable. Radio-phono (single play). 1947.
631	25-35	Table. Plastic. 1954. (GOR)
662	75-100	Console. Radio-phono. Open front, setback speaker. 1946.
682	30-40	Table. Wood. 1949.
861	100-125	Console (horizontal). Radio-phono-recorder-PA. 1947.
1063	150-200	Console (horizontal). Radio-phono-recorder-PA. 1947.

PAIGE

	150-175	1-tube. 1924.

PANDORA

	195	Crystal set.

PANASONIC

RF-811	20-25	Transistor. 1965.

PARAGON

Originally produced Adams-Morgan. In 1926, they sold out to Paragon Electric Co.

RA 10	400-500	Table. Battery. 1921.
RA 10 / DA 2	750-1000	Table. Battery. 1921. (VR-102) (B2-123)
RB 2	200-300	Table. Battery. 1923.

PARAMOUNT

Standard	90-100	Console. Battery. 1924.

PATHÉ

Universal Five	125-200	Table. Sloped front. Battery. 1925.

PEERLESS

600	20-30	Table. Very small. With box.

PENNY

6TP555	10-15	Transistor. Chrome grille. 1963.

PFANSTIEHL

Pfanstiehl began producing radios in 1924 and continued under that name until 1928. In 1928, they were known as Balkeit. Grigsby-Grunow-Hinds ("Majestic") bought them out. Later there were Fansteel radios, a more phonetic spelling of the original name.

7 "Overtone"	125-175	Table. Battery. 3 dial. 1924. (GOR)
10 "Overtone"	60-100	Table. Battery. Wood. 1924. (GOR)
20	50-100	Table. Battery. Wood. 1926.

PHILCO

Philco has been around a long time. It started in 1892 as the Helios Electric Co., then became the Philadelphia Storage Battery Co. It entered the home market with AC sets in 1927.

Note: Philco used the same model number with various suffixes to designate the style of the radio. For instance, 38-39 could end with a -B, -K, -T, or -X to show whether it was a table, cathedral, or console radio. Certain suffixes seem somewhat consistent: -B is often a cathedral; -CS a chairside; -L a lowboy; -H a highboy; -T a table. We have tried to include these suffixes, but may not always have succeeded. For more complete identification, refer to Grinder and Fathauer's *The Radio Collector's Directory and Price Guide* (Ironwood Press, 1986).

Philco used the prefix (37-, 38-, etc.) to refer to their model years. Even if the radio was produced at the end of 1936, if it was labeled a model 37-, it is identified as a 1937 model. Sometimes models were produced for more than one year, so it would be possible to find it listed as a 37-xxx and a 38-xxx. If you don't have the complete number, check a year or so either way to see if this is the case. They also reused their model numbers from time to time, which can cause confusion. Where we know this for sure, we've mentioned it. But there are probably more of these that we have missed.

Model Name/Number	Price Range($)	Description
Replica	75-125	Philco-produced miniature cathedral. 2/3 scale model of the 90B. Plastic cabinet. Transistors. Selling price was $49.95, which was the price of the 1931 original model. AM/FM. 1972. (Another reproduction is a Chinese copy of this 1972 Philco. AM/FM. Transistors. However, the cabinet is made of wood).
16B	250-300	Upright table. 1933. (FOS-118; GOR)
	200-300	Cathedral. 1933.
16X	175-250	Console. Sloped speaker board. 1933.
18B	300-350	Cathedral. AM/SW. 1933.
20B	250-300	Cathedral. First Philco cathedral. 1930. (FOS-117) (GOR)
20L	125-175	Lowboy. 1930.
21	300-400	Cathedral. 1930.
37-11	40-50	Console. 1937.
37-34	60-90	Table. 6 volt battery. 1937.
37-38	60-80	Upright table. Battery. 1937. (B2-125)
37-60	125-175	Cathedral. Wood. 1937.
37-61	125-175	Cathedral. AM/SW. 1937.
	100-150	Console. AM/SW. 1937.
37-84	100-150	Cathedral. 1937.
37-89	125-175	Cathedral. 1937.
37-93	100-150	Cathedral. Wood. 1937. (GOR)
37-116	200-300	Table. 1937.
37-610B	150-200	Table. Deco. Curved end. AM/SW. 1937.
37-620	100-150	Upright. Table. SM/2SW. 1937. (B2-126)
37-650B	100-200	Upright. Table. AM/SW. 1937.
37-670B	100-150	Upright. Table. AM/SW. 1937.

1938 Philco model 38-8.

ARR: *Antique Radios: Restoration and Price Guide* / ARR2: *Antique Radio Restoration Guide, Second Edition* /
B1: *Antique Radio Price Guide, First Edition* by Bunis / B2: *Antique Radio Price Guide, Second Edition* by Bunis /
FOS: *Flick of the Switch* / GOR: *Guide to Old Radios* / RGA: *Radios: The Golden Age* / RR: *Radios Redux* / VR: *Vintage Radio.*

Model Name/Number	Price Range($)	Description
37-670X	150-200	Console. AM/SW. 1937.
38B	75-100	Cathedral. Battery. 1930.
38-7	125-150	Console. Slant front. Inlaid veneer. 1938. (GOR)
38-7CS	125-150	Chairside. 1938.
38-8	100-125	Console. 1938. (FOS)
38-9	50-75	Table. 1938. (FOS-125)
38-10T	75-100	Table. AM/SW. Deco. 1938. (FOS-124)
38-12	30-50	Table. Deco. 1938.
38-14	30-40	Table. AM/SW. Plastic. 1938.
38-15CS	125-150	Chairside. Oval. 1938.
38-23T	75-100	Table. Deco. 1938.
38-34	60-80	Upright table. Battery. 1938.
38-35B	60-80	Cathedral. 6 volt battery. 1938.
38-38T	50-75	Table. Battery. 1938.
38-62T	35-60	Table. Deco. 1938.
38-93B	75-100	Upright Table. 1938.
38-116	200-250	Console. Large. AM/SW. 1938.
38-610	150-200	Table. Deco. Curved end. AM/SW. 1938.
38-620	100-150	Upright table. AM/2SW. Deco. 1938.
38-690X	750-1000	Console. Large. 1938.
39-30	75-100	Table. Slant front wood. Push-button. AM/SW. 1939.
39-70	80-100	Upright table. Battery. Wood. 1939. (AR-63)
39-116RX	200-350	Console. Push-button. Remote control. 13 tubes. 1939. (FOS-127) (B2-129)
40-120	15-25	Table. Wood. Handle. 1940. (GOR)
40-130	50-100	Upright table. Inlaid veneer. AM/SW. 1940.
40-150	60-80	Table. Push-button. AM/SW. 1940. (FOS-127)
40-155	60-90	Table. Wood. Push-button. Sloped front. AM/2SW. 1940. (GOR)
40-165	100-150	Console. 3 band. 1940.
40-180	100-150	Console. AM/2SW. Push-button. 1940.
	700	A totally restored example.
40-215RX	200-350	Console. Remote control. 1940.
40-510P	300-400	Console. Radio-phono. AM/SW. 1940.
41-221C	40-50	Table. Wood with swirled plastic grille. 1941.
41-226C	100-125	Table. Deco. 1941. (FOS-133)
41-240	40-50	Table. 1941.
41-250	75-125	Table. Wood. Push-button. 1941.
41-255	100-150	Table. Wood. Push-button. AM/SW. 1941.
41-265	60-100	Console. 3 band. 1941.
41-280	60-100	Console. 3 band. 1941.
41-285	100-150	Console. 1941.
41-1001	25-50	Table. Radio-phono. 1941.
42-22CL	40-60	Clock radio. 1942.
42-321	30-40	Table. Wood. 1942. (FOS-134; GOR)
42-345	100-150	Table. Wood. Push-button. 1942.
42-350	75-100	Table. Wood. 1942. (FOS-134; GOR)
42-390	100-175	Console. AM/old FM/SW. Push-button. 1942.
42-400	125-200	Console. Push-button. AM/old FM/SW. 1942.
42-1006	80-100	Console. Radio-phono. AM/SW. 1942.
42-KR3	30-50	Table. White painted wood. 1942. (GOR)
42PT7	30-40	Table. Wood. 1942.
42PT94	50-75	Table. Wood, plastic grille. Handle. 1942.
42-PT95	50-75	Table. Wood (light color). Ivory trim. 1942.
44B	200-250	Cathedral. 4 bands. 1934. (AR-52)

Model Name/Number	Price Range($)	Description
45C	100-125	Table. Wood. Deco. 1934.
45F	100-150	Console. 1934.
46-250	40-50	Table. Brown Bakelite. 1946.
46-350	25-40	Portable. AC/battery. Tambour top door. 1946.
46-420	35-50	Table. Plastic. Controls on top. 1946. (FOS-135)
46-427	35-50	Table. Wood. AM/SW. 1946.
46-480	100-150	Console. AM/FM/SW. 1946.
46-1201	60-80	Table. Radio-phono. Slide-in record player. Wood. 1946. (FOS-135)(GOR)
46-1209	100-150	Console. Radio-phono. 1946.
46-1213	75-100	Console (horizontal). FM/AM/SW. 1946.
46-1226	75-100	Console (vertical). Radio-phono. AM/SW. 1946.
47-204	30-40	Table. Wood with textured paint. 1947. (AR-66)
48-141	30-40	Table. Bakelite. Battery. 1948.
48-200	30-40	Table. Brown plastic. 1948.
48-206	30-40	Table. Leatherette. Ivory grille. 1948. (B2-134)
48-225	50-75	Table. Red. 1948.
48-200I	40-50	Same as 48-200. Ivory plastic.
48-206	40-50	Table. Wood, textured paint, plastic grille. 1948. (FOS-137)
48-214	30-40	Table. 1948.
48-225	30-40	Table. Maroon Bakelite. 1948.
48-230	60-80	Table. Plastic. 1948.
48-250	30-40	Table. Brown plastic. 1948. (GOR)
48-250I	30-40	Same as 48-250. Ivory plastic.
48-300	25-30	Portable. Wood. AC/battery. 1948.
48-360	40-50	Portable. Wood front, leatherette sides. Tambour door. AC/battery. 1948. **Note:** This style radio was produced for several years before this as the model 350.
48-460	40-60	Table. Brown plastic. Top controls. 1948.
48-460I	50-75	Same as 48-460. Ivory plastic.
48-461	40-50	Table. 1948.
48-475	40-60	Table. Blocky style. AM/FM. 1948.
48-482	75-150	Table. FM/AM/SW. Push-button. 1948.
48-1253	50-60	Table. Radio-phono. 1948.
48-1256	30-40	Table. Radio-phono. 1948.
48-1262	75-100	Console. Radio-phono. 1948.
48-1263	100-125	Console. Radio-phono. AM/SW. 1948.
48-1264	75-100	Console. Radio-phono. AM/FM. 1948. (FOS-137)
48-1266	70-90	Console. Radio-phono. AM/FM/SW. 1948. (FOS-137)
48-1286	75-100	Console (horizontal). Radio-phono. AM/FM. Open album storage on both sides. 1948. (FOS-138)
48-1401	100-150	Table. Radio-phono. Slide-in record player. Black plastic top, wood bottom. 1948. (FOS-140; GOR)
49-501	250-300	Table. Brown plastic. Highly curved. 1949. (FOS-140)
49-501I	250-300	Same as 49-501. Ivory plastic. (RR-79)
49-503	60-80	Table. Plastic. Light grille. 1949. (RR-82)
49-504	30-40	Table. Brown plastic. 1949.
49-504I	30-40	Same as 49-504. Ivory plastic.
49-505	40-50	Table. Plastic. Sculptured style cabinet. 1949. (FOS-140)

ARR: *Antique Radios: Restoration and Price Guide* / ARR2: *Antique Radio Restoration Guide, Second Edition* / B1: *Antique Radio Price Guide, First Edition* by Bunis / B2: *Antique Radio Price Guide, Second Edition* by Bunis / FOS: *Flick of the Switch* / GOR: *Guide to Old Radios* / RGA: *Radios: The Golden Age* / RR: *Radios Redux* / VR: *Vintage Radio.*

Model Name/Number	Price Range($)	Description
49-506	40-50	Table. Wood. 1949. (GOR)
49-601	20-25	Portable. 1949.
49-602	30-40	Portable. Handbag style. Brown plastic. 1949. (GOR)
49-603	40-50	Table. Knobs at top. Styled like portable. 1949.
49-605	25-30	Portable. AC/battery. 1949.
49-607	40-50	Portable. AC/battery. Wood grille, tambour top. 1949.
49-901	75-100	Table. Plastic. Single control—tap to change stations. 1949. (FOS-140)
49-902	30-40	Table. Plastic. White front. 1949.
49-904	25-30	Table. Lucite dial, grille. AM/SW. 1949.
49-905	30-40	Table. Plastic. AM/FM. 1949.
49-906	30-40	Table. Wood. AM/FM. 1949.
49-909	30-40	Table. Wood. Massive. AM/FM. 1949.
49-1401	100-150	Table. Radio-phono. Slot for record. 1949.
49-1405	40-45	Table. Radio-phono. 1949.
49-1602	60-90	Console. Radio-phono. 1949.
49-1606	60-90	Console (horizontal). Radio-phono. 1949.
49-1615	60-80	Console (horizontal). Radio-phono. FM/AM. 1949.
50	125-225	Cathedral. 1931. (ARR2-97)
50-522	20-30	Table. White painted. 1950.
50-621	10-30	Portable. AC/battery. 1950.
50-920	40-50	Table. Brown. 1950.
50-922	30-40	Table. Big top dial. Brown Bakelite. 1950.
50-925	25-30	Table. FM/AM. 1950.
50-1421	50-75	Table. Bakelite. Radio-phono. Large. 1950.
51-530	25-30	Table. Brown Bakelite with white knobs. 1951.
51-532	30-40	Table. Plastic. 1951.
51-537	40-50	Clock radio. 1951.
51-542	30-40	Table. Plastic. Clear eggcrate grille. 1951. (AR2-97)
51-930	25-35	Table. Big top dial. Brown or gray. 1951.
52	125-175	Cathedral. 1933.
51B	150-300	Cathedral. 1932. (FOS-117)
52-531	30-40	Clock radio. Brown. 1952.
52-540I	25-30	Table. Ivory. 1952.
52-542	30-40	Table. White with maroon dial and knobs. 1952. (GOR)
52-640	20-25	Portable. AC/battery. Maroon. 1952.
52-641	20-25	Portable. AC/battery. Maroon, red, blue, tan. 1952.
52-940	25-30	Table. Brown. Semicircular top dial. 1952.
52-941	25-30	Table. Ivory. Semicircular top dial. 1952.
52-1340	30-40	Table. Brown. Radio-phono. 1952.
53	40-50	Table. 1932.
53-560	30-40	Table. Plastic. 1953.
53-561	30-40	Table. Green, beige, ivory, or maroon plastic. 1953.
53-562	25-30	Table. Ivory, maroon, or dark green plastic. 1953.
	30-40	Tangerine plastic.
53-564	30-40	Table. Ivory plastic. 1953. (B2-137)
53-566	20-30	Table. Slant grille on top. Unusual. 1953.
53-652	20-30	Portable. AC/battery. Beige or green plastic. 1953.
53-658	20-25	Portable. AC/battery. 1953.
53-701	30-40	Clock radio. Brown. 1953.
53-950	20-30	Table. FM/AM. 1953.
53-956	20-30	Table. Bakelite. 1953.
53-1350	75-125	Drop-leaf end table. Radio-phono. 1953.
53-1750	75-125	Drop-leaf end table. Radio-phono. 1953.

Model Name/Number	Price Range($)	Description
53-1754	40-60	Radio-phonograph. Console. AM/SW. 1953.
54	50-75	Table. Wood. AM/SW. 1932.
60B	100-175	Cathedral. AM/SW. 1933. (FOS-118) **Note:** 60B was also made in both 1933 and 1936.
60MB	100-150	Upright table. Deco. AM/SW. 1934. (FOS-119—the model identified as a 60B is really the 60MB.)
65	150-175	Horizontal lowboy. 1929. (FOS-120)
66B	75-100	Upright table. AM/SW. 1934.
70	300-450	Grandfather clock. 1932. (FOS-122)
70B	300-400	Cathedral. 1932. (FOS-117)
	75-125	Upright table. 1938. (FOS-120) **Note:** same model number reused.
70L	125-175	Lowboy. 1932. (FOS-121)
71B	150-300	Cathedral. 1932.
80B "Philco Jr."	150-200	Cathedral. 1933. (FOS-118)
81 "Jr."	100-150	Cathedral. 1933. (FOS-118; GOR)
84B	125-200	Cathedral. 1934. (FOS-119; GOR)
	100-175	Cathedral. 1936. (FOS-119). **Note:** same model number reused.
86	125-150	Horizontal lowboy. Drop front desk. 1929. (VR-148)
89B	125-200	Cathedral. AM/SW. 1933. (FOS-119). Note: Other models were made in 1934-35 and 1936.
90B	300-450	Cathedral. This is the epitome of cathedral radios. 1931. (ARR-49; FOS-117; VR-263)
91B	300-350	Cathedral. 1932.
96H	150-175	Lowboy. 1930. (FOS-121)
105	40-50	Table. Radio-phono. 1939.
112	150-200	Console. 1931.
116	125-150	Upright table. 1935. (FOS-124)
118B	250-300	Cathedral. AM/SW. 1934.
501	150-200	Console. Radio-phono. AM/SW. 1934.
511	100-150	Table. Metal, with painted flowers on the front panel. 1928. (VR-147)
514	125-140	Table. Hand-painted flowers on front panel. 1928. (VR-127) (B2-140)
600C	75-100	Table. 1936.
610F	150-200	Console. 1936.
610T	60-90	Table. Deco. 1936.
620B	100-125	Upright table. 3 band. 1936. (FOS-120)
623	60-90	Upright table. 3 band. 1936.
A-801	125-150	Chairside. Deco. 1941.
B-569	20-30	Table. 1954.
B-570	25-30	Table. Red plastic. 1954.
	20-25	Sand plastic.
Beach radio	40-50	Portable. Flashlight built into side of radio.
C-584	25-40	Table. Maroon with white grille. 1955.
E-818	23-30	Table. Twin speakers. 1958.
E-670	25-30	Portable. AC/battery. 1957.
E-1370	25-30	Portable. Radio-phono. 1957.
H-1716M	50-60	Console. Phono. Stereo. 1960.

ARR: *Antique Radios: Restoration and Price Guide* / ARR2: *Antique Radio Restoration Guide, Second Edition* /
B1: *Antique Radio Price Guide, First Edition* by Bunis / B2: *Antique Radio Price Guide, Second Edition* by Bunis /
FOS: *Flick of the Switch* / GOR: *Guide to Old Radios* / RGA: *Radios: The Golden Age* / RR: *Radios Redux* / VR: *Vintage Radio*.

Model Name/Number	Price Range($)	Description
PT2	30-50	Table. Wood. Celluloid grille. 1940.
PT6	25-35	Table. 1940.
PT12	25-35	Table. 1940.
PT25 "Transitone"	25-40	Table. Brown Bakelite. Small. 1940. (FOS-126)
PT33 "Transitone"	30-50	Table. Brown Bakelite with handle. 1940. (GOR)
PT42	40-50	Table. Wood. 1940.
PT44	60-80	Table. Wood. Lyre cut back. 1940. (AR2-95)
PT87	30-40	Portable. Suitcase style. Battery. 1942. (FOS-132)
PT95	30-40	Table. Wood. Plastic dial. (AR2-10)
T-7K-128	100-125	Transistor. White. Philco's first transistor. 1959.
T-50-126	10-15	Transistor. 1961.
T-52-124	10-15	Transistor. Dark brick, gray, ivory. 1961.
T-64	30-35	Transistor. 1963.
T-74-124	15-20	Transistor. Leatherette back. 1961.
T-76B	15-20	Transistor. Leatherette. 1961.
T-802	10-15	Transistor. Leatherette. Strap. 1961.
"Transitone"		Philco used name to refer to many of their table models.

PHILHARMONIC

100C	50-75	Console (horizontal). Radio-phono. 1948.
100T	30-40	Table. Radio-phono. 1948.
249C	40-60	Console (horizontal). Radio-phono. 1949.
349C	60-80	Console (horizontal). Radio-phono. FM/AM. 1949.
8712	60-80	Console (horizontal). Radio-phono. AM/SW. 1947.

PHILIPS

Philips is a French company.

4A	50-65	Table. 3 band.
7851	150-200	Hi-fi. Receiver.

PILOT

Pilot was an extremely successful kit manufacturer during the 1920s and didn't produce their first complete, non-kit radio until 1930.

53	200-250	Upright table. 1934.
423	150-175	Cathedral. AM/SW. 1937.
G-184	100-150	Radio-phono. 1936.
T-411U	25-30	Table. Wood. AM/SW. Vertical dial. 1947.
T-500U	40-50	Table. Side speaker. Large dial. 1947.
T-511	30-40	Table. Wood. AM/SW. 1946.
T-521	35-40	Table. FM/AM. Perforated metal grille. 1947.
T-601	20-30	Table. Wood. FM tuner. 1947. (GOR)
T-741	25-40	Table. 1948.
T-1351	20-30	Table. 1939.

PITTSBURG

SP 2	125-150	Battery. 1922-1923.

POLICALARM

Policalarm radios were made by Regency Electronics.

PR8	25-30	Table. Plastic. Police band only. 1950. (GOR)

PORTOLA *(See Sentinel and Zenith. Made by United Air Cleaner.)*

PRECISION *(See also Crosley)*

Ace 3B	125-175	Table. Wood. Battery. 1923.
Ace type V	200	Table. Battery. 1922.

PURITAN

Gamble's stores sold Puritan radios.

Model Name/Number	Price Range($)	Description
504W	30-40	Table. AM/SW. 1948.
503	25-40	Table. Radio-phono. Wood. 1946. (GOR)
506	25-40	Table. White paint. Asymmetrical design. 1946.

PYE

Pye was an English company.

PE94MB9/LW	75-90	Table.

R

RADIO CRAFTSMAN

RC-8	40-50	Hi-fi. Chassis. Tuner. FM/AM. Chrome chassis. 1949.

RAYENERGY

SRB-1X	40-45	Table. Bakelite. 1946.

RAYTHEON

8TP2	100-150	Portable. Transistor. 1955.
T-2500	75-100	Transistor. Portable. 1956.

RCA (*Radio Corporation of America*)

RCA was formed by four other companies (General Electric, American Telephone & Telegraph, Western Electric, and the United Fruit Company) to keep control of overseas communication in the hands of the United States. (Later Westinghouse joined the group.) Although the RCA name was on the radios, they were simply the merchandiser for radios produced by General Electric and Westinghouse. In 1929, RCA merged with the Victor Talking Machine Co. in order to gain production facilities.

RCA was the founder of what became the National Broadcasting System in 1926. At that time, it controlled the Red Network and the Blue Network. In 1940, the government realized that NBC really was two networks—a definite breach of the anti-monopoly laws. NBC kept the stronger Red Network (what is now NBC). The Blue Network eventually became ABC.

Note: All RCA model numbers have been separated into number and letter groups with dashes between. RCA, in its service information, was not consistent in how they separated their model numbers. However, we hope this will help you find the information you need more easily.

Radio-phonographs use the suffix -C for crystal cartridges (high fidelity) and -M for magnetic cartridges. RCA radios were also supplied in Victor radio-phonographs. Look under Victor for several others.

I "Radiola"	300-500	Box. Crystal. 1923. (VR-109)
1-AX	20-25	Table. Plastic. 1941.
1-AX-2	20-25	Table. Ivory plastic. 1941.
1-R-81	30-40	Table. Black. Large. FM/AM. 1952.
1-RA-23	20-35	Table. Pink plastic. 1962.
1-T-5-J	25-30	Transistor. Aluminum front. 1960.
1-X-1-H	20-25	Table. Aqua plastic. 1961.
1-X-591	25-30	Table. Brown. Ripple grille. 1952.
1-X-592	25-30	Table. Ivory. Ripple grille. 1952.
II "Radiola"	250-300	Portable. 2 dial. Battery. 1923. (GOR; VR-109)
2-S-7	40-50	Console (horizontal). Radio-phono. 1953.
2-X-61	20-25	Table. Brown Bakelite. 1953.
2-X-62	30-40	Table. Ivory painted Bakelite. 1953.
2-XF-931	30-40	Table. Plastic. FM/AM. 2 dials. 1953. (ARR2-86)

ARR: *Antique Radios: Restoration and Price Guide* / ARR2: *Antique Radio Restoration Guide, Second Edition* / B1: *Antique Radio Price Guide, First Edition* by Bunis / B2: *Antique Radio Price Guide, Second Edition* by Bunis / FOS: *Flick of the Switch* / GOR: *Guide to Old Radios* / RGA: *Radios: The Golden Age* / RR: *Radios Redux* / VR: *Vintage Radio.*

Model Name/Number	Price Range($)	Description
III "Radiola"	100-150	Box. Battery. 1924. (ARR-9; GOR; VR-109)
III-A "Radiola"	150-200	Box. Battery. 1924. (ARR-10) (VR-110)
3-BX-51	20-25	Portable. Brown plastic. AC/battery. 1954.
3-BX-52	20-25	Portable. AC/battery. Tan plastic. 1954.
3-BX-53	20-25	Portable. Green plastic. AC/battery. 1954.
3-BX-54	25-30	Portable. Red plastic. AC/battery. 1954.
3-BX-671 "Stratoworld"	60-90	Portable. 7 bands. 1951.
3-RF-91	40-50	Table. Plastic. AM/SW. 1952. (GOR)
3-RG-14	10-15	Transistor. 1963.
3-RH-10	20-25	Transistor. NIB. 1961.
3-RH-21G	60-80	Transistor. 1961.
3-US-5	30-35	Radio-phonograph. Plastic table. 1955.
3-X-521	20-25	Table. Plastic. 1963. (ARR2-12)
IV "Radiola"	300-400	Table with doors. Battery. 3 dial. 1922. (VR-110)
4-C-532	20-25	Clock radio, ivory. 1954.
4-T	125-150	Cathedral. 1936.
4-X-551	30-40	Table. Black plastic. Top tuning knob. 1955. (ARR2-99)
4-X-641	20-25	Table. Black plastic. 1954.
4-Y-511	60-90	Radio-phonograph. 45 RPM only. Table. Plastic. 1954.
V "Radiola"	350-450	Table. Wood and metal. Battery. 2 dial. 1923. (VR-110)
5-A-410-A	350-400	Coca-Cola cooler.
5-Q-1	40-50	Upright table. AM/2SW. 1940.
5-Q-2	65-75	Upright table. AM/2SW. 1940.
5-Q-4	20-25	Table. Wood. 1940.
5-Q-5-A	20-25	Table. Plastic. AM/2SW. 1940.
5-Q-5-B	20-25	Table. Black plastic. AM/2SW. 1940.
5-Q-5-C	20-25	Table. Ivory plastic. AM/2SW. 1940.
5-Q-5-D	30-40	Table. Maroon plastic. AM/2SW. 1940.
5-Q-5-E	30-35	Table. Black plastic with metal grille. AM/2SW. 1940.
5-Q-6	20-25	Table. Plastic. AM/2SW. 1940.
5-Q-8	20-25	Table. Plastic. AM/2SW. 1940.
5-Q-12	20-25	Table. Plastic. 1940.
5-Q-55	40-50	Table. Plastic. AM/2SW. 1940. (FOS-153)
5-Q-56	20-25	Table. Plastic with ivory paint. AM/2SW. 1940.
5-T	100-150	Upright table. AM/SW. 1936. (FOS-152)
5-T-6	40-60	Table. Wood. AM/SW. 1936.
5-X-5	25-30	Table. Ivory plastic. 1939.
6-B-5-B	30-35	Portable. 1956.
6-BX-41-B	30-40	Portable. AC/battery. 1955.
6-BX-63	20-25	Portable. Gray plastic. 1952. (GOR)
6-Q-1	20-25	Table. Plastic. AM/2SW. 1940.
6-Q-4	20-25	Table. Plastic. AM/2SW/LW. 1940.
6-Q-4-X	20-25	Table. Plastic. AM/2SW/LW. 1940.
6-Q-7	30-35	Table. Wood. AM/2SW. 1940.
6-Q-8	20-25	Table. Wood. AM/2SW. 1940.
6-T	90-120	Upright table. AM/SW. 1936.
6-T-2	60-80	Table. 1936.
6-X-2	20-25	Table. Ivory plastic. 1942.
6-X-7-B	20-25	Table. Black plastic. 1956.
6-XD-5	25-30	Table. Eggcrate grille. Nipper logo. 1956.
7-BX-5-J	40-50	Portable. AC/battery. 1955.
7-BX-6-E	30-40	Portable. AC/battery. 1957.
7-BX-8-J	30-40	Portable. AC/battery. 1957.

Model Name/Number	Price Range($)	Description
7-BX-8-L	30-40	Portable. AC/battery. Green. 1957.
7-Q-4	25-30	Table. Wood. AM/2SW/LW. 1941.
7-Q-4-X	20-25	Table. Plastic. AM/2SW. 1940.
7-QB	20-25	Table. Wood. AM/2SW. 1941.
7-QBK	60-90	Console. AM/2SW. 1941.
7-QK-4	80-100	Radio-phonograph. Console. AM/2SW/LW. 1941.
VIII "Radiola"	400-500	Highboy. 2 dial. Battery. 1924.
8-BT-10-K	30-35	Portable. 1957.
8-BX-6	25-40	Portable. Aluminum and plastic. AC/battery. 1948. (FOS-157; GOR)
8-BX-6-L	40-50	Portable. AC/battery. 1957.
8-Q-1	50-65	Table. Wood. AM/2SW. 1940.
8-Q-2	30-40	Table. Wood. AM/2SW. 1940.
8-Q-4	50-60	Table. Wood. Curved grille. AM/2SW. 1940.
8-QB	30-50	Upright table. AM/2SW. 1940.
8-QBK	40-60	Console. AM/2SW. 1940.
8-QU-5-M	30-40	Table. Radio-phono. Wood. AM/2SW. 1940.
8-R-71	30-40	Table. Plastic. FM/AM. 1949.
8-R-76	40-50	Table. Painted blond finish. FM/AM. 1949.
8-RF-13	40-50	Table (on 1950s-style tapered legs). FM/AM. 1958.
8-V-90	50-60	Console (horizontal). Radio-phono. FM/AM. 1949.
8-V-111	100-125	Console (horizontal). Radio-phono. FM/AM. 1948.
8-X-53	30-40	Table. Wood. 1948.
8-X-71	25-30	Table. FM/AM. 1949.
	15-25	Table. Brown Bakelite. 1949. (GOR)
8-X-541	30-40	Table. Brown Bakelite. Center dial. 1949. (ARR2-50)
8-X-542	25-30	Table. White. Center dial. 1949.
8-X-545	40-50	Table. Burl grain paint. 1948. Center grille.
8-X-681	30-50	Table. Knobs in slots. 1949.
	30-50	Table. Brown Bakelite. 1950.
8-X-521	40-50	Table. Plastic. Top tuning dial. 1948.
IX "Radiola"	750+	Chassis with panel. Battery. Designed to be built into a phonograph. 1923.
9-EY-3	25-30	Phono (45 only). Bakelite. Open top. 1952.
9-INT-1	100-150	Table. Large. Blond wood. FM/AM/2SW. Euro-styling. 1958.
9-K-2	745	Console. Fully restored.
9-Q-1	40-50	Table. Wood. AM/6SW. 1940.
9-Q-4	30-35	Table. Wood. AM/3SW. 1940.
9-QK	75-100	Console. AM/6SW. 1940.
9-SX-1 "Little Nipper"	30-40	Table. Brown plastic with ivory knobs. AM/SW. 1939.
9-SX-2 "Little Nipper"	35-45	Same as 9-SX-1. Brown with ivory front and brown knobs.
9-SX-3 "Little Nipper"	35-45	Same as 9-SX-1. Ivory plastic with red knobs.
9-SX-4 "Little Nipper"	75-100	Same as 9-SX-1. Red with ivory front and red knobs.
9-SX-5 "Little Nipper"	50-60	Same as 9-SX-1. Black with marble-colored front and black knobs.
9-SX-7 "Little Nipper"	75-125	Same as 9-SX-1. Onyx plastic with maroon knobs.
9-SX-65 "Little Nipper"	80-10	Same as 9-SX-1. Blue plastic with onyx front and blue knobs.
9-SX-8 "Little Nipper"	70-90	Same as 9-SX-1. Marble-colored plastic with black knobs.
9-T	150-200	Upright table. AM/3SW. 1935.
9-TX-1	40-50	Table. Brown with mottled tan dial and knobs. 1939.

ARR: *Antique Radios: Restoration and Price Guide* / ARR2: *Antique Radio Restoration Guide, Second Edition* /
B1: *Antique Radio Price Guide, First Edition* by Bunis / B2: *Antique Radio Price Guide, Second Edition* by Bunis /
FOS: *Flick of the Switch* / GOR: *Guide to Old Radios* / RGA: *Radios: The Golden Age* / RR: *Radios Redux* / VR: *Vintage Radio*.

Model Name/Number	Price Range($)	Description
9-TX-2	25-30	Table. Ivory plastic. 1939.
9-TX-3	30-40	Table. Wood. 1939.
9-TX-4	700+	Table. Onyx Catalin with maroon dial and knobs. 1939.
9-TX-5	700+	Same as 9-TX-4. Green onyx Catalin with ivory dial and knobs.
9-TX-21	25-30	Table. Brown plastic with tan knobs. 1939.
9-TX-22	25-30	Table. Ivory plastic. 1939.
9-TX-23	50-75	Table. Wood. 1939.
9-TX-31	40-50	Table. Brown plastic with tan knobs. 1939. (FOS-153)
9-TX-32	20-25	Table. Ivory plastic. 1939.
9-TX-33	40-50	Table. Wood. 1939.
9-TX-50	60-80	Table. Wood. Handle. 1939.
9-W-106	60-75	Console (horizontal). Radio-phono. FM/AM. 1950.
9-X	25-35	Table. Wood. 1939.
9-X-1	750+	Table. Brazilian onyx and green Catalin. 1939.
9-X-2	750+	Table. Black Catalin. 1939.
9-X-3	750+	Table. Arizona onyx and cream Catalin. 1939.
9-X-4	500-1000	Table. Burl onyx and brown Catalin. 1939.
9-X-6	30-40	Table. Wood. 1939.
9-X-11	750+	Table. Brazilian onyx and green Catalin. 1939.
9-X-12	750+	Table. Black Catalin. 1939.
9-X-13	750+	Table. Arizona onyx and cream Catalin. 1939.
9-X-14	750+	Table. Burl onyx and brown Catalin. 1939.
9-X-561	25-40	Table. Beige or brown Bakelite. 1950. Same as 9-X-571.
9-X-571	40-50	Table. Brown plastic. Large brass horn grille. 1950. (FOS-161; GOR)
9-X-572	40-60	Table. Blond plastic. 1949. (GOR)
9-X-641	30-40	Table. Brown. AM/SW. 1950.
9-X-642	30-40	Table. Ivory. AM/SW. 1950.
9-Y-7	50-60	Table. Radio-phono. Bakelite. 45 RPM (only) changer. 1949.
9-Y-510	50-60	Table. Radio-phono. Bakelite. 45 RPM (only) changer. 1950.
X "Radiola"	250-350	Upright table. Battery. 2 dial. Enclosed speaker. 1924. (VR-111)
10-Q-1	50-60	Upright table. AM/2SW. 1940.
10-T	150-200	Upright table. AM/SW/LW. 1937.
10-X	20-25	Table. Plastic. 1941.
11-Q-4	50-75	Upright table. AM/2SW/LW. 1940.
11-QK	100-150	Console. AM/2SW/LW. 1940.
11-QU	125-150	Console (horizontal). Radio-phono. AM/2SW/LW. 1940.
11-X-1	20-25	Table. Plastic. 1941.
12-AX	20-25	Table. Plastic. Handle. 1942.
12-Q-4	60-90	Upright table. Wood. AM/2SW/LW. 1940.
12-QK	100-125	Console. AM/2SW/LW. 1940.
12-QU	125-150	Console (horizontal). Radio-phono. AM/2SW/LW. 1940.
12-X	20-25	Same as 12 AX.
13K	150-225	Console. AM/3SW. Tuning eye. 1936. (GOR)
14-AX	20-25	Table. Plastic. 1941.
14-AX-2	20-25	Table. Plastic. 1941.
14-X	30-40	Table. Plastic. 1941.
15-BP-4	20-30	Table. Wood. AC/battery. 1941.
15-BP-615E	20-30	Table. Wood. AC/battery. 1941.
15-BT	20-25	Table. AM/SW. AC/battery. 1941.
15-X	30-40	Table. Bakelite. 1940.
16 "Radiola"	75-100	Table. Battery. 1927. (VR-113)
16-K	50-60	Console. AM/SW. 1940.
16-T-2	30-40	Table. AM/SW. 1940.

RCA—*continued*

Model Name/Number	Price Range($)	Description
16-T-3	50-60	Table. Push-button. AM/SW. 1940.
16-T-4	60-75	Table. Push-button. AM/2SW. 1940.
16-X-1	10-15	Table. Push-button. 1941.
16-X-2	20-25	Table. Ivory plastic. 1941.
16-X-3	20-25	Table. 1941.
16-X-4	20-25	Table. Push-button. 1941.
16-X-11	20-25	Table. Plastic. AM/SW. 1941.
16-X-13	20-25	Table. Wood. AM/SW. 1941. (ARR-64)
16-X-14	25-30	Table. Push-button. AM/SW. 1941.
17 "Radiola"	75-100	Table. Wood. 1927. (VR-113)
17-K	60-80	Console. Push-button. AM/2SW. 1940.
18 "Radiola"	75-100	Table. Wood. 1927. (AR-22)
18-T	40-50	Table. Push-button. AM/2SW. 1940.
19-K	150-200	Console. Push-button. AM/2SW. 1940.
20 "Radiola"	150-200	Table. Slant front. 2 dial. Battery. 1925. (VR-113)
	200-250	Highboy or lowboy. Installed in a cabinet made by another manufacturer.
21 "Radiola"	125-150	Table. Battery. 1929.
22 "Radiola"	75-100	Console. Battery. 1929.
24 "Radiola"	250-300	Portable. Loop antenna. 2 dial. Battery. Superhet. 1925. (VR-112)
25 "Radiola"	150-200	Table. Loop antenna. 2 dial. 1925. (VR-112)
25-BP	25-30	Portable. Leatherette. AC/battery. 1942. (FOS-156)
26 "Radiola"	300-350	Portable. 2 dial. Battery. Loop in lid. Superhet. Gold colored dials. Wood. 1925. (GOR; VR-112)
26-BP	35-45	Portable. White and leatherette. AC/battery. Tambour door. 1942.
26-X-1	30-40	Table. Plastic. AM/SW. 1942. (FOS-156)
26-X-3	30-40	Table. AM/SW. 1942. (FOS-156)
26-X-4	40-50	Table. Push-button. AM/SW. 1942. (FOS-156)
27-K	50-60	Console. Push-button. AM/SW. 1942.
28 "Radiola"	250-300	Table radio with legs. 2 dial. Loop antenna. 1925. (B2-158)
28-D	100-150	Table. Wood. Tambour door. 1933. (ARR-51; FOS-147)
28-T	50-60	Table. Push-button. AM/2SW. 1942. (FOS-156)
28-X	40-50	Table. AM/SW. 1942. (FOS-156)
28-X-5	50-60	Table. Push-button. AM/SW. 1942. (FOS-156)
29-K	100-150	Console. AM/2SW. Push-button. 1942.
29-K-2	150-200	Console. Stepback top with horizontal knobs. AM/2SW. Push-button. 1942.
30 "Radiola"	200-250	Console. Battery. 1926.
32 "Radiola"	150-200	Console. Wood. 1927.
33 "Radiola"	75-100	Table. Metal. 1929.
34-X	20-25	Table. Wood. 1942.
35-X	30-40	Table. Wood. 1942.
36-X	30-40	Table. Wood. 1942.
40-X-30	20-25	Table. Plastic. 1940.
40-X-31	20-25	Table. Ivory plastic. 1940.
40-X-50	30-40	Table. Wood. Handle. 1940.
40-X-53	600-700	Table. "La Siesta" (Mexican street scene). 1939. (RR-51)
44 "Radiola"	75-100	Table. Wood. 1929. (ARR-42)
45-E	60-75	Bookcase with radio on top. Maple. 1940.

ARR: *Antique Radios: Restoration and Price Guide* / ARR2: *Antique Radio Restoration Guide, Second Edition* /
B1: *Antique Radio Price Guide, First Edition* by Bunis / B2: *Antique Radio Price Guide, Second Edition* by Bunis /
FOS: *Flick of the Switch* / GOR: *Guide to Old Radios* / RGA: *Radios: The Golden Age* / RR: *Radios Redux* / VR: *Vintage Radio.*

Model Name/Number	Price Range($)	Description
45-X	30-35	Table. Wood. 1940.
45-X-1	30-40	Table. Plastic, white. 1940. (FOS-155)
45-X-2	20-25	Table. Ivory plastic. 1940.
45-X-3	25-30	Table. Wood. 1940.
45-X-4	30-35	Table. Wood. 1940.
45-X-5	15-20	Table. Plastic. 1940.
45-X-6	20-25	Table. Ivory plastic. 1940.
45-X-11	30-40	Table. Plastic. 1940. (FOS-155; GOR)
45-X-12	40-50	Table. Ivory plastic. 1940.
45-X-13	30-40	Table. Wood. 1941. (FOS-155)
45-X-16	40-50	Table. Wood. 1940. (B2-151)
45-X-17	40-45	Table. Wood. 1940.
45-X-18	25-30	Table. Wood. 1941.
45-X-111	20-25	Table. Plastic. 1940.
45-X-112	20-25	Table. Ivory plastic. 1940.
45-X-113	30-35	Table. Wood. 1940.
46-X-1	20-25	Table. Plastic. 1940.
46-X-2	20-25	Table. Ivory plastic. 1940.
46-X-3	30-40	Table. Wood. 1940.
46-X-11	40-50	Table. Plastic. AM/SW. 1940. (FOS-155)
46-X-12	30-40	Table. Ivory plastic. AM/SW. 1940.
46-X-13	40-50	Table. Wood. AM/SW. 1940. (FOS-155)
46-X-21	25-30	Table. Plastic. AM/SW. 1940.
46-X-23	30-40	Table. Wood. AM/SW. 1940.
46-X-24	30-40	Table. Push-button. AM/SW. 1940.
48 "Radiola"	200-250	Lowboy. 1930. (FOS-146)
54-B-1	30-40	Portable (personal). 1947.
55-X	40-50	Table. Plastic. 2 speakers. 1942. (ARR-65; FOS-157)
56-X	30-40	Table, Brown Bakelite. 1946.
56-X-2	30-40	Table. Bakelite. 1946.
56-X-5	40-50	Table. 1946.
60 "Radiola"	75-100	Table. 1928. (ARR-31; VR-113)
60 "Radiola"	200-300	Lowboy. 1928.
61-1 "Radiola"	40-50	Table. Bakelite. 1946.
61-5 "Radiola"	30-40	Table. Wood. AM/SW. 1946.
64 "Radiola"	250-400	Console. Lowboy with doors. 1928.
65-AU	40-60	Table. Wood. Radio-phono. 1946. (FOS-157)
65-X-1	40-50	Table. Brown Bakelite. 1946. (FOS-158; GOR)
66 "Radiola"	175-200	Lowboy. Tapestry front. 1929.
66-E	60-80	Phono. Wood. Large. RCA dog on grille. Made for record store record playing. 1946.
66-X-1	50-65	Table. Brown Bakelite. Deco. AM/SW. 1946.
66-X-2	50-65	Table. Bakelite. AM/SW. 1948. (FOS-158)
66-X-8	350-450	Table. Catalin. Maroon. AM/SW. (B2-152)
66-X-11	40-60	Table. Brown Bakelite. 1947. (B2-152)
66-X-12	40-50	Table. Ivory plastic. Deco. 1947.
68-R-1	30-40	Table. Bakelite. AM/FM. 1947. (FOS-158)
68-R-3	30-40	Table. Bakelite. AM/FM. 1947.
75-X-11	50-75	Table. Walnut plastic. Brass front. 1948.
75-X-12	50-75	Same as 75-X-11. Ivory plastic.
75-X-16	50-75	Same as 75-X-11. Golden-brown "fine woods" plastic. (GOR)
75-X-17	60-90	Same as 75-X-11. Black Oriental, hand painted.
75-ZU "Radiola"	40-50	Radio-phonograph. Table. Wood. 1948.
76-ZX-11 "Radiola"	30-40	Table. Plastic. 1948.

Model Name/Number	Price Range($)	Description
77-U	35-40	Table. Radio-phono. Wood. 1948. (FOS-158)
77-X-1	60-70	Console (horizontal). Radio-phono. 1948.
85-T-1	30-40	Table. Wood. 1936. (FOS-152)
85-T-2	40-60	Table. Wood. Red finish. 1936. (FOS-152)
86 "Radiola"	300-400	Console. Radio-phonograph-recorder. 1930.
86-K-7	575	Console. Fully restored.
86-T	60-75	Table. Wood. Left side curves into top. AM/SW. Deco. 1938. (GOR)
86-T-6	50-60	Table. Wood. Curved top. AM/2SW. 1938.
87-T	40-50	Table. Wood. AM/SW. 1937. (GOR)
91-BT-61	25-30	Upright table. Wood. 6 volt battery. 1938.
94-BK	30-40	Console. Battery. 1938.
94-BP-1	20-30	Portable. Leatherette. Battery. 1941. (FOS-157)
94-BT	25-30	Table. Wood. Battery. 1938.
94-X	30-40	Table. Wood. 1938.
94-X-1	40-45	Table. Wood. Push-button only. No tuning dial. 1938.
94-X-2	40-45	Same as 94-X-1. Blond wood.
95-T	30-35	Table. Wood. 1938.
95-T-5	40-50	Table. Wood. Push-button. 1938. (FOS-153)
95-T-5-LW	40-50	Table. Wood. Push-button. 1940.
95-X-1	30-40	Table. Wood. Push-button. 1938.
95-X-11	25-30	Table. Wood. Push-button. 1938.
95-XLW	25-30	Table. Wood. AM/SW. 1940.
96-E	100-125	Chairside. Push-button. 1938.
96-E-2	125-150	Chairside. Push-button. AM/2SW. 1939.
96-K	100-125	Console. Push-button. AM/SW. 1938.
96-K-5	75-100	Console. Push-button. AM/2SW. 1939.
96-K-6	100-150	Console. Push-button. AM/2SW. 1939.
96-T	40-50	Table. Wood. Push-button. 1938.
96-T-1	45-60	Table. Wood. Push-button. 1938. (FOS-153)
96-T-2	40-50	Table. Wood. AM/SW. Push-button. 1938.
96-T-3	40-50	Table. Wood. Push-button. AM/2SW. 1938.
96-T-4	50-60	Table. Wood. AM/SW. Push-button. 1937.
96-T-7	30-45	Table. Wood. Push-button. AM/2SW. 1939.
96-X	30-40	Table. Wood. Push-button. 1938.
96-X-1	100-150	Table. Brown. Wrap-around grille. AM/SW. 1939. (B2-154)
96-X-2	30-40	Table. Black plastic. Wrap-around grille. AM/SW. 1939.
96-X-3	35-40	Same as 96-X-2. Brown and ivory plastic.
96-X-4	30-40	Same as 96-X-2. Ivory plastic.
96-X-11	30-40	Table. Brown plastic. Wrap-around grille. Push-button. AM/SW. 1939.
96-X-12	30-40	Same as 96-X-11. Black plastic.
96-X-13	35-45	Same as 96-X-11. Brown and ivory plastic.
96-X-14	30-40	Same as 96-X-11. Ivory plastic.
97-E	100-175	Chairside. Push-button. AM/2SW. 1938.
97-K	75-90	Console. Push-button. AM/SW. 1939.
97-K-2	85-100	Console. Push-button. AM/2SW. 1939.
97-KG	100-125	Console. Push-button. AM/2SW. 1938.
97-KT	60-90	Console. Push-button. AM/2SW. 1938.

ARR: *Antique Radios: Restoration and Price Guide* / ARR2: *Antique Radio Restoration Guide, Second Edition* / B1: *Antique Radio Price Guide, First Edition* by Bunis / B2: *Antique Radio Price Guide, Second Edition* by Bunis / FOS: *Flick of the Switch* / GOR: *Guide to Old Radios* / RGA: *Radios: The Golden Age* / RR: *Radios Redux* / VR: *Vintage Radio*.

Model Name/Number	Price Range($)	Description
97-T	50-60	Table. Wood. Push-button. AM/2SW. 1938.
97-T-2	45-50	Table. Wood. Push-button. AM/2SW. 1939.
97-T-4	30-40	Table. Wood. Push-button. AM/SW. 1939.
97-T-5	30-40	Table. Wood. Push-button. AM/SW. 1939.
97-T-6	30-40	Table. Wood. Push-button. AM/SW. 1939.
97-X	40-50	Table. Wood. Push-button. 1938.
97-Y	60-80	Console. Push-button. AM/2SW. 1938.
98-EY	125-150	Chairside. Push-button. AM/2SW. 1938.
98-K	125-150	Console. Push-button. Curved dial. AM/2SW. 1938.
98-K-2	125-150	Console. Push-button. AM/2SW. 1939.
98-T	40-50	Table. Wood. Push-button. AM/2SW. 1939.
98-T-2	40-50	Table. Wood. Push-button. AM/2SW. 1940.
98-X	50-60	Table. Wood. Push-button. AM/2SW. 1938. (B1-129)
98-YG	75-100	Console. Push-button. AM/2SW. 1938.
99-K	100-150	Console. Push-button. Curved dial. AM/2SW. 1938.
99-T	40-50	Table. Wood. Push-button. AM/2SW. 1938.
100	100-150	Upright table. Wood. AM/SW. 1932.
103	75-100	Upright table. Wood. AM/SW. 1934.
110	150-250	Cathedral. AM/SW. 1933.
110-K	200-250	Console. Push-button. AM/3SW. 1941. (FOS-155)
110-K-2	200-250	Console. Push-button. AM/3SW. 1941.
111	75-100	Upright table. 1933.
111-K	150-200	Console. Push-button. AM/3SW. 1941.
118	100-125	Upright table. AM/SW. 1934.
119	75-100	Upright table. AM/SW. 1935.
120	150-250	Cathedral. AM/SW. 1933. (B2-155)
128	200-250	Upright table. AM/2SW. 1934.
140	200-250	5 band. 1933.
143	200-250	Upright table. AM/3SW. 1934. (AR-53; FOS-148)
211-K	100-150	Console. AM/3SW. 1942.
224	125-175	Console. 6-legged. AM/SW. 1934.
380	75-90	Console. Radio-phono. 1934.
500 "Radiola"	25-30	Table. Plastic. 1941.
501 "Radiola"	25-30	Table. Ivory plastic. 1941.
510 "Radiola"	20-25	Table. Marbled brown plastic. 1939.
	20-25	Ivory plastic.
511 "Radiola"	25-30	Table. Plastic. 1941.
	25-30	Ivory plastic.

1941 RCA Radiola model 512; wood table.

512 "Radiola"	25-35	Table. Wood. 1941. (GOR)
513 "Radiola"	25-35	Table. Wood. 1941.
515 "Radiola"	25-30	Table. Wood. AM/SW. 1941.
516 "Radiola"	20-25	Table. Plastic. Handle. 1942.

RCA—*continued*

Model Name/Number	Price Range($)	Description
517 "Radiola"	20-25	Table. Wood. Nipper on dial. 1942.
520 "Radiola"	25-30	Table. Wood. 1942. (GOR)
522 "Radiola"	20-25	Table. Wood. 1942.
526 "Radiola"	20-25	Table. Plastic. Handle. 1942.
527 "Radiola"	20-25	Table. Wood. 1942.
612-V-3	100-150	Console. Radio-phono. Push-button. FM/AM/SW. 1947.
710-V-25	60-80	Console (horizontal). Radio-phono. FM/AM. 1948.
810-K-1	100-150	Console. Deco. 1938. (FOS-153)
811-K	100-150	Console. Wood. Push-button. 1937. (GOR)
910-KG	150-200	Console. AM/2SW. 1938.
911-K	150-200	Console. AM/4SW. 1938.
AA-1400	100-150	Detector, amplifier, battery. 1922.
Aeriola	175-200	Box. Amplifier. 2 tube. 1922.
Aeriola Jr.	250-300	Box. Crystal. 1922. Westinghouse made. (VR-106)
Aeriola Sr.	150-200	Box. 1 tube. 1922. Westinghouse made. (VR-107)
AR-812	100-125	Panel with chassis. Battery. 1924.
	235	Complete with loop antenna and horn speaker. 1924.
B-411	50-70	Table. Brown swirl and chrome trim. 1951.
BP-10	40-50	Portable. Small. 1941. (FOS-156,157)
BT-6-5	70-90	Upright table. AM/SW. Battery. 1935.
BT-40	20-25	Table. Wood. Battery. 1939.
BX-6	30-40	Portable. AC/battery. Aluminum front, cover. (ARR2-99)
C-13-2	125-200	Radio-phonograph. Console. AM/LW/3SW. 1935. (FOS-151)
C-15-3	150-200	Console. AM/3SW/LW. 1935.
Coca-Cola 5-A-410-A	300-350	Cooler.
DA	150-200	Box. Detector-Amplifier. 3 tube. Battery. 1923.
D-22-1	500	Console (large). Radio-phono-recorder. AM/LW/3SW. Mike. 1935.
HF-1	150-200	Console. Modern 6-leg style. 1938.
HF-2	150-200	Horizontal console. 1938.
HF-4	150-200	Horizontal console. AM/4SW. 1938.
HF-6	200-250	Console. AM/6SW. 1938.
HF-8	200-250	Console. AM/6SW. 1938.
K-50	60-90	Console. Push-button. 1940.
K-60	100-126	Console. Push-button. AM/2SW. 1940.
K-61	75-100	Console. Push-button. AM/SW. 1940.
K-62	60-90	Console. Push-button. AM/2SW. 1940.
K-80	100-150	Console. Push-button. AM/2SW. 1940.
K-80	595	Console. Fully restored.
K-81	100-150	Console. Push-button. AM/2SW. 1940.
K-82	60-90	Console. Push-button. AM/2SW. 1940.
K-105	60-90	Console. AM/2SW. 1940.
K-130	150-200	Console. AM/2SW. Push-button. 1939.
Nipper Dog	55	Chalk figure.
P-5 "Radiola"	20-25	Portable. AC/battery. 1941.
PCR-5	550	Pepsi Cooler.
Q-11	20-25	Table. Wood. AM/2SW. 1942.
Q-12	20-25	Table. Plastic. AM/2SW. 1942.
Q-14	20-25	Table. Wood. AM/2SW. 1942.

ARR: *Antique Radios: Restoration and Price Guide* / ARR2: *Antique Radio Restoration Guide, Second Edition* /
B1: *Antique Radio Price Guide, First Edition* by Bunis / B2: *Antique Radio Price Guide, Second Edition* by Bunis /
FOS: *Flick of the Switch* / GOR: *Guide to Old Radios* / RGA: *Radios: The Golden Age* / RR: *Radios Redux* / VR: *Vintage Radio*.

Model Name/Number	Price Range($)	Description
Q-14-E	20-25	Same as Q-14.
Q-15	20-25	Table. Wood. AM/2SW. 1942.
Q-15-E	20-25	Same as Q-15.
Q-16	40-50	Table. Wood. AM/4SW. 1942.
Q-17	40-50	Table. Wood. AM/4SW. 1942.
Q-18	20-25	Table. Wood. AM/2SW. 1942.
Q-20	20-25	Table. Plastic. AM/SW. 1940.
Q-21	25-30	Table. Wood. AM/SW. 1940.
Q-23	30-40	Table. Wood. AM/4SW. 1942.
Q-24	45-60	Table. Wood. AM/4SW. 1941.
Q-25	30-35	Table. Wood. AM/4SW. 1941.
Q-26	30-40	Table. Wood. AM/4SW. 1942.
Q-27	30-40	Table. Wood. AM/4SW. 1942.
Q-30	40-50	Table. Wood. AM/5SW. 1942.
Q-31	40-50	Table. Wood. AM/5SW. 1942.
Q-33	40-50	Table. Wood. AM/4SW. 1942.
Q-44	40-60	Table. Wood. AM/7SW. 1941.
QB-2	20-25	Table. Plastic. Battery. 1941.
QK-23	60-80	Console. AM/4SW. 1941.
QU-2-M	75-100	Console. Radio-phono. AM/4SW. 1941.
QU-3-M	20-25	Table. Radio-phono. Wood. AM/4SW. 1941.
QU-5	100-125	Console (horizontal). Radio-phono. AM/4SW. 1941.
QU-7	200-250	Console (horizontal). Radio-phono-recorder. AM/7SW. 1942.
QU-8	300-350	Console (horizontal). Radio-phono-recorder. AM/7SW. Top of the line. 1941.
QU-51-C/QU-51-M	75-100	Console (horizontal). Radio-phono. Push-button. AM/4SW. 1942.
QU-52-C/QU-52-M	75-100	Console (horizontal). Radio-phono. AM/4SW. 1942.
QU-55	60-90	Console (horizontal). Radio-phono. AM/4SW. 1942.
QU-56-C/QU-56-M	30-40	Table. Radio-phono. AM/2SW. 1942.
QU-72	40-45	Radio-phono. AM/SW. 1947.
R-5 "Radiolette"	150-200	Cathedral. 1931.
R-7	75-100	Table. 1931.
R-8	100-150	Table. Wood. 1932.
R-28-P	100-150	Table. Wood. 1932.
R-73	100-150	Table. 1933.
R-560-P "Radiola"	25-30	Table. Wood. Radio-phono. 1942.
R-566-P "Radiola"	25-30	Table. Wood. Radio-phono.
RA/DA	200-250	Regenerating receiver/amplifier combination. First commercial receiver sold by RCA. 2 boxes. 1921.
"Radiola"		This was a model name often used by RCA. Where possible, radios in this list are located under their model numbers, and also identified as "Radiola."
Radiola III		
"Balanced Amplifier"	150-200	Box. Amplifier. 2 tube. Battery. 1924.
"Radiola Grand"	400-500	Box with lid. Battery. 1923. (VR-113)
"Radiolette"	See model R-5.	
RAE-26	150-200	Console. Radio-phono. 1931.
RC-608	25-30	Table. Wood. FM/AM. 1947.
RC-1023-C		
(chassis number)	30-60	Metal hotel/motel radios.
RFA-15-V	20-25	Clock radio. White. 1965.
RGD-30-E	20-25	Table. Gray plastic. 1966.
RHM-19-J	20-25	Transistor. 1967.
RS "Radiola"	200-275	Box. Battery. Combined the RA/DA in one box. 1923. (VR-109)
RV-151	100-125	Console (horizontal). Radio-phono. FM/AM/SW. 1949.

RCA—*continued*

Model Name/Number	Price Range($)	Description
Super VIII "Radiola"	400-500	Console. Battery. 1924.
T-1-EH	10-15	Transistor. 1960.
T-2-K	10-15	Transistor. 1960.
T-4-8	50-60	Upright table. Wood. 1934.
T-6-1	60-75	Upright table. AM/2SW. 1935.
T-6-7	75-125	Upright table. AM/2SW. 1935.
T-8-14	80-120	Upright table. AM/2SW. 1935.
T-55	40-50	Table. Wood. Push-button. 1940.
T-56	40-50	Table. Wood. Push-button. 1940.
T-60	50-60	Table. Wood. Push-button. AM/SW. 1940.
T-62	50-60	Table. Wood. AM/SW. 1940. (FOS-155)
T-63	30-40	Table. Wood. Push-button. AM/SW. 1940.
T-64	40-50	Table. Wood. Push-button. AM/2SW. 1940.
T-65	40-60	Table. Wood. AM/2SW. 1940.
T-80	50-75	Table. Wood. AM/2SW. 1940.
U-8	30-40	Table. Radio-phono. 1939.
U-9	20-25	Table. Radio-phono. 1940.
U-10	20-25	Table. Radio-phono. 1940.
U-20	100-125	Console (horizontal). Radio-phono. AM/SW. 1940.
U-25	60-90	Console (horizontal). Radio-phono. AM/2SW. 1940.
U-26	60-90	Console (horizontal). Radio-phono. AM/2SW. 1940.
U-30	75-100	Console (horizontal). Radio-phono. AM/2SW. 1939.
U-40	60-90	Console (horizontal). Radio-phono. 1940.
U-42	100-125	Console with doors. Radio-phono. Tuning eye. 1940.
U-43	75-100	Console (horizontal). Radio-phono. Tuning eye. 1940.
U-44	60-90	Console (horizontal). Radio-phono. AM/2SW. 1940.
U-45	60-90	Console (horizontal). Radio-phono. AM/2SW. 1940.
U-46	100-150	Console (horizontal). Radio-phono. AM/2SW. 1940.
U-50	30-40	Table. Radio-phono. AM/2SW. Leatherette. 1939.
U-104	25-30	Table. Radio-phono. Push-button. 1939.
U-111	30-40	Table. Radio-phono. 1938.
U-112	30-40	Table. Radio-phono. 1938.
U-115	30-45	Table. Radio-phono. Wood. Push-button. 1939.
U-119	40-50	Table. Radio-phono. Wood. Push-button. AM/2SW. 1938.
U-121	60-90	Console (horizontal). Radio-phono. Push-button. 1939.
U-122-E	100-150	Chairside. Radio-phono. AM/2SW. Push-button. 1938.
U-123	75-90	Console (horizontal). Radio-phono. Push-button. 1939.
U-124	75-90	Console. Radio-phono. AM/2SW.
U-125	100-125	Console. Radio-phono. AM/2SW. Push-button. 1939.
U-126	60-90	Console (horizontal). Radio-phono. AM/2SW. 1938.
U-127-E	125-150	Chairside. Radio-phono. Push-button. 1939.
U-128	60-80	Console (horizontal). Radio-phono. AM/2SW. 1938.
U-129	60-80	Console (horizontal). Radio-phono. AM/2SW. 1939.
U-130	60-80	Console (horizontal). Radio-phono. 1938.
U-132	125-200	Console (horizontal). Radio-phono. AM/6SW. 1938.
U-134	125-200	Console (horizontal). Radio-phono. AM/6SW. 1938.
UY-122-E	125-150	Chairside. Radio-phono. Push-button. AM/2SW. 1942.
UY-124	75-100	Console. Radio-phono. Push-button. AM/2SW. 1942.
V-100	30-40	Table. Radio-phono. 1940.

ARR: *Antique Radios: Restoration and Price Guide* / ARR2: *Antique Radio Restoration Guide, Second Edition* /
B1: *Antique Radio Price Guide, First Edition* by Bunis / B2: *Antique Radio Price Guide, Second Edition* by Bunis /
FOS: *Flick of the Switch* / GOR: *Guide to Old Radios* / RGA: *Radios: The Golden Age* / RR: *Radios Redux* / VR: *Vintage Radio.*

Model Name/Number	Price Range($)	Description
V-101	35-40	Table. Radio-phono. 1940.
V-104	40-45	Table. Radio-phono. Push-button. 1941.
V-105	30-40	Table. Radio-phono. 1942.
V-135	30-40	Table. Radio-phono. 1942. (B1-133)
V-140	25-30	Table. Radio-phono. 1942.
V-170	60-90	Console (horizontal). Radio-phono. Push-button. AM/SW. 1941.
V-175	60-90	Console (horizontal). Radio-phono. Push-button. AM/SW. 1942.
V-200	50-60	Console (horizontal). Radio-phono. Push-button. AM/SW. 1941.
V-201	60-80	Console (horizontal). Radio-phono. Push-button. AM/SW. 1941.
V-205	75-100	Console (horizontal). Radio-phono. AM/2SW. 1941.
V-209	75-100	Console (horizontal). Radio-phono. AM/SW. 1942.
V-210	75-100	Console (horizontal). Radio-phono. AM/SW. 1942.
V-215	85-100	Console (horizontal). Radio-phono. AM/2SW. 1942.
V-219	100-125	Console (horizontal). Radio-phono. AM/2SW. 1942.
V-221	100-125	Console (horizontal). Radio-phono. AM/2SW. 1942.
V-225	100-150	Radio-phonograph. Horizontal console. AM/2SW. 1942.
V-300	100-125	Console (horizontal). Radio-phono. AM/2SW. Push-button. 1941.
V-301	85-100	Console (horizontal). Radio-phono. AM/2SW. Push-button. 1941.
V-302	100-125	Console (horizontal). Radio-phono. AM/2SW. Push-button. 1941.
V-405	100-125	Console (horizontal). Radio-phono. AM/2SW. 1941.
VA-20	20-30	Record player. Brown Bakelite.
VHR-202	90-120	Console (horizontal). Radio-phono-recorder. AM/2SW. 1941.
VHR-207	100-125	Console (horizontal). Radio-phono-recorder. AM/2SW. 1941.
VHR-212	125-150	Console (horizontal). Radio-phono-recorder. AM/2SW. 1942.
VHR-307	125-150	Console (horizontal). Radio-phono-recorder. AM/2SW. 1941.
VHR-407	100-125	Console (horizontal). Radio-phono-recorder. AM/2SW. 1941.
Wings	750+	Wings cigarette pack. 8-by-12-by-10 inch.
X-2-JE	20-25	Table. White and gray. 1959.
X-5-HE	20-25	Table. White and gray. 1954.
X-55	40-50	Table. Wood. Push-button. 1942.
X-60	30-40	Table. Wood. Push-button. 1942.
X-551	30-40	Table. Plastic. 1947. (GOR)

RECORDIO

Recordio radios were made by Wilcox-Gay.

7D44	60-85	Console (horizontal). Radio-phono-recorder. AM/FM. Blond wood. 1948.

REGAL

747	30-40	Portable. Metal case with plastic lid and back. Flip up lid. 1947.
777	30-40	Portable. Metal. Plastic flip-up lid. 1949.
7251	40-50	Table. Plastic. 1948.

REALISTIC

Realistic was and is the Radio Shack house brand

90-L-696	10-15	Transistor. 1961.
T-1V	25-30	Hi-fi. Table. Receiver. 1961.

REALTONE

TR-861	50-60	Transistor. White. 1962.

REGAL

1049	20-25	Table. Plastic. AM/SW. 1947.
7162	20-25	Table. AM/SW. 1949.
7163	20-25	Table. AM/2SW. 1949.
FM78	25-30	Table. FM/AM. 1949.

REGAL—*continued*

Model Name/Number	Price Range($)	Description
W800	20-25	Table. Brown Bakelite. 1947.
W901	20-25	Table. Brown Bakelite. 1946.

REGENCY

TR-1	250-350	The first transistor radio! Red. 1955.
TR-4	100-150	Transistor. 1957.

REINHARTZ

Reinhartz radios were made by Elgin Radio Co.

2L0	400-500	Table. Battery. Wood. 1925.

RELIABLE

Reliable Radio Co. of New York sold Reliable radios.

Treasure Chest	60-80	Chest. 1934. (GOR)

REMLER

9 Tube Super	150-200	Kit. Battery. 1925. (VR-145)
5310	25-30	Table. Radio-phono. Wood. 1948.
5500 "Scottie Pup"	125-150	Table. 1949. (RR-61)

REX

Masterdyne	75-100	Table. Battery. 3 dial. 1924.

RIPPNER

	100-125	Crystal.

RME

45	100	Table. Communications receiver. Metal. 6 band. Speaker separate. 1946.
84	60-80	Table. Communications receiver. Metal. 5 band. 1947.

ROLAND

5T5	20-25	Table. Plastic. 1954.
5T14	25-30	Table. White and Pink. 1959.
5X3	25-30	Radio-phonograph. Table. 1954.
8XF1	25-30	Radio-phonograph. Table. 1953.

ROSS

RE-711	25-30	Desk pen set and radio. Black. 1967.

ROTH DOWNS

Orpheus	75-90	Console (small).

S

SAINT JAMES

Twin 4	300	Kit. Battery. 1927.

ST. REGIS

CM	200-250	Cathedral. Miniature. Mid-1930s. (Likely made by International). (GOR)

SARKES TARZIAN

723-502	25-30	Table. FM only. 1960.

ARR: *Antique Radios: Restoration and Price Guide* / ARR2: *Antique Radio Restoration Guide, Second Edition* /
B1: *Antique Radio Price Guide, First Edition* by Bunis / B2: *Antique Radio Price Guide, Second Edition* by Bunis /
FOS: *Flick of the Switch* / GOR: *Guide to Old Radios* / RGA: *Radios: The Golden Age* / RR: *Radios Redux* / VR: *Vintage Radio*.

E.H. SCOTT

This is not the same company as H.H. Scott. H.H. Scott was primarily a producer of high-fidelity equipment and components. When people refer to a Scott, however, E.H. is the company they mean. This was the company that chrome-plated not only its chassis, but also its tube shields. Because of this, many Scotts were not enclosed in cabinets, but stayed out in the open for everyone to admire.

As in the 1930s, even today Scott's radios are sold as chassis and speaker only or as a chassis in a particular model cabinet. The names of the cabinets are impressive, such as the "Sheraton" or the "Chippendale Grande." Scott's slogan was "The Stradivarius of Radio Receivers."

Model Name/Number	Price Range($)	Description
16	300-500	(FOS-167)
16A	300-500	Chassis and speaker. 28 tubes. AM/FM. 1948.
800-B	200-400	Chassis and speaker. 1946. (FOS-169)
	500+	Chippendale cabinet. Console.
Allwave 2 volt	200-350	Chassis and speaker. Battery. 1934.
Allwave 12 "DeLuxe"	200-350	Chassis and speaker. 1 or 2 dial tuning. 1931. (FOS-168)
Allwave 15	250-400	Chassis and speaker. 1934.
Allwave Imperial	250-400	Chassis and speaker. 1935. Also known as the "Full range High Fidelity Receiver." (FOS-168)
FM Tuner	125-200	FM only. Old FM (pre-1943) band only.
Phantom	400-500	Chassis and speaker. 1940. (FOS-168)
Philharmonic	300-500	Chassis and speaker. 30 tubes. 1937. (FOS-168)
	600+	Chippendale cabinet. Console.
	750+	Chippendale Grande. Horizontal console.
	900+	Warrington cabinet. Console.

H.H. SCOTT

200B	75-100	Hi-fi amplifier.
299	100-150	Hi-fi amplifier. 1959.
344B	100-125	Hi-fi. Stereo receiver (transistor). 1971.
350	150-200	Hi-fi. Tuner.
382C	100-125	Hi-fi. Receiver (transistor). 1968.

SENTINEL

Sentinel radios were made by the United Air Cleaner Co.

1U-342	25-30	Table. Radio-phono. Leatherette. 1952.
1U-343	20-25	Table. Black Bakelite. 1952. (GOR)
11	125-175	Lowboy. Wood. Deco. 1930. (GOR)
15	125-200	Lowboy. Wood. Gothic panels. 1930. (GOR)
195ULT	1500++	Table. Butterscotch and maroon Catalin. (Sentinel called it onyx.) Push-button. 1939. (GOR)
238V	150-200	Large book. 1941.
282K	25-30	Table. Radio-phono. 1947.
284GA	30-40	Table. Radio-phono. Wood. Phonograph automatically plays the record when the top is closed. 1947.
284I	40-50	Table. Ivory. Top front controls. 1946.
284W	30-45	Table. Brown. Top front controls. 1946.
286PR	40-50	Portable. Metal top. AC/battery. 1947.
302I	40-50	Table. Plastic. AM/FM. 1948.
305I	40-50	Table. Plastic. AM/3SW. 1948.
309I/309W	30-40	Table. Plastic. 1947. (GOR)
313W	30-40	Table. Plastic. 1948.
314I/314W	30-40	Table. Plastic. 1948.
315I/315W	30-40	Table. Plastic. 1948.
332	30-40	Table. Plastic. 1949. (GOR)
338	25-30	Table. 1947.
343	20-30	Table. Brown Bakelite. 1952.

SENTINEL—*continued*

Model Name/Number	Price Range($)	Description
344	30-40	Table. Black plastic. 1953. (GOR)
Portola	150-200	Chairside. 1930.

SETCHELL-CARLSON

55	20-40	Portable. AC/battery. Cloth covered. 1938. (GOR)
416	60-80	Table. Plastic. Top knobs. 1946.

1938 Setchell-Carlson; cloth-covered portable case; AC/battery operation.

447	40-50	Portable. Leatherette, plastic grille. AC/battery. 1948. (GOR)
458R	30-40	Intercom-radio. Ivory or black plastic. 1950. (GOR)
570	150-200	Table. Tubular shape. Handle. Orange. 1950.
588	40-50	Table. Wood. 1939. (GOR)

SHERWOOD

S-1000	50-60	Hi-fi. Control amplifier. 1957.
S-1000-II	40-50	Hi-fi. Control amplifier. 1958.

SHOWERS

Consolea	100-150	Table. Wood. Gold decoration. Battery. 1926. (GOR)

SIGNAL

These radios, from the late 1940s, were made by Signal Electronics Co. of New York. Previously this trade name was used by the Signal Radio and Electric Corp. in 1923 and the Signal Electric Mfg. Co. in 1926.

341-A	25-35	Portable. Imitation snakeskin. AC/battery. 1948.
AF252	50-60	Plastic. Table. AM/FM. 1948.

SILVER MARSHALL

620 "Cockaday"	100-125	Table. Battery. 1928.
720	100-125	Table. Wood. Battery. 1929.
F4	150-250	Cathedral.
Q	150-200	Console with doors. 6 legs. 1931.

SILVERTONE

Silvertone radios were sold by Sears Roebuck.

1	60-80	Table. Metal. Brown, with white knob and dial. 1949. (RGA-100)
11	30-40	Clock radio. White. 1951.
15	25-30	Table. Brown Bakelite. 1951.
90	30-35	Table. Metal. Battery. 1935.
107	25-30	Table. Metal. 1934.

ARR: *Antique Radios: Restoration and Price Guide* / ARR2: *Antique Radio Restoration Guide, Second Edition* /
B1: *Antique Radio Price Guide, First Edition* by Bunis / B2: *Antique Radio Price Guide, Second Edition* by Bunis /
FOS: *Flick of the Switch* / GOR: *Guide to Old Radios* / RGA: *Radios: The Golden Age* / RR: *Radios Redux* / VR: *Vintage Radio.*

Model Name/Number	Price Range($)	Description
101.567	100-150	Table. Black with white push-buttons. 1939.
132.857	30-40	Table. Brown Bakelite. 1949. (FOS-173; GOR)
132.878	30-40	Table. Brown or white metal. 1950.
132.881	30-40	Table. Brown Bakelite. 1951. (GOR)
1058	25-30	Table (with legs to stand on). Radio-phono. FM/AM 1961.
1215	10-15	Transistor. 1961.
1217	10-15	Transistor. 1961.
1252	100-150	Upright table. 1931.
1561	40-60	Table. AM/SW. 1940.
1809	50-75	Upright table. Deco. AM/SW. 1934.
1845	50-75	Console. AM/SW. 1934.
1853	150-200	Console (vertical). Battery. 1934. Century of Progress Model (Chicago World's Fair).
2001	40-50	Table. Brown metal. 1950. (GOR)
2004	25-30	Table. Wood. 1953.
2016	40-50	Table. Ivory. 1956.
2028	20-25	Table. Wood. Battery. 1953.
3001	25-30	Table. Brown Bakelite. Dial on top. 1954.
3004	25-30	Table. Big dial. 1954.
3040A	35-40	Table. Radio-phono. Plastic. 1955.
3068	50-60	Console (horizontal). Radio-phono. AM/FM. 1955.
3215	20-25	Portable. Maroon plastic. AC/battery. 1954.
3216	20-25	Same as 3215. Green plastic.
3217	20-25	Same as 3215. Gray plastic.
3561	80-100	Table. White mottled plastic. Push-button. 1947. (RR-63)
4016	25-30	Radio-phonograph. Table. Plastic. 1955.
4032	30-40	Radio-phonograph. Table. Plastic. 1955.
4046A	25-30	Radio-phonograph. Table. 1955.
4215	20-25	Transistor. 1977.
4408	25-30	Table. Battery. Airplane dial. 1935.
4500	75-100	Table. Black Bakelite, silver grille cloth. First plastic radio offered by Sears. 1936. (GOR)
6012	25-30	Table. White painted. Handle. 1947.
6050	40-50	Table. Wood. Plastic grille. 1947. (FOS-172)
6051	25-30	Table. Wood. 1947.
6057	50-75	Console (horizontal). Radio-phono. 3 speed phonograph. Blond wood. 1956. (GOR)
6068A	50-60	Console. Radio-phono. FM/AM. 1961.
6071	30-40	Table. Wood (plastic grille). Radio-phono (single play). 1947.
6072	25-30	Table. Wood. Radio-phono (single play). 1946.
6178A	200-300	Table. White, red knobs. 1938. (RR-27)
6200A	20-25	Table. 1949.
6220A	30-40	Table. Battery. 1946.
6230	40-50	Upright table. AM/3SW. Battery. 1946.
6440	686	Console. Fully restored.
7004	25-30	Table. 1956.
7006	20-25	Table. Brown plastic. 1941.
7013	20-25	Table. Black plastic. 1957. (GOR)
7021	25-30	Table. White painted plastic. Push-button. 1946.
7022	50-60	Table. White metal, red knobs. 1942.
7025	30-50	Table. Brown Bakelite. Deco. 1946. (GOR)
7038	50-60	Upright table. Push-button. 1941.
7048	150-200	Cathedral. 1933. **Note:** A console was made with this number in 1941.

SILVERTONE—*continued*

Model Name/Number	Price Range($)	Description
7054	30-40	Table. Blond wood. Push-button. 1949. (GOR)
7080	25-30	Table. Wood. Radio-phono. 1947.
7090	50-60	Console (vertical). AM/SW. Push-button. 1947.
7100	40-50	Console (vertical). Radio-phono. 1947.
7115	60-80	Console (vertical). Radio-phono. FM/AM. 1947.
7116	60-80	Console (horizontal). Radio-phono. FM/AM. 1947.
7200	20-25	Table. Wood. FM/AM. 1957.
7224	40-50	Portable (large). Transistor. 4 band. AC/battery. 1957.
7226	40-50	Portable (large). Transistor. 8 band. AC/battery. 1958.
8002	25-30	Table. Plastic. Ivory. 1957.
8003	50-60	Table. Metal. 1949.
8005	30-40	Table. Plastic. 1948. (FOS-172)
8010	40-50	Clock radio. Plastic. 1948.
8013	30-40	Table. Brown. 1958. (GOR)
8025	20-25	Clock radio. Brown. Large clock. 1958.
8026	20-25	Clock radio. Ivory. Large clock. 1958.
8027	20-25	Clock radio. Pink. Large clock. 1958.
8050	25-30	Table. Wood. 1948.
8052	25-30	Table. Wood. Push-button. 1949.
8055A	40-50	Radio-phono. Horizontal console. AM/FM. 1958.
8072	20-25	Table. Radio-phono. Wood. 1948.
8080	30-40	Table. Radio-phono. Bakelite. 1948.
8086	40-50	Table. Wood. Radio-phono-wire recorder. 1949.
8100	40-50	Console (small). Radio-phono. 1948.
8101C	40-50	Console. Radio-phono. 1949.
8103	40-50	Console (horizontal). Radio-phono-wire recorder. 1949.
8105A	50-60	Console (horizontal). Radio-phono. AM/SW. 1948.
8108A	50-60	Console (horizontal). Radio-phono. FM/AM. 1949.
8115B	50-60	Console (horizontal). Radio-phono. FM/AM. 1949.
8210	20-25	Portable. Brown. Large center dial. 1958.
8211	20-25	Portable. Blue. Large center dial. 1958.
8212	20-25	Portable. Red. Large center dial. 1958.
8218	20-25	Portable. Side tune. 1958.
8230	20-25	Table. Wood. AC/battery. AM/3SW. 1949.
8270A	25-30	Portable. Plastic and aluminum. AC/battery. 1949.
9000	30-45	Table. White plastic. 1950.
9005	20-25	Table. Brown plastic. 1949.
9022	40-60	Table. White painted Bakelite. 1949.
9028	20-25	Clock radio. Ivory. 1959.
9054	40-50	Table. Wood. 5 band. Eurostyle. 1949.
9260	20-30	Portable. Plastic with metallic front. AC/battery. 1948.
G	35-45	Table. Metal. Battery. 1932.
R1181	60-80	Table. AM/3SW. 1940.

SIMPLON

WVV-2	25-30	Table. Wood. Curved side and top. 1947.

SIMPLEX

N	100-150	Cathedral. 1932.

ARR: *Antique Radios: Restoration and Price Guide* / ARR2: *Antique Radio Restoration Guide, Second Edition* /
B1: *Antique Radio Price Guide, First Edition* by Bunis / B2: *Antique Radio Price Guide, Second Edition* by Bunis /
FOS: *Flick of the Switch* / GOR: *Guide to Old Radios* / RGA: *Radios: The Golden Age* / RR: *Radios Redux* / VR: *Vintage Radio*.

SIMPLI-DYNE

Model Name/Number	Price Range($)	Description
Jr	50	Table. Battery. 1920.

SKY KNIGHT

CB-500P	25-30	Table. Wood. Battery. 1947.

SLEEPER

54	225-300	Table. Sloped front panel. Battery. 1925.
3300	75-100	Table. Battery. 1920. (VR-119)
Imperial 68	125-150	Console. Battery. 1927.
Serenader	75-100	Table. Battery. 1926. (VR-138)

SOMERSET

Somerset radios were produced by National Airphone in 1924. The company failed in 1925 (although their ads continued in radio magazines). Another attempt was made to produce radios in 1926 under the Somerset brand. After three months, the new owner dropped the brand in favor of his own.

5	80-100	Table. Slant front panel. Battery. 3 dials. 1926. (GOR)

SONIC

TR-500	15-20	Transistor. Leatherette. 1958.

SONORA

102	25-30	Portable. Plastic. AC/battery. 1949.
335	20-25	Portable. Plastic. AC/battery. 1954.
A30	85-100	Table. Radio-phono. 1928.
C	35-40	Table. Battery. 3 dial. 1924.
RBU-176	40-50	Table. Ivory Bakelite. 1946.
RDU-209	40-50	Table. 1946.
RMR-219	80-100	Console (horizontal) Radio-phono. AM/SW. 1947.
RQU-222	100-150	Table. 1946.
RX-223	20-25	Table. Wood. Battery. 1947.
RZU-222	40-50	Table. Brown Bakelite with beige knobs. 1947.
TV-48	50-60	Table. White. Pink center knobs. 1940. (ARR2-52)
WBRU-239	30-40	Table. Radio-phono. Wood. 1947.
WCU-246	50-75	Bedlamp radio. 1948.
WDU-249	35-40	Portable. Plastic covered. AC/battery. 1948.
WEU-262	40-50	Table. Plastic. AM/FM. 1948.
WJU-252	60-80	Table. Plastic. 1948.
WKRU-254A	50-60	Console (horizontal). Radio-phono. AM/FM. 1948.
WLRU-219A	60-80	Console (horizontal). Radio-phono. AM/FM. 1948.

SONY

TR-630	40-60	Transistor. 1963.

SORRENTO

T-666	20-25	Transistor.

SPARTON

6-66A	20-25	Table. Leatherette. AM/SW. 1948.
6-AW-26-PA	25-30	Table. Wood. Radio-phono. AM/SW. 1947.
6-AM-06	25-30	Portable. AC/battery. Leatherette. 1948.
7-46	60-90	Console. Wood. 1946. (GOR)
10-BW-76-PA	100-150	Console (horizontal). Radio-phono. FM/AM/SW. 1947.
65	85-100	Upright table. AM/SW. 1934.
79	80-100	Console. 1928.
100	30-40	Table. Ivory plastic. 1948.
109	80-100	Console. 1928.
141XX	20-40	Table. Wood. AM/FM. 1951. (GOR)

SPARTON—*continued*

Model Name/Number	Price Range($)	Description
235	200-250	Console. Radio-phono. 1930.
301 "Equasonne"	500-600	Highboy with doors. Elaborate decoration. 1929. (GOR)
301	20-25	Portable. Brown plastic over metal. AC/battery. 1953.
305	20-25	Same as 301. Green plastic.
309	25-30	Same as 301. Ivory plastic.
351	40-50	Table. Blond wood with green knobs.
500 "Cloisonne"	2000+	Table. Mirror. 1939.
506 "Bluebird"	3000+	Table. Mirror. Chrome trim. AM/SW. 1935.
557	2500+	Blue or peach mirror. 3 knob. AM/SW. 1936.
558	2500+	Blue or peach mirror. 4 knobs. AM/SW. 1937.
930	100-150	Console. 1929.
1003	60-70	Console (horizontal). Radio-phono. FM/AM/SW. 1949.
1010	60-70	Console (horizontal) Radio-phono. 1948.
1030A	50-60	Console. Radio-phono. 1948.
1040	50-60	Console (horizontal). Radio-phono. FM/AM. 1949.
1051	40-50	Console (horizontal). Radio-phono. AM/SW. 1949.
1059	40-50	Console (horizontal). Radio-phono. 1949.
1068	150-200	Console. Wood. Push-button. 1937. (GOR)
1186 "Nocturne"	20,000+	Floor model. Large round mirror. 46" high. Deco. Chrome trim. AM/SW. Extremely rare! Available with blue or rose mirror or crystal glass. 1936.
5218	80-90	Table. Push-button. AM/SW. 1938.
AC-62	100-125	Table. Early AC set.

SPLENDID

	300	1-tube.

SPLITDORF

R-500 "Polonaise"	150-200	Table. Battery. 1925.
R-560	80-100	Table. Battery. 3 dial. 1926.

STANDARDYNE

B5	60-100	Table. Wood. Battery. 3 dial. 1925. (GOR)
BH	100-150	Lowboy. Drop front. Enclosed speaker above radio panel. Cabinet below. 1925. (GOR)

STEELMAN

3AR5U	20-25	Portable. Radio-phono. 1956.
4AR11	30-35	Console (horizontal). Radio-phono. FM/AM. 1959.
595	25-30	Portable. Radio-phono. Leatherette. 1952.
603	50-60	Console (horizontal). Radio-phono. FM/AM. 1961.
704	30-40	Console (horizontal). Radio-phono. FM/AM. 1961.
705	60-75	Console (horizontal). Radio-phono. FM/AM. Stereo. 1961.

STEINITE

	50-250	Crystal. 1925.
26-1	125-175	1 tube. 2 dial. 1925.

STERLING

DeLuxe	125-150	Table. Marbleized plastic with chrome top. (RR-33)

STEWART WARNER

Until 1925, Stewart Warner manufactured auto parts. They discontinued making radios and televisions in 1954.

Model Name/Number	Price Range($)	Description
01-6G1	150-200	Upright table. Push-button. AM/2SW. 1939.
03-5C1-WT	30-40	Table. Wood. 1939. (GOR)
07-5B3	75-125	Table. Plastic. 1939.
07-5B3Q "Dionne Quintuplets"	800-1000	Table. Decals on model 07-5B3. 1939. (FOS-176)
07-51H	40-50	Table. White paint with red knobs. 1938.
07-513 "Gulliver's Travels"	500-700	Table. Decals on model 07-513. 1939.
07-513Q "Dionne Quintuplets"	800-1000	Table. Decals on model 07-513. 1939. (FOS-176) (RR-33)
07-713Q "Dionne Quintuplets"	700-800	Table. Ivory plastic. Decals on model 07-713. Top controls. 1939.
07-514H	50-60	Table. Wood, small. horizontal grille. 1938.
51T56	20-30	Table. Wood. 1948.
51T136	25-30	Table. Wood. 1937.
62T36	500-700	Table. Catalin. AM/SW. 1946.
72CR26	100-150	Console (horizontal). Radio-phono. AM/SW. 1947.
300	80-100	Table. Battery. 3 dial. 1925. (VR-138)
305	150-200	Table. Battery. 1925.
325	80-100	Table. Battery. 3 dial. 1925.
525	50-60	Table. Battery. 1927.
751H	30-40	Table. Plastic. Left side curved from top to bottom. 1940. (GOR)
900	100-150	Lowboy. Wood. 1929. (GOR)
9000B	30-35	Table. Wood. AM/SW. 1946.
9002A	30-40	Table. Plastic. 1948.
9005A	20-30	Table (big). Wood. Battery. 1947.
9160AU	20-30	Table. Brown plastic with tan knob and dial. 1952.
9160BU	40-45	Same as 9160AU. Yellow plastic with green knob and dial.
9160CU	30-40	Same as 9160AU. Blue plastic with blue knob and dial.
9160DU	25-30	Same as 9160AU. Rust plastic with tan knob and dial.
9160EU	20-25	Same as 9160AU. Tan plastic with rust knob and dial.
9170-B	10-15	Portable. Green plastic. AC/battery. 1954.
9170-C	10-15	Same as 9170-B. Gray plastic.
9170-D	10-15	Same as 9170-B. Maroon plastic.
9170-J	20-25	Same as 9170-B. Red plastic. (ARR2-99)
9178-C	25-30	Table. Radio-phono. 1955.

1937 Stewart Warner model R-180A; side speakers.

STEWART WARNER—*continued*

Model Name/Number	Price Range($)	Description
9187-B	25-30	Clock radio. Green plastic with ivory knobs. 1954.
9187-E	40-45	Same as 9187-B. Chartreuse plastic with black knobs.
9187-J	30-35	Same as 9187-B. Red plastic with tan knobs.
A51T2	50-65	Table. Brown Bakelite. Top controls. 1947.
A51T3	50-65	Table. Ivory Bakelite. Top controls. 1947.
A61CR3	40-60	Radio-phonograph. Console. 1948.
A61P1	30-40	Portable. AC/battery (rechargeable). 1947.
A72T3	35-40	Table. Wood. AM/FM. 1947.
B51T1	40-50	Table. Brown Bakelite. Top controls. 1949.
B61T1	30-40	Table. White. Asymmetrical. 1949.
B61T2	30-40	Table. Brown. Asymmetrical. 1949.
B92CR1	50-60	Console (horizontal). Radio-phono. 1947.
C51T1	40-50	Table. Ivory Bakelite. 1948. (GOR)
R-180A	30-50	Table. Wood. Speakers on sides of cabinet. 1937. (GOR)
St. James	200-300	Highboy. Solid walnut front. 1930. (GOR)

STROMBERG-CARLSON

Stromberg-Carlson was originally a manufacturer of telephone equipment.

Model Name/Number	Price Range($)	Description
1A	125-175	Table. Battery. 3 dial. 1924. (VR-133)
61Y	30-40	Table. Wood. Deco. 1935.
68	125-200	Console. Deco. AM/SW. 1935.
130J	50-100	Table. Deco. 1937.
231R	200-350	Chairside (semi-circular). Mirror top. AM/SW. 1937. (FOS-180)
240R	300-500	Console with doors. Semi-circular. Deco. Push-buttons. AM/4SW. 1937. (FOS-180; GOR)
320H	40-50	Table. AM/FM. 1938. (FOS-180)
400H	30-35	Table. 1939.
410H	40-60	Table. Wood. AM/SW. 1939.
420L	75-100	Console. Push-button. AM/SW. 1939.
520H	45-60	Table. Wood. AM/SW. 1940.
635 "Treasure Chest"	150-200	Table. Wood. AC. 1928
900G	30-40	Table. Brown with ivory front. 1941
1100H	20-25	Table. Wood. 1947.
1101	40-50	Table. Ivory. 1946.
1105	30-40	Portable. Leatherette. White grille. AC/battery. 1947.
1110-HW	60-80	Table. Wood. Push-button. Vertical dial. AM/SW. 1947.
1121	100-150	Console. 1946.
1202	50-60	Table. Radio-phono. 1949.
1204	40-50	Table. Plastic. AM/FM. 1948.
1210PLM	80-100	Console (horizontal). Radio-phono. AM/FM. 1948.
1400	40-50	Table. Ivory plastic. Full wrap-around grille. 1949.
1407-PFM	40-60	Console (horizontal). Radio-phono. FM/AM. 1949.
1409-PGM	40-60	Console (horizontal). Radio-phono. FM/AM. 1949.
1500	40-50	Table. Red plastic. 1950. (GOR)
AR-411	25-30	Hi-fi. Amplifier with controls. 1957.
C-1	25-30	Clock radio. 1951.

SYLVANIA

Model Name/Number	Price Range($)	Description
4P14	15-20	Transistor. Blue or white front. 1961.
4P19W	20-25	Transistor. Tan. 1962.

ARR: *Antique Radios: Restoration and Price Guide* / ARR2: *Antique Radio Restoration Guide, Second Edition* /
B1: *Antique Radio Price Guide, First Edition* by Bunis / B2: *Antique Radio Price Guide, Second Edition* by Bunis /
FOS: *Flick of the Switch* / GOR: *Guide to Old Radios* / RGA: *Radios: The Golden Age* / RR: *Radios Redux* / VR: *Vintage Radio*

Model Name/Number	Price Range($)	Description
5C13B	20-25	Clock radio. 1961.
55C13	40-50	Console (horizontal). Radio-phono. FM/AM. 1961.
454BR	20-25	Portable. Brown plastic. Battery. 1954.
454GR	20-25	Same as 454BR. Green plastic.
454H	20-25	Same as 454BR. Ivory plastic.
454RE	20-25	Same as 454BR. Red plastic.
511B	20-25	Table. Black. 1952.
511H	20-25	Table. Ivory. 1952.
511M	20-25	Table. Brown. 1952.
512RE	25-30	Table. Red. 1952.
512YE	25-30	Table. Yellow. 1952.
512BR	25-30	Table. Brown. 1952.
512CH	25-30	Table. Chartreuse. 1952.
512GR	25-30	Table. Green. 1952.
512BR	25-30	Table. Brown. 1952.
542CH	25-30	Clock radio. Chartreuse. Large clock. 1952. (AR2-61)
542GR	25-30	Clock radio. Green. Large clock. 1952.
542YE	25-30	Clock radio. Yellow. Large clock. 1952.
542BR	25-30	Clock radio. Brown. Large clock. 1952.
542RE	25-30	Clock radio. Red. Large clock. 1952.
649-1	15-20	Transistor. Metal. "Golden Shield." 1961.
1107	20-25	Table. Black.
2101TU	20-25	Table. Turquoise plastic. 1957.

SYMPHONIC
124	30-40	Console. Radio-phono. FM/AM. 1962.

T

TATRO
CR-557	60-70	Lowboy. 6 legs. Wood. About 1930. (GOR)

TELE-TONE
111	25-30	Table. Wood. 1948.
134	25-30	Portable. Leatherette. Radio-phono. 1946.
135	20-25	Table. 1947.
150	25-30	Table. Ivory plastic. 1948.
159	20-25	Table. Plastic. 1948.
160	40-45	Table. 2-tone plastic. 1948.
190	20-25	Portable. AC/battery. 1949.
195	40-50	Table. Black with white knobs. 1949.
198	25-30	Table. Wood. FM/AM. 1949.

TELEFUNKEN
535IW "Jubilate"	30-40	Table. Multi-band. 1950s.
5346W "Contessa"	70-90	Console. Small. AM/2SW.
Andante 8	35-40	Table. AM/FM/SW. 1950s.
Jubilee	40-60	Table. 2 band. 1956.

TELECHRON
8H59	50-60	Clock radio. Red. 1948.
8H67	20-25	Clock radio. Tan painted. 1948.

TELEKING
RK-41	25-30	Table. Plastic. 1953.
RKP-53-A	25-30	Portable. Plastic. AC/battery. Tapered shape. 1954.

TELESONIC

Model Name/Number	Price Range($)	Description
1635 "Medco"	25-30	Table. Blond wood. 1947.
1642 "Medco"	25-30	Table. Plastic. 1947.

TEMPLE

Began in 1928.

E-511	25-30	Table. Wood. Radio-phono. 1946.
E-514	40-45	Table. Wood. 1946.
F-616	25-30	Table. Wood. 1946. (GOR)
F-617	25-30	Table. Wood. Radio-phono. 1947.
G-418	50-60	Table. Metal. 1947.
G-419	30-40	Table. Metal. 1947.
G-515	20-25	Table. Wood. Cloth grille. 1947.
G-516	20-25	Table. Wood. Radio-phono. 1947.
G-724	25-30	Table. Wood. AM/FM. 1948.
G-725	50-70	Console (horizontal). Radio-phono. 1948.

THERMIODYNE

TF-5	60-70	Table. Battery. 1925.
TF-6	75-125	Table. Battery. 1925.

THOMPSON

Thompson began producing radios and speakers in 1923, and went into receivership in 1926.

Neutrodyne 5	75-150	Table. Battery. Wood. 1924.
S70 "Concert Grand"	75-125	Table. Battery. Sloped front panel. 3 dial. 1925.
V-50	100-125	Table. Battery. Sloped front panel. 3 dial. 1925.

TOSHIBA

6P-15	30-40	Transistor. 1962.
6TP-309A	70-80	Transistor. White. 1959.
6TP-357	20-25	Transistor. 1961.
7TP-3525	25-30	Transistor. AM/SW. 1960.

TPI

4081	40-50	Coke Dispenser, modern style.

TRANCEL

TR81	20-25	Transistor. 1962.

TRAV-LER

Trav-Ler radios were made by the Trav-Ler Karenola Radio & Television Corp., Chicago.

1937 Trav-Ler, no model information; AM/SW (Ed and Irene Ripley).

ARR: *Antique Radios: Restoration and Price Guide* / ARR2: *Antique Radio Restoration Guide, Second Edition* /
B1: *Antique Radio Price Guide, First Edition* by Bunis / B2: *Antique Radio Price Guide, Second Edition* by Bunis /
FOS: *Flick of the Switch* / GOR: *Guide to Old Radios* / RGA: *Radios: The Golden Age* / RR: *Radios Redux* / VR: *Vintage Radio*.

Model Name/Number	Price Range($)	Description
5000-I	25-30	Table. Ivory plastic. 1946.
5002-I	25-30	Table. White painted. 1946.
5015	30-40	Table. Plastic. 1948.
5020	20-25	Portable. AC/battery. Leatherette. 1946.
5022	30-40	Portable. 1946.
5028	25-30	Portable. Leatherette. AC/battery. 1948.
5030	30-35	Table. Radio-phono. Leatherette. 1947.
5036	25-30	Table. Radio-phono. Cloth. 1949.
5049	30-40	Portable. Alligator. White plastic grille. 1948.
5051	40-50	Table. Plastic. 1947.
5054	50-60	Table (small). Cream color plastic. 1948.
5056A	30-40	Table (small). Bakelite. 1950.
5066	30-40	Table. Brown plastic. 1946. (GOR)
5091	30-45	Table. Wood. 1953.
5372	20-25	Portable. Radio-phono. Leatherette. 1954.
8103	20-25	Table. Radio-phono. Wood. 1949.

TRESCO *(See also Tri-City)*

W	200	Receiver and amplifier. (GOR)

TRI-CITY *(See also Tresco)*

Tri-City produced radios for Montgomery Ward in 1923. They also sold radios under their own brand, "Tresco."

W2	75-150	Box. Battery. Made for Wards. 1923.
W6	75-150	Box. Battery. Made for Wards. 1923.

TROY

100	40-60	Table. Wood. Telephone dial. 1937. (GOR)

TRUETONE

Truetone was Western Auto's house brand.

4DC-5945A	40-50	Console (horizontal). Radio-phono. FM/AM. Stereo. 1961.
D-711	50-60	Table. 1938.
D-1181	40-50	Table. 1941.
D-1644	25-30	Table (on legs). Radio-phono. 1946.
D-1747	75-100	Console (horizontal). Radio-phono. AM/4SW. 1947.
D-1752	75-125	Console. Radio-phono. AM/FM. 1948.
D-1846A	75-125	Console. Radio-phono. AM/FM. 1948.
D-1850	75-100	Console (horizontal). Radio-phono. AM/FM. 1948.
D-2017	75-100	Table. Boomerang shape. 1951.
D-2018	75-100	Table. 1951.
D-2027A	30-40	Table. Wood. FM-AM. 1950.
D-2210	75-100	Table. Metal. Deco. 1941.
D-2270	20-25	Portable. Radio-phono. Leatherette. 1953.
D-2386	20-25	Table. Black plastic. 1954.
D-2387	20-25	Same as D-2386. White plastic.
D-2388	25-30	Same as D-2386. Red plastic.
D-2413A	20-25	Table. Beige. 1953.
D-2418A	25-30	Clock radio. Black plastic with bright grille. 1954.
D-2419A	40-45	Same as D-2418. Red plastic.
D-2420A	20-25	Same as D-2418. White plastic.
D-2603	25-30	Table. Wood. Radio-phono (single play). 1946.
D-2613	25-30	Table. White plastic. 1947.
D-2615	75-100	Table. White painted. Push-button. Side tuning knob. 1946.
D-2620	40-50	Table. Wood. 1946.
D-2622	30-40	Table. Wood (curved sides). 1947.

TRUETONE—*continued*

Model Name/Number	Price Range($)	Description
D-2623	25-30	Table. Wood. 1946.
D-2626	30-40	Table. Wood. AM/SW. 1948.
D-2634	25-30	Table. Wood. 1946.
D-2644	25-30	Table. Wood. Battery. 1946.
D-2663	20-25	Table. Wood. Battery. 1946.
D-2691	30-40	Table. Metal. 1947.
D-2692	25-30	Table. Wood. Plastic grille. 1948.
D-2710	30-40	Table. Brown Bakelite. 1947.
D-2810	30-40	Table. Plastic. 1948.
D-2815	40-60	Violin shape. Brown Bakelite. 1948.
D-2815	50-75	Violin shape. White Bakelite. 1948.
D-2819	30-40	Table. Plastic. AM/FM. 1948.
D-2851	25-30	Table. Radio-phono. 1948.
D-2857A	25-30	Table. Ivory. Twin speakers. 1958.
D-2858A	25-30	Table. Turquoise. Twin speakers. 1958.
D-2906	20-25	Table. Brown. 1949.
D-2907	20-25	Table. Ivory. 1949.
D-2910	20-25	Table. 1949.
D-2919	25-30	Table. FM-AM. 1949.
D-3120A	20-25	Portable. Plastic. AC/battery. 1953.
D-3130/D-3130B	20-25	Portable. Plastic. AC/battery. 1953.
D-3210A	30-40	Portable. Plastic. AC/battery. 1953.
D-3490	25-30	Portable. Plastic. Battery. 1955.
D-3615	20-25	Portable. AC/battery. Two-tone leatherette. 1947.
D-3630	30-35	Portable. AC/battery. Two-tone leatherette. 1947.
D-3721	20-25	Portable. 1947.
D-3722	25-30	Portable. Leatherette with plastic grille. AC/battery. 1948.
D-3789A	20-25	Portable. Leatherette. AC/battery. 1957.
D-3810	25-30	Portable. Leatherette. AC/battery. 1948.
DC-3166	100-125	Transistor. Pink. "Lady Truetone" 1962.

TUSKA

One of the early radio companies, Tuska incorporated in May 1920 and had their first radios advertised and for sale in August of the same year.

224	300-350	Table. Battery. 2 dial. 1922. (VR-121)
225	200-300	Table. Battery. 2 dial. 1923. (VR-121) (B2-190)
301 "Superdyne Junior"	200-250	Table. Battery. 1925.
305 "Superdyne"	150-200	Table. Battery. 2 dial. 1925.

U.S. APEX

8A	150-200	Cathedral. 1931.

ULTRADYNE

Ultradyne radios were made by the Lacault Co.

L2	60-90	Table. Battery. 1924.

ARR: *Antique Radios: Restoration and Price Guide* / ARR2: *Antique Radio Restoration Guide, Second Edition* /
B1: *Antique Radio Price Guide, First Edition* by Bunis / B2: *Antique Radio Price Guide, Second Edition* by Bunis /
FOS: *Flick of the Switch* / GOR: *Guide to Old Radios* / RGA: *Radios: The Golden Age* / RR: *Radios Redux* / VR: *Vintage Radio*.

VALLEYTONE

Model Name/Number	Price Range($)	Description
	50-100	Table. 6 tube. 1925.

VICTOR *(See also RCA)*

The Victor Talking Machine Co. believed in phonographs, not radio. After the company was sold in 1926, and recognizing that radio was hurting the sales of phonographs and records, it brought out a radio-phonograph using an RCA Radiola 28 for the radio. It appears they were ready to start designing their own radios when they merged instead with RCA in 1929.

Note: The VV designation stands for a spring-wound motor. VE means an electric motor.

RE-45	200-300	Console. Radio-phono. 1929. (ARR-41)
RE-57	100-150	Console. Radio-phono. 1930.
VE-9-55	1000+	Console (horizontal). Radio-phono. Uses a Radiola 28. An automatic changer turned the record over. 1927.
VV-7-1	175-225	Console (highboy). Radio-phono. Uses a Radiola 18. Acoustic phonograph. 1928.
VV-9-1	500	Console (horizontal lowboy). Radio-phono. "Florenza" with doors. Uses a Radiola 25. Acoustic phonograph. 1926.

VICTOREEN

Victoreen was a pioneer in kit radios. It got involved in the nasty, long-drawn-out patent fights of the 1920s, but managed to sell out before the fights came to court.

	150	Kit. 5-tube.
	125-150	9 tube.
	150-175	Superhet.

VICTORIA

TR-650	10-15	Transistor. 1961.

VIEWTONE

RRC-201	25-30	Portable. Leatherette. Radio-phono. 1946.

VIZ

RS-1	80-100	Table. Mottled plastic. 1946.

WARE

Ware produced radios until 1925. At that time, a major disagreement with Music Master (about 15,000 radio sets that were, or were not, delivered) forced them to quit. It is reported that most of the Ware radios were then unloaded in New York City department stores.

T	175-250	Table. Battery. 3 dial. 1924. (VR-124) (B1-157)

WATTERSON

4790	25-30	Table. Wood (two-toned). 1947.
ARC-4591A	25-30	Table. Wood. Radio-phono. 1947.
RC-4581	25-30	Table. Wood. Radio-phono (single play). 1947.

WEBCOR

1068-1	40-50	Console (horizontal). Radio-phono. FM/AM. 1961.
1098-1	40-50	Console (horizontal). Blond wood. Radio-phono. FM/AM. 1961.

WELLS-GARDNER

108A1-704	40-60	Table. Telephone dial. Wood. 1937. (GOR)
WG-30A8-A-496	60-90	Console (horizontal). Radio-phono. AM/FM. 1954.

WESTERN COIL

Model Name/Number	Price Range($)	Description
Lewis	1250	1922.
WC-15-JR		
"Radiodyne"	150-200	Table. Battery. 1926.
WC17	100-150	Table. Battery. 2 dial. 1924.

WESTERN ELECTRIC

4B	300-400	Table. Battery. 2 dial. 1923.
7A	150-250	Amplifier.
14A	100-150	Amplifier.

WESTINGALE

	100-125	Table. Scenic front. 1926-1927. (GOR)

WESTINGHOUSE

There were Westinghouse radios in 1921 and again in 1930. In between, they continued to make radios that were sold under the RCA name. As a member of the patent-pool that included RCA, they produced 40 percent of the radios sold under the RCA name during that period, namely the Aeriola Jr. and the Aeriola Sr. (General Electric manufactured the other 60 percent). Westinghouse was not only a developer of radios, it also was a strong supporter of broadcasting. Station KDKA (the first licensed broadcasting station in the U.S.) was started in October 1920. Their first broadcasting studio was a tent on top of one of their buildings.

52R11	20-25	Table. Brown plastic with black dial and knob. 1952.
52R12	20-25	Same as 52R11. Ivory plastic with ivory dial and knobs.
52R13	25-30	Same as 52R11. Maroon plastic with black dial and knobs.
52R14	20-25	Same as 52R11. Gray plastic with black dial and knobs.
52R15	25-30	Same as 52R11. Green plastic with black dial and knobs.
52R16	30-40	Same as 52R11. Red plastic with black dial and knobs.
Aeriola Jr.	1000	Box. Crystal. 1922 (like new).
Aeriola Sr.	150-200	Box. 1 tube. 1922.
H-M1400	40-50	Console (horizontal). Radio-phono. FM/AM. 1961.
H-117	80-100	Console (vertical). Radio-phono. FM/AM/SW. 1946.
H-122	60-90	Chairside. Radio-phono. Radio can be removed from cabinet to use elsewhere. 1946.
H-122A	40-45	Table. Brown plastic. 1946. Radio from H-122.
H-124	100-125	Table. Green painted with gold grille. 1945. (RGA-63)
	100-125	Table. Brown painted with gold grille. 1945. (RGA-63)
H-130	40-50	Table. Wood. 1946. (GOR)
H-133	20-25	Table. Wood. Battery. 1947.
H-146	50-75	Refrigerator radio.
H-147	30-40	Table. Brown Bakelite. 1947.
H-157	25-30	Table. Wood. 1948.
H-161	40-50	Table. Wood. AM/FM. 1948.
H-165	15-25	Portable. AC/battery. 1947.
H-166	80-100	Console (horizontal). Radio-phono. Curved front. 1948.
H-168	50-75	Console (horizontal). Radio-phono. AM/FM. 1948.
H-169	150-200	Console (horizontal). Radio-phono. 2-way speaker. Large. AM/FM/2SW. 1948.
H-171	100-150	Chairside. Radio-phono. Blond wood. Radio is plastic and can be removed from wood cabinet base. 1948. (ARR-66)
H-182	35-40	Table. Plastic. Metallic trim. 1949.
H-185	15-20	Portable. Maroon plastic. AC/battery. 1949. (FOS-182)

ARR: *Antique Radios: Restoration and Price Guide* / ARR2: *Antique Radio Restoration Guide, Second Edition* /
B1: *Antique Radio Price Guide, First Edition* by Bunis / B2: *Antique Radio Price Guide, Second Edition* by Bunis /
FOS: *Flick of the Switch* / GOR: *Guide to Old Radios* / RGA: *Radios: The Golden Age* / RR: *Radios Redux* / VR: *Vintage Radio.*

Model Name/Number	Price Range($)	Description
H-188	100-150	Table. Plastic "Pagoda" top and grille. 1948.
H-191	100-150	Console (horizontal). Radio-phono. FM/AM. 1949.
H-195	20-25	Portable. Leatherette. AC/battery. 1949.
H-199	50-60	Console. Radio-phono. FM/AM. 1949.
H-203	40-50	Console (horizontal). Radio-phono. FM/AM. 1949.
H-204	50-60	Table. Plastic. Deco. 1948.
H-211	40-50	Table (vertical). Handle. Vertical dial on right. 1949.
H-307T7	25-30	Table. Brown. FM/AM. 1950.
H-308T7	25-30	Table. Ivory. FM/AM. 1950.
H-310T5	25-30	Table. Brown plastic. 1950.
H-311T5	25-30	Table. Ivory plastic. 1950.
H-331P4U	20-25	Portable. Green plastic. AC/battery. 1952.
H-333P4U	30-40	Portable. Brown plastic. AC/battery. 1952.
H-345T5	20-25	Table. Brown with gold front. 1951.
H-350T7	25-30	Table. Brown. FM/AM. Center dial. 1949.
H-351T7	25-30	Table. Ivory. FM/AM. Center dial. 1949.
H-354C7	50-60	Console. Radio-phono. FM/AM. 1952.
H-382T5	20-25	Table. Brown plastic. 1954.
H-384T5	20-25	Table. Maroon Bakelite. 1953.

1953 Westinghouse model H393T6; maroon plastic.

H-393T6	25-30	Table. Maroon plastic. 1953. (GOR)
H-397T5	40-50	Clock radio, Gold dial on Maroon. 1954. (ARR2-56)
H-435T5	20-25	Table. White, gold dial. 1955.
H-436T5	30-40	Table. Maroon, gold dial. 1955.
H-494P4	25-30	Portable. 1955.
H-495P4	50-60	Portable. 1955.
H-598P4	20-25	Portable. Beige and red plastic. AC/portable. 1957.
H-648T4	20-25	Table. White plastic. 1955.
H-702T5	25-30	Clock radio. Aqua. 1958.
H-710T5	40-50	Clock radio. Bright pink and white. 1959.
H-716T5	20-25	Table. FM/AM. 1960.
H-743T4	25-30	Table. White. Dark dials with gold center. 1955.
H-825T5	20-25	Table. 1959.
H-852N6	20-25	Table. Light blue and white. 1964.
Refrigerator radio	See model H-146	
WR-8-R "Columaire"	250-300	Grandfather clock. 1929.
WR-15	200-250	Grandfather clock. 1931.
WR-22	75-100	Upright table. AM/SW. 1934.
WR-28	120-150	Upright table. AM/SW. 1934.
WR-166LW	60-80	Table. 1938.
WR-274	50-60	Table. AM/SW. Push-button. 1939.

WESTONE

Model Name/Number	Price Range($)	Description
30	20-25	Table.

WILMAK (See Denchum)

WINDSOR

6T-220	100-125	Transistor. Blue with case. 1961.

WOLPER

RS5	100-120	Table. Slant front. Stepped back enclosed horn. Mid-1920s. (GOR)

WOOLAROC

Woolaroc radios were sold by Phillips Petroleum.

3-15A	40-50	Table. Metal. 1948.
3-17A	40-50	Table. Plastic. 1948.
3-71A	60-100	Console (horizontal). Radio-phono. 1948.

WORKRITE

Air Master	100-150	Table. Wood. Slant front. Battery. 3 dials. 1924. (GOR)
Aristocrat	200-250	Horizontal highboy. Slant front panel. 2 end compartments with doors, 1 with enclosed speaker. 3 dials. Battery. 1924. (GOR)
Chum	200-250	Table. Slant front panel. 2 dials. Battery. 1925. (GOR)

ZENITH

Chicago Radio Laboratories began in 1918 to supply amateur equipment. CRL's call letters were 9ZN. So, in 1919, they installed a new receiver at the station and called it a Z-Nith. From there it became Zenith. Zenith has been innovative: the first portable (1924), the first major production of AC sets (1926), and the first push-button tuning (1927).

Note: Because of the long, complicated sequences in Zenith model numbers, they are separated by hyphens into letter and number groups. This was done with RCA also, and for the same reasons. This does not mean that the groups are broken up like this by Zenith.

—	150	Turning display stand for console. Dark blue.
1R/2R	650	Table. Battery. 3 dial. 1922.
3R	350-400	Table. Battery. 1923. (VR-115)
4-B-231	30-60	Table. Battery. 1936.
4-B-314	60-80	Table. 1937.
4-G-800	35-40	Portable. Plastic. Flip up cover. AC/battery. 1948.
4-G-800-Z	30-40	Portable. Plastic. Flip up cover. Metallic front. AC/battery. 1948.
4-K-400	75-125	Portable (miniature). Black. 1941.
4-K-422	60-75	Table. Battery. Bakelite. 1939.
4R	300-400	Table. Battery. 1923. (VR-116)
5-D-611	40-45	Table. Wood.
	30-40	Table. Plastic. (B2-199)
5-D-810	30-40	Table. Plastic. Metal grille. 1949.
5-D-811	30-40	Table. 1948.
5-E-01	20-25	Table. White. 1949.
5-F-134	100-150	Upright table. Battery. AM/3SW. 1941. (GOR) (Cabinet same as 7-D-127 in FOS-193)

ARR: *Antique Radios: Restoration and Price Guide* / ARR2: *Antique Radio Restoration Guide, Second Edition* /
B1: *Antique Radio Price Guide, First Edition* by Bunis / B2: *Antique Radio Price Guide, Second Edition* by Bunis /
FOS: *Flick of the Switch* / GOR: *Guide to Old Radios* / RGA: *Radios: The Golden Age* / RR: *Radios Redux* / VR: *Vintage Radio*.

Model Name/Number	Price Range($)	Description
5-G-003	30-35	Portable. AC/battery. Semi-circle grille, dial. 1947.
5-G-01	20-25	Table. Brown. 1950.
5-G-03	25-30	Clock radio. Brown. 1950.
5-G-41	40-50	Portable. AC/battery. Flip lid. 1951. (FOS-196) (ARR2-70)
5-G-617	25-50	Table. Bakelite. Push-button. 1941.
5-R-135	75-100	Upright table. 1937.
5-R-216	75-100	Table. Wood. 1937.
5-R-236	75-100	Chairside. Magazine storage. 1937. (GOR)
5-R-312	100-150	Table. Bakelite. Push-button. (ARR-61; RGA-71)
5-R-337	75-100	Chairside. Push-button. 1938.
5-S-29	100-175	Upright table. AM/2SW. 1936. (FOS-192)
5-S-127	100-175	Upright table. AM/SW. 1936.
5-S-228	125-175	Upright table. AM/2SW. 1938.
5-S-319	75-100	Table. Push-button. AM/SW 1938.
5-S-338	125-150	Chairside. 1937.
6-B-129	125-150	Upright table. 6 volt battery. 1936. (FOS-191; GOR)
6-C-05 (chassis)	30-40	Table. Wood. Small. 1946.
6-C-40	30-40	Portable. AC/battery. 1946.
6-D-015	50-75	Table. Brown plastic. 1946. (RGA-71)
6-D-015-Z	50-75	Table. Green plastic. 1946.
6-D-029	40-60	Table. Wood. 1946. (FOS-195; GOR)
6-D-030	50-60	Table. Wood. Deco. 1946. (B1-166)
6-D-411G	75-100	Table. 1939.
6-D-414	40-60	Table. Brown Bakelite. Inverted Bakelite chassis. 1939. (GOR)
6-D-510	20-25	Table. Bakelite. 1941. (B2-201)
6-D-525	75-100	Table. Wood. Black dial. 1941. (B2-201)
6-D-610	40-50	Table. Brown Bakelite. Handle. 1941.
6-D-614	40-50	Table. 1940.
6-D-615W	40-50	Table. Deco. 1941.
6-D-621	40-50	Table. 1941.
6-D-628	50-60	Table. 1941.
6-D-815	30-35	Table. Plastic. Gold grille with dial on it. Handle. 1949. (B2-202)
6-D-2615	20-25	Table. 1941.
6-G-001 "Universal"	30-40	Portable. Black leatherette. 1946.
6-G-004Y	50-60	Portable. AC/battery. Black. 1947.
6-G-05	20-25	Table. Brown. 1950.
6-G-038	40-50	Table. Wood. AC/battery. Whip antenna. 1947.
6-G-501-F/-L/-M	30-50	Portable. AC/battery. 1940.
6-G-581-M	30-35	Table. Ship on grille.
6-G-601-M	40-50	Portable. AC/battery. Cloth covered. 1941. (GOR)
6-G-801	30-40	Portable. Plastic. Front doors open. AC/battery. 1949. (FOS-196)
6-H-02	25-30	Table. Radio-phono. Bakelite. Large center. 1951.
6-J-05	30-40	Table, brown with brass trim. 1952.
6-J-230	100-150	Upright table. AC/battery. 1941.
6-R-084	25-30	Table. Wood. Radio-phono. 1947.
6-R-631	50-75	Table. Wood. Push-buttons. 1941. (GOR)
6-R-886	30-40	Table. Radio-phono. Blond wood. 1947. (GOR)
	80-100	Same Radio-phono with matching table. (GOR)
6-S-128	200-250	Upright table. AC/SW. 1936. (FOS-191)
6-S-229	150-200	Upright table. AM/SW. 1937. (GOR)
6-S-254	200-250	Console. AM/2SW. 1936.
6-S-321	75-125	Table. AM/LW/SW. Push-button. 1937.
6-S-511	50-60	Table. Brown Bakelite. Push-button. Handle. 1940.
6-S-511W	50-60	Table. White. 1949. (B2-204)

Model Name/Number	Price Range($)	Description
6-V-27	100-150	Upright table. AM/SW. 6 volt battery. 1935. (ARR-59) (FOS-192)
7-E-01 (chassis)	30-40	Table. Brown. FM/AM. 1948.
7-E-02 (chassis)	30-40	Table. Brown. FM/AM. 1949.
7-E-022	20-25	Table. Brown plastic. AM/FM. 1949.
7-G-605		
"Trans-oceanic"	150-225	Portable. First Trans-oceanic. Multi-band. Airplane on grille. 1941. (FOS-194; GOR)
7-H-02Z (chassis)	60-70	Table. Brown. FM/AM. Gold dial. 1951.
7-H-04Z2	30-40	Table. Brown. FM/AM. 1951.
7-H-820	50-60	Table. AM/2FM. 1948.
7-H-820W	50-60	Table. White. AM/2FM. 1948.
7-H-822	25-30	Table. Plastic. AM/FM. 1949.
7-H-921	40-50	Table. Bakelite. 1949.
7-J-03	75-100	Table. Black and white plastic. 1953.
7-J-232	300-500	Upright table. AC/6v. AM/SW. 1937. The "Waltons" radio, from the TV show.
7-J-368	125-175	Console (vertical). 1938.
7-R-070	40-50	Table. Radio-phono. Wood with textured paint. Plastic grille. 1948.
7-R-887	100-150	Console. Radio-phono. 1949.
7-S-240	200-250	Chairside. Walnut wood. Large black dial. AM/2SW. 1938. (GOR)
7-S-258	250-350	Console. 1938.
8-G-005		
"Transoceanic"	75-125	Portable. AC/battery. Multi-band. 1948.
8-H-034	40-60	Table. Plastic. AM/2FM. 1946.
8-H-061	100-150	Console. AM/2FM. 1946.
8-H-861	40-50	Table. Wood. AM/2FM. 1948.

1939 Zenith model 8S463. Here is one of the reasons Zenith has a reputation for making big, impressive console radios. It's a large radio that becomes the focal point of the room.

ARR: *Antique Radios: Restoration and Price Guide* / ARR2: *Antique Radio Restoration Guide, Second Edition* / B1: *Antique Radio Price Guide, First Edition* by Bunis / B2: *Antique Radio Price Guide, Second Edition* by Bunis / FOS: *Flick of the Switch* / GOR: *Guide to Old Radios* / RGA: *Radios: The Golden Age* / RR: *Radios Redux* / VR: *Vintage Radio.*

Model Name/Number	Price Range($)	Description
8-S-154	150-200	Console (vertical). 3 band. 1936.
8-S-226	150-200	Chairside. 1939. (FOS193)
8-S-463	200-250	Console. Push-button. 1939. (GOR)
8-S-661	125-175	Console. 1941.
8-T-01Z	30-40	Table. Brown. FM/AM. 1955.
9-H-984-LP	80-100	Console (vertical) Radio-phono. FM/AM. 1949.
9-S-262	200-300	Console. AM/SW. 1939.
9-S-263	200-300	Console (vertical) 3 band. 1936.
10-H-571	300-350	Looks like a spinet piano. Push-button. AM/FM/SW. 1941.
10-H-573	200-250	Console. AM/SW/old FM. 1940.
10-S-153	300-350	Console. 1936.
10-S-160	200-250	Console. AM/3SW. 1936. (FOS-191)
10-S-443	100-150	Table. Wood. AM/SW. Push-button. 1940.
10-S-464	250-300	Console. 1941.
10-S-567	200-250	Console. 1940.
10-S-669	150-200	Console. 1941.
11	75-100	Table. Battery. 1927. (GOR) **Note:** Also available as a lowboy in 1931.
11-E	100-125	Table. Wood. AC. 1927.
11-S-474	200-250	Console. AM/2SW. 1939.
12-S-265	400-450	Console. AM/2SW. 1937.
12-S-266	800	Console (vertical). Restored. 1936.
12-S-370	300-350	Console (vertical). 1937.
12-S-568	300-400	Console. AM/2SW. Push-button. 1940.
12-U-158	300-250	Console (vertical). 1936.
15-U-271	1000+	Console. Big. 15 tube. 1937.
33-X	150	Table. 1928.
34-P	100-150	Console. Drum dial. 1928.
40A	500-600	Console (horizontal). Elaborate. Wood. Push-button. 1930. (GOR)
60	100-125	Console. Wood. Small. 1929. (GOR)
64	300-500	Lowboy with doors. Wood. Push-button. 1931. (GOR)
230	150-200	Upright table. 1930. (FOS-190)
250	250-300	Cathedral. 1932.
807	150-200	Upright table. 1935.
1000-Z "Stratosphere"	2000+	Console. Big. 23 tube. Multi-band. Multi-speaker. 1934.
1005 (chassis)	300	Console. Push-button. 1939.
5416 (chassis)	30-40	Portable. Cloth covered. Battery. 1939. (GOR)
A-402L	25-30	Portable. AC-battery. 1958.
A-513F	30-35	Table. Large center oval grille. 1958.
A-600 "Transoceanic"	60-80	Portable. AC-battery. Multi-band. 1957.
B-508R	30-40	Table. Maroon and white front. 1957. (ARR2-92)
B-509	20-25	Table. Red and white plastic. 1968.
B-513-V	20-25	Table. Plastic. 1959. (GOR)
B-600	60-80	Portable. AC-battery. Multi-band. 1957.
C-724L	20-25	Table. Plastic. FM/AM. 1960.
C-730	20-25	Table. AM/FM. 1955.
D-6015	30-40	Table. Brown. Foldup handle.
F-510B	20-25	Table. Aqua and White. 1964.
G-500 "Transoceanic"	75-125	Portable. AC/battery. Multi-band. 1950.
G-510	20-25	Table. Black plastic. 1949.
G-515	20-25	Clock radio. Yellow and white front. 1963.
G-723	25-30	Table. 1950.
G-725	30-40	Table. Bakelite. FM/AM. 1950.
H-500 "Transoceanic"	75-100	Portable. AC/battery. Multi-band. 1951 (common).

Model Name/Number	Price Range($)	Description
H-503	30-40	Portable. AC/Battery. Brown alligator and gold trim. 1951. (AAR2-92)
H-511W	35-60	Table. White, walnut, or ebony plastic. 1954. (GOR)
H-615	30-40	Table. Burgundy plastic. Large dial. 1951. (GOR)
H-724	40-50	Table. Bakelite. FM/AM. 1951.
H-725	30-40	Table. Black plastic. AM/FM. 1950. (GOR)
H-742Z1	30-40	Table. Brown. FM/AM. Cloth grille, gold dial, handle. 1952. (ch 7-H-02-Z-1)
HFM-1184-E	50-55	Radio-phonograph. Horizontal console. AM/FM. 1955.
J-402-G	30-40	Portable. Plastic. 1952.
J-506C	20-25	Table. Gray and white. 1963.
J-509-C	20-25	Table. Green plastic. 1961. (GOR)
J-615	25-30	Table. Brown. Handle. 1952. (ch. 6-J-05)
K-410	25-30	Portable. Plastic. Heavily chromed. Assorted colors. Battery. 1954.
K-412-W	20-25	Table. White plastic. 1953.
K-477-E	40-45	Console (horizontal). Radio-phono. 1953.
K-510	20-30	Table. Brown. Large dial. 1952.
K-510W	20-30	Table. White. Large dial. 1952.
K-510Y	20-30	Table. Yellow. Large dial. 1952.
K-515	30-40	Clock radio. Brown. 1952. (AAR2-52)
K-518	25-30	Clock radio. Plastic. 1952.
K-526	20-25	Table. Brown. Large dial. 1953.
K-622/-F/-G/-W	40-45	Clock radio. Plastic. Assorted colors. 1953.
K-666-R	50-60	Table. Radio-phono. Bakelite. 1953.
K-725	30-40	Table. FM/AM. Green. 1953.
L-403	30-40	Portable. Variety of colors. 1953.
L-410	25-30	Portable. Plastic. Heavily chromed. Assorted colors. Battery. 1954.
L-600 "Transoceanic"	45-60	Portable. AC/battery. Multi-band. 1954.
L-622 /-F/-G /-W	40-45	Clock radio. Plastic. Assorted colors. Contrasting grille. 1953. (B1-173)
M-403	30-40	Portable. Red and black plastic with chrome. (Other colors available.) 1953. (RR-98)
Portola	125-150	Chairside. Wood. Manufactured by United Air Cleaners for Zenith. 1936. (GOR)
R-50	10-15	Transistor. 1963.
R-511F	40-50	Table. Green. 1955.
R-640	10-15	Transistor. 1966.
R-755	10-15	Transistor. 1963.
Royal 20	50-60	Transistor. In box. 1967.
Royal 50	25-30	Transistor. 1963.
Royal 80	50-60	Transistor. In box. 1966.
Royal 250	25-30	Transistor. 1960.
Royal 275	40-50	Transistor. Two-tone green. 1960.
Royal 275	30-40	Transistor. Two-tone brown. 1960.
Royal 280	20-25	Transistor. 1968.
Royal 400	50-60	Transistor. Black. 1963.
Royal 500	100-125	Transistor. Black. 1956.
Royal 500-H	100-150	Transistor. Oval grille. 1962.
Royal 500-WI	70-80	Transistor. White. 1962.

ARR: *Antique Radios: Restoration and Price Guide* / ARR2: *Antique Radio Restoration Guide, Second Edition* /
B1: *Antique Radio Price Guide, First Edition* by Bunis / B2: *Antique Radio Price Guide, Second Edition* by Bunis /
FOS: *Flick of the Switch* / GOR: *Guide to Old Radios* / RGA: *Radios: The Golden Age* / RR: *Radios Redux* / VR: *Vintage Radio.*

Model Name/Number	Price Range($)	Description
Royal 670	10-15	Transistor. 1964.
Royal 675G	30-40	Transistor. 1960.
Royal 760 "Navigator"	20-25	Transistor. 1959.
Royal 780	30-40	Transistor. 2 band. 1960.
Royal 3000 "Transoceanic"	100-150	Transistor. Multi-band. 1964.
Royal 7000	100-150	Transistor. 1975.
SFD-660-C	25-30	Portable. Radio-phono. Leatherette. 1961.
SFD-2503-W	40-50	Console (horizontal). Stereo phono. 1961.
Super VII	150-200	Table. Battery. 2 dial. 1924. (GOR; VR-116)
Super VIII	200-250	Horizontal highboy. Spinet desk style. 2 dial. Battery. Super VII with legs. 1924. (GOR; VR-114,148)
Super-Zenith X	150-250	Horizontal highboy. Slant front panel. 2 end compartments with doors. Enclosed speaker above radio panel. 2 drawers in base. 1925. (GOR)
T-600 "Transoceanic"	60-90	Portable. AC/battery. Multi-band. 1954.
T-723	25-30	Table. Brown Bakelite. AM/FM. 1956.
T-825	30-50	Table. Plastic. Big dial. 1955.
"Transoceanic"		Portable. Early models were cloth; grille cloth had embroidered picture of airplane or sailboat. See 7-G-605 for first model. Later models were black leatherette. All had flip-up lid. Whip antenna for shortwave. AM/5 or 6 SW. These prices are for the more common black leatherette sets. Within these, model differences do not seem to affect the prices noticeably. (ARR-68)
X-316	25-30	Table. Light blue and white. AM/FM. 1968
X-323	25-30	Table. AM/FM. 1968.
XD-50-G	20-25	Table. Green. 1961.
XD-50-R	20-25	Table. Red. 1961.
XD-50-W	20-25	Table. White. 1961.
Y-723	30-40	Table. White plastic. AM/FM. 1956.
Y-725	25-30	Table. Brown Bakelite. AM/FM. 1956.

ZEPHER

Model Name/Number	Price Range($)	Description
5003	20-25	Table. Small. Japanese. Gray.
ZR-620	100-125	Transistor. White. 1962.

RADIO-RELATED AND NOVELTY ITEMS

Many of the items in this section have only single prices. This is because they came primarily from classified ads. Often there was only one ad for an item, which means this section will give you a general idea of what prices may be doing. Someone certainly was trying to sell these radios at these prices. Whether or not they got it, we don't know. Nevertheless, it may give you an idea of what is happening in radio-related fields.

NOVELTY RADIOS

Alcohol, Smoking, and Accessories

Name and Description	Price Range ($)
Bar-radio. White French provincial floor model by Philco.	400
Porto Baradio. Model PB520. Bakelite and clear plastic. With glasses. Used Stewart-Warner chassis 9008-B. (FOS-177)	250-400
Beer keg. Magic Tone Model 508.	125-175
Beer keg. Made by Radiokeg. 1934.	125-200
Beer-keg radio-lamp. Magic Tone Model 900.	250-300
Bottle radio. Made by Mackt-Tone.	90-100
Beer bottle. Large. Tubes. (RGA-17)	175-225
Beer bottle. Made by Magic Tone.	350
Budweiser radio. AM/FM.	40-50
Coors beer can. New in box. Hong Kong.	45
Gin bottle. Fleishman's. Clear plastic. AM. (Hong Kong). Like new.	60-90
Grain Belt signboard radio.	60-100
Marlboro cigarette pack. Transistor.	55
Pabst Blue Ribbon beer can. Transistor.	15
Rainier beer can. Transistor. New in box.	25
Rum bottle. "Malibu" FM/AM. 11 inches high. Transistor.	60
Smokerette. Pipe stand with 3 tobacco compartments. AM. Made by Porto. 1947.	125-175
Wings cigarettes. Pack. 8-by-12-by-10 inches. Made by RCA.	750+

Animals

Horse radio with saddle and blanket. (Abbotware model Z-477.)	150-225
Mouse on cheese. Transistor.	20
Owl. Jeweled eyes. Transistor	65

Automotive

Amalie oil can. Transistor.	30
Champion spark plug.	75
Champion spark plug. New in box.	175
Ford, car tire. Promotional piece. AM.	150
Havoline oil can. Transistor.	40

ARR: *Antique Radios: Restoration and Price Guide* / ARR2: *Antique Radio Restoration Guide, Second Edition* / B1: *Antique Radio Price Guide, First Edition* by Bunis / B2: *Antique Radio Price Guide, Second Edition* by Bunis / FOS: *Flick of the Switch* / GOR: *Guide to Old Radios* / RGA: *Radios: The Golden Age* / RR: *Radios Redux* / VR: *Vintage Radio*.

Hubcap. Wall mounted. Transistor. Made by Toshiba.	45
Lincoln town car. 1928. Transistor. New in box. Hong Kong.	30
Marathon Ultra D oil can. Transistor.	40
Rolls Royce car. Transistor.	20
Simplex car. 1912. Transistor. New in box. Hong Kong.	35
Sinclair gas pump. Transistor.	15-20

Bed Accessories

Lamp radio. Made by Mitchell. Model Lullaby 1250.	50-75
Lamp radio. Made by Mitchell. Model Lullaby 1251.	50-75
Lamp radio. Sonora. Model WCU-249.	50-75
Pillow Radio. Coin-op. Hung from headboard to make it easier to use while lying down. Pillow speaker. Pink or white. Dahlberg model 430-D1. c1955. (RGA-101)	100-200

Boats and Ships

Cabin Cruiser with stand. Transistor.	100
Chris Craft motor boat. Transistor. 1960s.	75
Melody Cruiser. Ship with metal sails. Made by Majestic. (RGA-73)	300-400

Books

Crosley. Bookcase model. 1932.	100-125
Sentinel model 238V. 1941.	100-150

Boxes, Chests, and Jewelry Cases

Atwater Kent model 555. 1933.	250-350
Majestic	75-125
Emerson model L-559.	125-175
Jewelry box. Emerson model 238.	200-250

Children, Radio, TV, Movies

Batman. Transistor. Original box.	40
Big Bird. (Holding 1930s radio). Transistor.	35
Bugs Bunny. Transistor	35
Cabbage Patch. Transistor.	15
Casper the friendly ghost. With box. Transistor.	40
Charlie McCarthy. Majestic model 1. Tube type. (FOS-108; RGA-35)	500+
Dick Tracy wrist radio.	50-75
Gulliver's travels. Stewart-Warner model 07-513. Tube type.	500-700
Holly Hobby standing next to cathedral radio. Transistor.	25
Hopalong Cassidy plastic table radio with foil front. Tube type. Foil must be in good condition. 1950. Arvin model 441T. (FOS-61; RGA-91)	125-250
Incredible Hulk. Transistor.	30
Michael Jackson. Transistor.	30
Mickey Mouse molded wood (model 411) or wood with metal trim (model 410). Made by Emerson. (RGA-12,13) (Tube type)	1000+
Mickey Mouse Clock radio. White plastic. 3 dimensional Mickey head. Made by General Electric.Tube type.	40-60
Mickey head. 2 dimensional. Transistor.	30-40
Mork from Ork. Transistor.	45
Mork from Ork egg ship. Transistor.	50
Raggedy Ann and Andy. AM. Transistor. (Hong Kong.)	40-75
Sesame Street with two Muppets.	30
Six-Million Dollar Man backpack/radio. New in box.	40
Snoopy. Transistor.	40
Snow White. Molded wood cabinet, hand-painted by Disney artists. Emerson, model Q-236.	750+

Children, Radio, TV, Movies—*continued*

Strawberry Shortcake. Transistor.	15
Superman bust. Transistor. New in box.	75
Superman phone booth. Transistor.	175

Dionne Quintuplets. Made by Stewart-Warner.

There are at least three different models with decals of the quintuplets.
    Identified under Stewart-Warner.

Food and Household

Campbell's Soup mix. Transistor.	55
Cheeseburger. Transistor. The size of a Whopper.	20
Green Giant corn can. Transistor.	45
Heinz Ketchup bottle. Transistor.	55
Lipton's Cup-a-Soup box. Transistor.	45
Little Sprout. Transistor.	20
Pet milk can. Transistor.	55
Polaroid 600 film box (blue). Transistor. Made in China.	25
Raid. Sick-looking bug leaning on dial.	195
Raisin man. Transistor. New in box.	85
Safegard Soap bar. Transistor. New in box.	75
Stanley tape measure. Transistor.	45

Globes

World globe. Made by Marc.	40-50
Globe with plane on top of radio.	90
Globe. "New World" by Colonial. (RGA-15)	1700

Grandfather Clocks

Crosley, model 126-1.	200-300
Crosley, Oracle model.	300-400
Philco model 70.	300-450
Philco model 53-706. Clock radio. Shaped like 13-inch-high grandfather clock.	60-80
Same as above but made by Silvertone.	250-350
Made by Simplex.	300-400
Made by Westinghouse.	200-325

Lamp-Radios

Rocket-ship shape. "Lumitone" Mitchell model 1260. (RGA-55)	75-125
Knight in armor shape.	40-50
Same, made by Radio Lamp Co. of America (RGA-55)	150-200
Lantern. "Town Crier" Made by Guild.	75

Microphones

Little Wonder Microphone (attached to radio).	55
"On the Air Mike." Plastic.	90-100
"Radio USA." Velocity-type microphone. Transistor. FM/AM. New in box.	50

Musical Instruments

Juke Box by Audiosound (JB1939C). FM/AM/cassette.	80
Grafanola. Made by Guild. Radio-phonograph. AM/FM.	200
Piano. Made by Continental. (RGA-49)	125-150
Piano (Made by General Radio).	125-150

ARR: *Antique Radios: Restoration and Price Guide* / ARR2: *Antique Radio Restoration Guide, Second Edition* /
B1: *Antique Radio Price Guide, First Edition* by Bunis / B2: *Antique Radio Price Guide, Second Edition* by Bunis /
FOS: *Flick of the Switch* / GOR: *Guide to Old Radios* / RGA: *Radios: The Golden Age* / RR: *Radios Redux* / VR: *Vintage Radio.*

Record player. Looks like Volkswagen van. Drives in circles playing LP record that lays on table top. "Soundmobile." — 60

Violin shape. Truetone, model D-2815. — 50-75

Patriotic

Liberty Bell. Transistor. — 55

Statue of Liberty. Transistor. — 50

Statue of Liberty. Scene on radio made by Radiovision. — 200-300

SOFT DRINKS

Coca-Cola

Coca-Cola bottle. Made by Crosley. — 1500+

Coke bottle. Transistor. AM. — 10-15

Coke bottle. Transistor. AM. New in box. — 40

Coke can. 1978. — 10

Coke cooler. Point of purchase model 5-A-410-A. (FOS-185) (RGA-89) 1949. Tube type. — 400-600

Coke cooler. Transistor. — 30-50

Coke dispenser. TPI 4081. Transistor. — 45

Coke insulated bag with built-in radio. Transistor. — 25

Coke logo on usual transistor AM-FM radio. 1970s. General Electric model CL-500. — 20-25

Coke vending machine. AM/FM. Transistor. — 50-80

Mountain Dew can. Transistor. — 35

Pepsi Cola

Pepsi bottle. 28 inches high. With original labels. Bakelite. 1940s? — 300-400

Pepsi bottle. Plastic. Transistor. Recent. — 10-15

Pepsi can. 1960s. — 15-20

Pepsi can. 1970s. — 10-15

Pepsi cooler. Plastic. 1950s. — 200-300

Pepsi fountain dispenser. Plastic. 1960s. — 150-250

Pepsi vending machine (horizontal). Dispenser. Plastic. 1960s. — 150-300

Pepsi vending machine (upright). "Say Pepsi please." Plastic. 1960s. — 50-75

Pepsi vending machine (upright). "Vending Machine radio." Plastic. Transistor. AM/FM. Recent. — 15-25

Pepsi Vending machine (upright). Plastic. AM/FM. Transistor. — 15-25

Reproductions of Classic Radios

Cathedral. Made by Philco. — 140-150

Tombstone. JVC model JR-120 — 30-35

Telephones

Country Belle wall telephone radio. Made by Guild. — 50-60

French telephone (white and gold). Transistor. — 50-60

Other Novelties

Knights in armor head. Transistor. Japan. — 45

"British Paint" can. Transistor. — 20

Camera and radio. Made by Cameradio. Tube type. — 100-150

Cookie Jar (aqua) with salt and pepper. Styled to look like RCA 65X1 radio. — 50

Desk pen set. Black. Continental TR-630. Transistor. 1961. — 30

Football and tee. Wilson. Transistor. — 20

Stained glass. Green and white. Made by RadioGlo. — 1000

Sunglasses. Transistor. Original box. Made by Ross. — 25-30

Other Novelties—*continued*

Name and Description	Price Range ($)
Teapot. The porcelain/wood cabinet sits on a potmetal "hottray" which, in reality, is the power supply. Made by Guild.	100-125
Toilet. Blue and white. "Little John" Transistor. Hong Kong.	30
Women's shoe. Red. FM only.	30

ADVERTISING ITEMS

Admiral
Neon clock, restored.	300

Atwater Kent
Lamp, no shade.	125-150
Lamp, with shade.	350-400
Playing cards, per deck.	40-75
Sign.	100

Bendix
Sign	25-40

Clarion
Lit sign	150

Crosley
Coloradio lit sign. (RGA-97).	500
"Magic Chef" timer. Deco style.	25-30

Cunningham Tubes
Postcard	2-3

Day-Fan
Small sign painted Gold and black on blue "Day-Fan radio A year ahead."	40

Fada
Advertising sign.	50-60

Farnsworth
Advertising banner.	50-75

Majestic
Calendar. 1931. 26 by 48 inches. Framed. Eagle and plane over mountains.	350
Street car headliner	50

Motorola
Sign. Tin. 3 color. 14 by 6 inches.	110

Old Gold
Window card advertising Fred Waring and His Pennsylvanians on CBS. Black and white.	40

Philco
Clock advertising Philco tubes.	75
Outdoor advertising sign.	65-75

RCA
Cardboard display. Mickey Mouse and Pluto.	20
Clock. Reverse painting. "RCA Radio Batteries for Extra Listening Hours." 1950s.	150

ARR: *Antique Radios: Restoration and Price Guide* / ARR2: *Antique Radio Restoration Guide, Second Edition* /

B1: *Antique Radio Price Guide, First Edition* by Bunis / B2: *Antique Radio Price Guide, Second Edition* by Bunis /

FOS: *Flick of the Switch* / GOR: *Guide to Old Radios* / RGA: *Radios: The Golden Age* / RR: *Radios Redux* / VR: *Vintage Radio*.

Name and Description	Price Range ($)
Clock. Plastic. 1950s. RCA Tubes.	120
Clock. Radiotron.	90
Counter display. Metal. RCA Tubes.	50
Counter clock display. RCA Electron Tubes.	45
Curtain for showroom. 8 by 15 feet. Overall pattern of Nipper.	200-275
Display case. Lit. Radiotron.	300
Fan. Radiola.	30-40
Lighter. Made by Zippo.	10
Map of world. Prewar. 4 by 8 feet.	125
Sign. Plastic. 24 inches in diameter.	35-50
Tapestry advertising Radiola.	250

Stromberg-Carlson

Desk sign. Brass. "Stromberg-Carlson Authorized Radio Apparatus."	145
Display sign. Brass.	62.50

Westinghouse

Advertising clock.	75-100

Zenith

Trans-oceanic display.	30-50
Turning display stand for console radios. Zenith blue.	150

Other Advertising

Cookbook. KDKA station promotion.	20
KLPR ashtray (Oklahoma City). Frankoma pottery.	50
Stein, stoneware. Advertising Wennersten's radio store.	65

ANTENNA

Bodine.	50
Clapp-Eastham antenna switch.	90
Philco. New in box. Antenna kit.	20
RCA Radiola AG-814.	55

CRYSTAL SETS

Name	Model	Price Range ($)
Airchamp		15-25
Amrad	Model A	250-300
Aurora	Kit	20-25
Beaver	Baby Grand	175-200
Blair		100-125
Crosley Harko		250-450
DeForest	DT600 Everyman	250-300
Echophone		200-250
Ericson		130
Fada		150-200
Fellows		250-300
Flyver		150
Gecophone (England)	Model 1	250
	Model BC 1501	400
General Electric	Model ER-753	175-225
Henry Hyman		70
Homemade (various ones)		20-100
Howe		75-125
Ken-Rad		150-200
Lemco	340 (VR-68)	85-90

CRYSTAL SETS—*continued*

Name	Model	Price Range ($)
Martian	Big 4	100-150
	Special	200-250
Mengele		200
Meteor		150
Midget	Blue	45
	Black	55
Monarch		160
O-So-EZ		150
Pandora		65
Philmore	Model 336	50-75
	Blackbird	100-125
Polytran		15-20
Rapid Radio		45-65
RCA	Radiola I (VR-109)	300-500
Spenser		45
Steinite		150-250
Telefunken		250
Uncle Al Miracle		150
Volta		150-175
Weco	Used	40-50
	Unused	90
World		135

SPEAKERS

Name/Model	Type	Price Range ($)
Amplion AR-19	Horn	100
Amplion AU-5	Horn	125
Atwater Kent E	Cone	25-50
Atwater Kent E2	Cone	40-55
Atwater Kent F2	Cone	50-60
Atwater Kent F4A	Cone	25-35
Atwater Kent H	Horn	60-80
Atwater Kent L	Horn	50-70
Atwater Kent M	Horn	80-100
Baldwin A	Cone	45
Baldwin Concert Grand	Horn	80
Brandes H	Horn	30-55
Brandes Table Talker	Cone	10-20
Bristol Baby Audiophone	Horn	95
Crosley type D	Cone	40-50
Crosley Dynacone F	Cone	30-40
Crosley Musicone	Cone	15-25
Dictogrand	Horn	80-100
Farrand Junior 20	Cone	60-80
Jewett Super Speaker	Horn	30-40
King Am-pli-tone	Horn	250-300
Kodel	Horn	225
Kolster K-6	Cone	30-35

ARR: *Antique Radios: Restoration and Price Guide* / ARR2: *Antique Radio Restoration Guide, Second Edition* /
B1: *Antique Radio Price Guide, First Edition* by Bunis / B2: *Antique Radio Price Guide, Second Edition* by Bunis /
FOS: *Flick of the Switch* / GOR: *Guide to Old Radios* / RGA: *Radios: The Golden Age* / RR: *Radios Redux* / VR: *Vintage Radio*.

Name/Model	Type	Price Range ($)
Magnavox A2R	Horn	125-150
Magnavox "Beverly"	30-40	
Magnavox M1	Horn	75-125
Magnavox M4	Horn	100-150
Magnavox M20	Horn Cabinet	60-70
Magnavox R2	Horn	130
Magnavox R2C	Horn	175
Magnavox R3	Horn	50-75
Magnavox R3 (type B)	Horn	75-100
Meistersinger	Horn	70-80
Music Master	Horn	60-120
Na-Ald Midget	Cone	125
Pathé	Cone Cabinet	20-30
RCA Radiola 100	Cone	20-40
RCA Radiola 100A	Cone	25-50
RCA Radiola 103	Cone	40-75
RCA Radiola 106	Cone floor model (Tapestry front)	45-65
RCA Radiola UZ-1325	Horn	40-85
Radialamp	Cone	400-500
Rola	Cone	160
Rola	Horn	50-75
Saal	Horn	45-60
Stewart-Warner 435	Cone	45
Thompson Magnaphone	Horn	15-20
Thorola Junior	Horn	70-125
Timmons Ship	Cone	60-75
Tower Meistersinger	Cone	85-125
Trimm L38	Cone	40-50
Truetone	Horn	30
Utah Acorn	Horn	50-65
Victor Lumiere	Cone	100-150
Voice of the Sky	Horn	250-425
WLS Silvertone	Horn	35
Western Electric 10-D	Horn	60
Western Electric 10-F	Horn	50
Western Electric 521-W	Horn	100
Western Electric 540-AW	Cone	85-100
Westinghouse 518W	Horn	25-40

TEST EQUIPMENT

Name	Type	Model	Price Range ($)
B & K	Tube tester	600	30-40
Conair	5-inch oscilloscope		40-50
EICO	Audio generator	377	15-20
EICO	Oscilloscope	460	30-50
EICO	Signal generator	324	20-25
EICO	Signal generator	330	25-35
EICO	Audio generator	379	25-35
EICO	Signal tracer	147A	25-30
EICO	Tube tester	625	20-25
EICO	VTVM	1050	15-25
Heathkit	Condenser tester	C3	15-25
Heathkit	Oscilloscope	0-8	25-30

TEST EQUIPMENT—*continued*

Name	Type	Model	Price Range ($)
Heathkit	Signal generator	SG-6	25-30
Heathkit	Signal generator	SG-7	25-30
Heathkit	Signal tracer	T-1	20-25
Heathkit	Signal tracer	T-3	30-35
Heathkit	Tube tester	TC-1	20-35
Heathkit	VTVM	1M18	15-20
Heathkit	VTVM	1M38	10-15
Heathkit	VTVM	WV77B	30-35
Hickock	Oscilloscope	677	20-25
Hickock	Tube tester	533A	100-125
Hickock	VTVM	209A	75-90
Knight	Tube tester	KG-600B	30-35
Paco	Electrolytic capacitor tester	C-25	10-15
Precision	Signal generator	200C	30-45
RCA	Audio generator	WA44B	30-40
RCA	3-inch oscilloscope	W057B	25-40
RCA	Signal generator	WR49A	30-35
RCA	Sweep generator	WR679A	40-50
RCA	VTVM	WV98C	40-65
Superior	VOM	670A	20-30
Triplett	Signal generator	2432	30
Weston	Ohm meter	689	15-20
Weston	Tube tester	777	20-30

L I T E R A T U R E

BOOKS

Fiction

Title	Author	Price Range ($)
Bert Wilson, Wireless Operator	Duffield	8
Motor Rangers Wireless Station	Marvin West	8
Motor Road Club and the Wireless	Hancock	8
Radio Boys books		each 6-10
Radio Girls books		each 9
Tom Swift and His Photo Telephone	Appleton	10
Tom Swift and His Wireless Message	Appleton	10

Technical Engineering

Title	Author	Price Range ($)
Audel's Radioman's Guide. 1940.		12
Cathode Ray Tube at Work. 1935	Rider	8

Title	Author	Price Range ($)
Drakes Radio Cyclopedia. 1931.		7
Electricity for Boys. 1914.	Zerbe	6
Electricity One-Four.	H.C. Mileaf	9
Elements of Radio.	Marcus	8
Experimental Radio.	Ramsey	10
Frequency Modulation. 1942.	Hund	10
Fundamentals of Radio.	Jordan	8
Fundamentals of Radio.	Terman	8
Fundamentals of Vacuum Tubes. 1941.	Eastman	6
Hawkins Electrical Guide.		each 10
ICS Radio Handbook.		10
Leutz' Modern Radio Reception. 1924.		50
Leutz' Modern Radio Reception. 1928.		40
Look and Listen, The TV Handbook. 1939. Introduction to TV and instructions for building the Andrea TV receiver kit. The KT-E-5, the first cathode ray TV kit ever.	Sleeper	60
New Catechism of Electricity. 1897.	Hawkins	20
Operator's Wireless Telephone and Telegraph Handbook, First Edition. 1909. Library copy.	V. H. Laughter	45
Pictorial Album of Wireless and Radio. 1961.	Greenwood	12
Principles of Radio Communication. 1927.	Morecraft	15
Radio Amateurs Handbook. ARRL. 1935.		30
Radio Encyclopedia. 1927.	Gernsback	20-30
Radio Engineering, Third Edition. 1947.	Terman	10
Radio Engineers Handbook. 1943.	Terman	10
Radio Experimenter and Builder. 1934.		10
Radio for Everybody. 1922.	Lescarboura	12
Radio for the Amateur. 1922.	Packer	10
*Radio Laboratory Handbook. ca.*1925.	Scroggie (British)	11
Radio Manual, Third Edition. 1940.	Sterling	12
Radio Master's Encyclopedia. 1941.		25
Radio Operating Questions and Answers. 1929.	Nilson & Hornung	7
Radio Physics Course. 1934.	Ghirardi	15
Radio Simplified. 1923. *(Fair condition)*	Kendall and Koehler	10
Radio Telephone for Amateurs. 1922.	Ballantine	13
Radio Telephony. 1918.	Goldsmith	16
Radio Up to the Minute. 1927.	Nilson	10
Radiotron Designer's Handbook, Third Edition. 1941. Australian.	F. Langford-Smith	40
Radiotron Designer's Handbook, Fourth Edition. 1952. Australian.	F. Langford-Smith	50
Restoration and Preservation of Scientific Apparatus for Collections. 1987. In French and English.	Guy Bira	20
Romance of Modern Electricity. 1906.	Gibson	20
Saga of the Vacuum Tube. 1977. Hardcover.	Tyne	25-30
Shortwave. 1930.	Leutz and Gable	70
Sound Recording. 1949.	Frayne & Wolf	15
Super Heterodyne. 1926.	Lacault	10
Television. 1940.	Zworykin & Norton	50
Textbook on Wireless Telegraphy. 1917.	Stanley	12

Technical Engineering—*continued*

Title	Author	Price Range ($)
Theory of Radio Communications. 1929.	Filgate	10
Vision of Radio.	Jenkins	200
Wireless Experimenter. 1919.	Bucher	25

Servicing

Title	Author	Price Range ($)
Atwater Kent (Complete, reprint)		70
General Electric Service Data, 1946-1961.		6
Gernsback's Official Radio Service Manual. 1930.		25
Mallory Radio Service Encyclopedia, 1937.		8
Modern Radio Servicing.	Ghirardi	10-15
Philco Service Notes, 1928-1937.		10
RCA HB-3 Tube Manual (5 vol.)		35
RCA Receiving Tube Manual. 1937.		4
RCA Service Manual. v.1		75-85
RCA Service Data. vv.1, 2. 1923-1942.		each 30
RCA Service Notes. 1931-32.		25
RCA Service Notes. 1933.		15-25
Radio Circuit Manual. 1941, 1942.		each 15
Radio Field Service Data. 1935.	Ghirardi	15
Radio Service Man's Handy Book, vol. 1. 1931.		20-25
Radio Servicing Theory & Practice. 1949.	Marcus	8
Rider's Record Changer Service. 1941.		5
Rider's Record Changer Service. 1949-1950. (v. 3)		12
Rider's Manual, vv. 1-5, abridged		35-50
Rider's Manual (v. 1)		40-60
Rider's Manual (vv. 2, 3)		35-40
Rider's Manual (v. 4)		15-20
Rider's Manual (vv. 5-22)		10-15
Rider's Manual (v. 23)		75
Sam's Photofacts (sets 100-1210)		each .10-.25
Sam's Record Changer Manual, 1951-52 (v. 2)		15
Sam's Record Changer Manual, 1954-55 (v. 7)		15
Servicing Superheterodynes. 1934.	Rider	10
Supreme (Most-often-needed radio diagrams). 1939-on.		each 10-12
Sylvania Radio Tubes Technical Manual. 1951.		5
Zenith Service Manual (#2)		15
Zenith Schematic Service Manual, 1929-1939.		19

Broadcasting

Title	Author	Price Range ($)
A Tower in Babel. (volume 1 to 1933).	Barnouw	25
Golden Web. (volume 2 from 1933 to 1953)	Barnouw.	25
Big Broadcast. 1920-1950.	Buxton. Programs and performers. 1972	20
Radiotron Designer's Handbook, Fourth Edition.		50

Title	Author	Price Range ($)
David Sarnoff. 1966.	Lyons	10
In Search of Light. The Broadcasts of Edward R. Murrow. 1938-1961. 1967.		15
Inventing American Broadcasting. 1899-1922. 1987.	Susan Douglas	15
On the Air. 1937.	Floherty	5
Pictorial History of Radio. 1960.	Settel	25
Pictorial History of Radio in Canada. 1975.	Stewart	8
Story of Radio (3 volumes). 1975	Dalton	set 20
Where the Melody Lingers on. WNEW. 1934-1964. Anniversary book.		8

CATALOGS

Allied Catalog. 1934.		10-15
Allied Catalogs (1940s)		8-10
Allied Catalogs (1950s)		6-8
(Other radio supply general catalogs are sold at about the same prices.)		
Beckley-Ralston Catalog. Early 1920.		75
J.H. Bunnell Catalog #29. 1924.		35
Bunnell Wireless Catalog (#44). 1922.		15
Clapp Eastham Radio Telegraph Apparatus Catalog. 1914-1915.		40
Wm. B. Duck Catalog #9 (1915) (wireless section)		30
Wm. B. Duck Catalog #16		50
E.I. Catalog #19		50
Grebe Radio Receivers. Fair condition. 1923.		10
MESCO Catalog. 1922.		25
Philco Yearbook. 1942.		5
Pilot Catalog. 1927.		15
Radio Enters the Home. Original ed. (has been reprinted).		30-50
RCA Radio Apparatus, First Edition. Fair condition. 1921.		35
RCA Radio Apparatus, Fifth Edition. Good condition. 1921.		32
RCA Radiola, First Edition. 1927.		15-20

INSTRUCTIONS

Atwater Kent World Wide Radio Station Directory.		8
How to Conduct a Radio Club.	Bucher	60
Grebe Synchrophase. 1912.		35
Remler Operating Instructions for the 330/331/333.		15

MAGAZINES

(Per issue, unless otherwise noted.)

Popular Radio. 1925-1926. Each.		5
QST. 1917.		22.50
QST. 1928-1930.		3
QST. 1931-1936.		2
QST. 1927-1931. Complete sets, by year.		175
Radio. 1922-1926. Issues 1-60		290
Radio Broadcast. 1927. Complete set.		175

Title	Author	Price Range ($)
Radio Broadcast. 1928. Complete set.		165
Radio Broadcast. 1929. Complete set.		175
Radio Broadcast. 1927-1930.		2.50
Radio Craft. 1939-1947.		2.50-3
Radio News. 1927-1929.		4
Radio News. 1930-1935.		2-3
Radio News. 1936-1940.		2.50
Radio News. 1945-1958.		2
Wireless Age. 1916.		22
Wireless News. 1912.		15

M I S C E L L A N E O U S

Company	Model	Description	Price Range ($)
Electro-Voice	950	High impedance cardiod crystal microphone. Used for public address.	30
RCA	Slimline	Microphone.	35
RCA	"Junior Velocity"	Microphone. (ARR-66) Used in radio and public address.	250
Shure	5B.	Crystal microphone.	75
Stromberg-Carlson		Remote control box with cable and plug.	200
Turner	101C	Cardiod microphone. Used in public address and recording.	30
Universal		Double-button microphone.	55
Western Electric	522-W	Phonograph attachment.	40-50
Wizard		Microphone (working toy).	20
Zenith		Earphone accessory. Connected earphone to radio with separate volume control.	40

ARR: *Antique Radios: Restoration and Price Guide* / ARR2: *Antique Radio Restoration Guide, Second Edition* / B1: *Antique Radio Price Guide, First Edition* by Bunis / B2: *Antique Radio Price Guide, Second Edition* by Bunis / FOS: *Flick of the Switch* / GOR: *Guide to Old Radios* / RGA: *Radios: The Golden Age* / RR: *Radios Redux* / VR: *Vintage Radio.*

FURTHER READING

Radio Repair and Restoration

Johnson, David. *Antique Radio Restoration Guide, 2nd edition*. Radnor, PA: Wallace-Homestead, 1992

General Information

Bunis, Marty and Sue. *The Collector's Guide to Antique Radios, 3rd edition*. Paducah, KY: Collector Books. This is a fine source of pictures and prices. Only the latest edition is in print.

Collins, Philip. *Radios: The Golden Age*. San Francisco: Chronicle Books, 1987. This work primarily features photographs of Catalin and Bakelite sets of the 1930s and 1940s.

Collins, Philip. *Radios Redux*. San Francisco: Chronicle Books, 1991. A second book of great pictures like *Radios: The Golden Age*.

Lane, David and Robert. *Transistor Radios, A Collector's Encyclopedia and Price Guide*. Radnor, PA: Wallace-Homestead, 1994.

McMahon, Morgan E. *A Flick of the Switch, 1930-1950*.

McMahon, Morgan E. *Radio Collector's Guide*.

McMahon, Morgan E. *Vintage Radio, 1887-1929*.

These three books by McMahon are still among the most useful ones on identifying old radios. They are being republished by Antique Electronic Supply, 6221 S. Maple Ave., Tempe, AZ 85283.

Paul, Floyd A. *Radio Horn Speaker Encyclopedia*. Glendale, CA, 1986.

Broadcast Information

Barnouw, Erik. *A Tower in Babel: A History of Broadcasting in the United States to 1933*. Volume 1. New York: Oxford University Press, 1966.

Barnouw, Erik. *The Golden Web: A History of Broadcasting in the United States, 1933-1953*. Volume 2. New York: Oxford University Press, 1968. More and more histories of specific radio stations are being written. Station histories can be very enjoyable, combining history with stories by and about the early broadcasters. The information about KMA, for instance, came from one of these local histories.

Birkby, Robert. *KMA Radio: The First Sixty Years*. Shenandoah, Iowa: May Broadcasting Co., 1985.

INDEX